Adobe Photoshop, Illustrator, and InDesign Collaboration and Workflow

Adobe

Classroom in a Book®

The official training workbook from Adobe

Bart Van de Wiele

Adobe Photoshop, Illustrator, and InDesign Collaboration and Workflow Classroom in a Book®

Writer: Bart Van de Wiele
Adobe Press Executive Editor: Laura Norman
Development Editor: Victor Gavenda
Senior Production Editor: Tracey Croom
Technical Reviewer: Mike Rankin
Keystroke Reviewer: Megan Ahearn
Copyeditor: Scout Festa
Proofreader: Kelly Kordes Anton
Compositor: Kim Scott, Bumpy Design
Indexer: Valerie Haynes Perry
Cover Illustration: E Larson
Interior Designer: Mimi Heft

ISBN-13: 978-0-13-790846-2
ISBN-10:   0-13-790846-6

1 2022

WHERE ARE THE LESSON FILES?

Purchase of this Classroom in a Book in any format gives you access to the lesson files you'll need to complete the exercises in the book.

1 Go to adobepress.com/DesignCIB.

2 Sign in or create a new account.

3 Click Submit.

Note: If you encounter problems registering your product or accessing the lesson files or web edition, go to adobepress.com/support for assistance.

4 Answer the questions as proof of purchase.

5 The lesson files can be accessed through the Registered Products tab on your Account page.

6 Click the Access Bonus Content link below the title of your product to proceed to the download page. Click the lesson file links to download them to your computer.

Note: If you purchased a digital product directly from adobepress.com or peachpit.com, your product will already be registered. However, you still need to follow the registration steps and answer the proof of purchase question before the Access Bonus Content link will appear under the product on your Registered Products tab.

Pearson's Commitment to Diversity, Equity, and Inclusion

Pearson is dedicated to creating bias-free content that reflects the diversity of all learners. We embrace the many dimensions of diversity, including but not limited to race, ethnicity, gender, socioeconomic status, ability, age, sexual orientation, and religious or political beliefs.

Education is a powerful force for equity and change in our world. It has the potential to deliver opportunities that improve lives and enable economic mobility. As we work with authors to create content for every product and service, we acknowledge our responsibility to demonstrate inclusivity and incorporate diverse scholarship so that everyone can achieve their potential through learning. As the world's leading learning company, we have a duty to help drive change and live up to our purpose to help more people create a better life for themselves and to create a better world.

Our ambition is to purposefully contribute to a world where:

- Everyone has an equitable and lifelong opportunity to succeed through learning.
- Our educational products and services are inclusive and represent the rich diversity of learners.
- Our educational content accurately reflects the histories and experiences of the learners we serve.
- Our educational content prompts deeper discussions with learners and motivates them to expand their own learning (and worldview).

While we work hard to present unbiased content, we want to hear from you about any concerns or needs with this Pearson product so that we can investigate and address them.

- Please contact us with concerns about any potential bias at https://www.pearson.com/report-bias.html.

CONTENTS

GETTING STARTED

Welcome to *Adobe Photoshop, Illustrator, and InDesign Collaboration and Workflow Classroom in a Book.* The goal of this book is to challenge the status quo when working with, and combining, the primary Adobe design applications: Adobe Photoshop, Adobe Illustrator, and Adobe InDesign. The nine lessons in this book will take you on a journey that explores how to get the most out of these applications and how multi-app workflows will forever change the way in which you approach a design project.

This book is aimed at graphic designers, print designers, illustrators, web designers, and anyone else who is working on a project in which you might bump into the limitations of a single design application. For example, InDesign is a great solution for typesetting and building multipage layouts, but it can't do image retouching. Photoshop is amazing at image retouching but lacks the drawing tools in Illustrator. And while Illustrator can be used for typesetting single-page layouts, it lacks the advanced type features, image placement options, and automation features in InDesign.

Each of the Adobe design apps comes with unique strengths, but they often need each other to fulfill a specific task as part of a larger process. It's important to understand how the interaction among these applications will allow you to deliver impressive work. However, success is guaranteed only when you know what you're doing. Failing that, you might find yourself struggling to make changes to an existing design, as some components of the file might have been flattened, text might have been outlined, or individual elements might have passed out of your control. Because you expect these three apps to work together smoothly, it can be very frustrating when you have to lose time backtracking your steps.

This book is here to help you make the right decisions, teach you how to ask the right questions before taking a specific course of action, and support the synergy between Photoshop, Illustrator, and InDesign.

About Classroom in a Book

Adobe Photoshop, Illustrator, and InDesign Collaboration and Workflow Classroom in a Book is part of the official training series for Adobe. The lessons are designed so that you can learn at your own pace. A basic understanding of Photoshop, Illustrator, and InDesign is required to successfully complete all lessons in this book. But all collaboration and workflow techniques taught in this book are easy to master and are aimed at designers who have no prior knowledge of this particular subject.

Although each lesson provides step-by-step instructions for creating a specific project, there's plenty of room for exploration and experimentation. The review questions at the end of each lesson will help you test your newly acquired knowledge and give you the confidence to apply these new techniques in the field.

Prerequisites

This book focuses on teaching you the value of multi-app workflows. This includes learning how to correctly set up a variety of files and documents and which factors need to be considered before choosing a course of action. Teaching how to start using Photoshop, Illustrator, or InDesign is beyond of the scope of this book; it is recommended that you consult other titles in the Classroom in a Book series for that purpose.

To get full value from the exercises in this book it is recommended that you have some prior knowledge of Photoshop, Illustrator, and InDesign. This will ensure that you finish every exercise successfully without losing time searching for basic features and functionalities.

When working with Photoshop, you should have some experience with the following features:

- Creating and managing layers
- Using the basic selection tools
- Creating and applying layer styles like drop shadows and other effects
- Creating and using adjustment layers
- Understanding the basics of layer masks
- Working with text and shape layers

For Illustrator, it is recommended you should have some experience with the following features:

- Using the basic selection tools
- Creating and managing layers
- Creating and using artboards
- Applying swatches

For InDesign, you should be familiar with the following features:

- Applying basic text formatting options and styles
- Placing, moving, and transforming images
- Using the Links panel to relink or update links

Preference settings

As part of every exercise, you will be asked to reset your program preferences. Resetting a program's preferences brings it back to its "factory settings." This ensures that the interface of the program corresponds to the screenshots that guide you through the exercise. However, keep in mind that reverting a program's settings to their default values also discards any custom settings that have been set up—for example, InDesign custom workspaces or Photoshop color settings. If you are unsure how resetting your preferences might affect your saved settings, it is recommended to skip this step.

Changing interface settings

Resetting the application preferences changes the user interface color to the Medium Dark theme. However, all screenshots in this book are taken using the Medium Light theme. If you want your interface brightness to match that of the images in this book, change the interface settings after each time you reset the preferences.

1 Start your application, and choose [name of application] > Preferences > General (macOS) or Edit > Preferences > General (Windows).

2 Click the Interface category (named User Interface in Illustrator).

3 Click the third Color Theme swatch from the left.

4 Click OK to close the preferences.

Activating fonts

Many of the lesson files use fonts that are provided by Adobe as part of a Creative Cloud membership.

If you open a lesson file and the Missing Fonts dialog box opens, click Activate. This downloads the required font from the Creative Cloud and makes it available on your computer.

Updating InDesign links

When you place an image in InDesign, the file path to the placed image is saved as part of the link to the file. If you move the InDesign file (and its links) to another location, the links to the placed images are broken because the paths to the placed images has changed.

If you open an InDesign file and the Issues With Links dialog box opens, click Update Modified Links to restore the broken links.

Saving locally versus saving to the cloud

When you save a file from Photoshop or Illustrator for the first time, the application offers you the choice between saving your document on your computer and saving it to the cloud. In this book, we intend for you to save every work file to the Desktop unless a step specifies that you should save it to the cloud. Because saving to the Desktop is such a basic action, most exercises don't even mention this dialog box. You can select Don't Show Again to hide it, but resetting the preferences at the start of every lesson brings it back to life every time you save a new document.

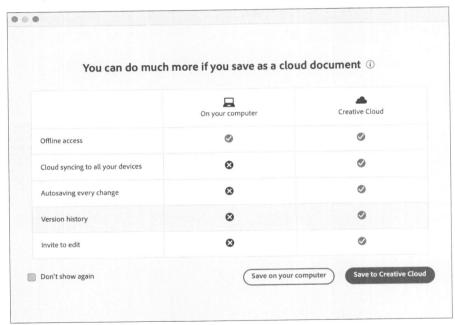

File-saving preferences

Every time you save a new file in Illustrator or save a file using the Save As command, the Illustrator Options dialog box opens. Simply click OK to accept the default settings.

If the Photoshop Format Options dialog box opens when you save a file in Photoshop, make sure that Maximum Compatibility is selected and select Don't Show Again, then click OK.

Online content

Your purchase of this Classroom in a Book includes online materials provided by way of your Account page on adobepress.com.

Lesson files

To work through the projects in this book, you will need to download the lesson files by following the instructions in the "Accessing the lesson files and Web Edition" section.

Web Edition

The Web Edition is an online interactive version of the book, providing an enhanced learning experience. Your Web Edition can be accessed from any device with a connection to the internet, and it contains the following:

- The complete text of the book
- Hours of instructional video keyed to the text

Accessing the lesson files and Web Edition

You must register your purchase on adobepress.com in order to access the online content.

1 Go to adobepress.com/DesignCIB.

2 Sign in, or create a new account.

3 Click Submit.

4 Answer the question as proof of purchase.

5 The lesson files can be accessed from the Registered Products tab on your Account page. Click the Access Bonus Content link below the title of your product to proceed to the download page. Click the lesson file links to download the lessons to your computer.

The Web Edition can be accessed from the Digital Purchases tab on your Account page. Scroll down to the Web Edition section of that page and click the Launch link to access the product.

● **Note:** If you encounter problems registering your product or accessing the lesson files or Web Edition, go to adobepress.com/support for assistance.

● **Note:** If you purchased a digital product directly from adobepress.com or www.peachpit.com, your product will already be registered. However, you still need to follow the registration steps and answer the proof of purchase question before the Access Bonus Content link will appear under the product on your Registered Products tab.

Additional resources

Adobe Photoshop, Illustrator and InDesign Collaboration and Workflow Classroom in a Book is not meant to replace documentation that comes with any of the applications or to be a comprehensive reference for every feature. Only the commands and options used in the lessons are explained in this book. For comprehensive information about Photoshop, Illustrator, and InDesign features and tutorials, refer to the following resources, which you can reach by choosing commands from the Help menu in each application.

Adobe Learn & Support: Choose Help > [application name] to find and browse Help and Support content on adobe.com. On the Learn & Support page, click User Guide for documentation on individual features.

Tutorials: For a wide range of interactive tutorials on the features of each application, click Learn on the Home screen or choose one of the following:

- In Photoshop, choose Help > Hands-on Tutorials. The Discover panel opens, displaying a catalog of in-app tutorials and other learning resources.

- In Illustrator, choose Help > Tutorials. Just as in Photoshop, the Discover panel opens, guiding the reader to a rich array of learning resources.

- In InDesign, choose Help > InDesign Tutorials to open helpx.adobe.com/indesign/tutorials.html.

Adobe blog: blog.adobe.com brings you tutorials, product news, and inspirational articles about using Adobe Creative Cloud products.

Creative Cloud tutorials: For inspiration, key techniques, cross-application workflows, and updates on new features, go to the Creative Cloud tutorials page, helpx.adobe.com/creative-cloud/tutorials.html.

Adobe Community: Tap into peer-to-peer discussions, questions, and answers on Adobe products at the Adobe Support Community page at community.adobe.com. Click the link for a particular application to visit the community for that app.

Adobe Creative Cloud Discover: This online resource offers thoughtful articles on design and design issues, a gallery showcasing the work of top-notch designers and artists, tutorials, and more. Check it out at creativecloud.adobe.com/discover.

Resources for educators: adobe.com/education and edex.adobe.com offer a treasure trove of information for instructors who teach classes on Adobe software. Find solutions for education at all levels, including free curricula that use an integrated approach to teaching Adobe software and that can be used to prepare for the Adobe Certified Associate exams.

Adobe Creative Cloud product home page: adobe.com/creativecloud.html has more information about the features and functionality of the applications.

Adobe Authorized Training Centers

Adobe Authorized Training Centers (AATCs) offer instructor-led courses and training on Adobe products, employing only Adobe Certified Instructors. A directory of AATCs is available at learning.adobe.com/partner-finder.html.

1 WORKFLOWS AND FILE FORMATS

Lesson overview

In this lesson, you'll learn the following:

- The goals and rewards of this book.
- The value of established file formats like JPEG, EPS, and TIFF for graphic designers.
- The importance of using native file formats.

 This lesson will take about 30 minutes to complete. Please log in to your account on adobepress.com/DesignCIB to download the files for this lesson, or go to the "Getting Started" section at the beginning of this book and follow the instructions under "Accessing the lesson files and Web Edition." Store the files on your computer in a convenient location.

Your Account page is also where you'll find any updates to the lesson files. Look on the Lesson & Update Files tab to access the most current content.

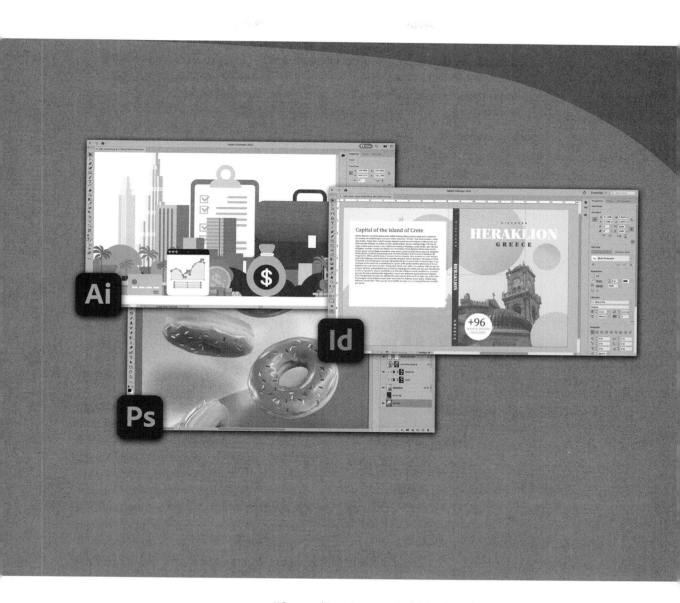

When used together properly, Adobe Photoshop, Illustrator, and InDesign form a powerful team that empowers you to build flexible workflows for any design project.

Workflows

Every lesson in this book teaches you how to work with two, or sometimes three, design apps at the same time.With each workflow described, you need to follow a specific sequence of operations to build the project from the ground up. Following that sequence ensures the success of the project you're building.

A dictionary would describe a workflow as "The sequence of industrial, administrative, or other processes through which a piece of work passes from initiation to completion."

This definition applies to every exercise in this book. There is a reason behind every step in these exercises and the order in which you perform them, just like in real life. In fact, our lives and daily schedules can also be described as workflows. We set an alarm every night to make sure we're up at the proper time. We freshen up, have breakfast, and make sure we're ready for the next step—which is usually getting to work, or at least making sure we don't miss the bus or train that will take us to work. Every step of our daily schedule, or "flow," is planned in anticipation of the next step.

But as you go through your day, you might encounter disruptions caused by clients who ask you to make changes to the latest version of a design you've been working on. Applying basic text modifications probably won't ruin your day. But what if the same client asks you to go back to a version from two weeks ago, or wants you to change a graphic that was also used in five different files across two different apps? These can be simple requests from the client's point of view. But to you, they can be big demands that you didn't count on when planning your project or your day. And before you know it, you end up having to re-create work you had overwritten two weeks ago, or trying to find a font you used in a flattened version of your file. In other words, you must recover (or re-create) work for which you no longer possess the initial building blocks. And the reason you no longer have the original building blocks is that you made a decision. Somewhere along the way, you decided that it was probably all right to:

- Overwrite a Photoshop file on your server
- Flatten a few layers
- Keep only one of six Illustrator artboards placed in Photoshop
- Copy and paste an image into InDesign instead of placing it
- Or any number of other things

The driver behind these decisions was probably your desire to take a shortcut while working. But sometimes we must avoid the path of least resistance when working on complex designs.

We can't predict the future, and we need to be prepared for disruptions while taking our design projects from initiation to completion. Using native integrations allows us to make a change to almost any detail of a complex design at any given moment. And it's thanks to these integrations that our digital workflows will stop disrupting our personal daily schedules.

Interoperability

Workflows define the process of going from initiation to completion. This process can be interpreted as a framework for designers. It's how we envision our day and our projects and what we do to bring them to a successful end. See workflows as *what* you're doing. And if workflows are the *what*, then interoperability can be the *how*.

Interoperability between applications

The goal of interoperability is the seamless, frictionless movement of assets across applications. To achieve this, we need a fundamental understanding of how applications like Photoshop, Illustrator, and InDesign work—more specifically, to understand for which purposes they can be used and what their limitations are.

Let's say you are working in InDesign, where you need to use the drawing tools to create a specific shape on a parent page. You need to combine and intersect five or six different shapes to accomplish this, but you run into a few problems:

- When selecting the shapes, you accidentally include other objects, such as text frames, in your selection. So you end up losing time making basic selections.

- The boundaries of the pasteboard area around your parent page are too small to comfortably work in.

- It dawns on you that InDesign might be missing the complex vector-editing capabilities that would allow you to easily achieve the shape you're looking for. Using the Pathfinder panel might work, but it's a slow process that involves drawing many different shapes.

Some designers might realize they should have built the shape in Illustrator and then brought it into InDesign. Others might soldier on to get the job done using only InDesign. In reality, most designers want to stay in the main app they've chosen to build a project in, but realize they sometimes need to leave that application in order to perform specialized tasks. This creates the need to better understand how design assets can travel bidirectionally between different applications.

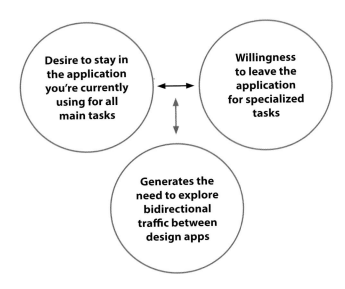

Case study

Let's explore a common scenario in which you would need to combine Illustrator with InDesign. Say you need to bring artwork from Illustrator into InDesign. There are a variety of ways to do so. The quickest way is by copying the Illustrator artwork and pasting it into InDesign.

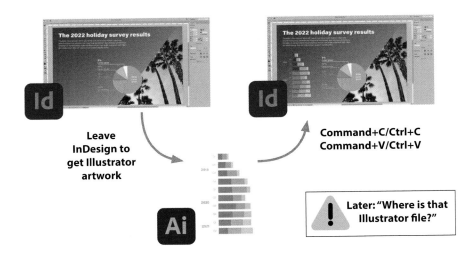

You could also place the Illustrator file by using the Place command in InDesign. This diagram shows the pros and cons of placing files at two stages of the workflow: when you import the artwork into InDesign, and when edits are required:

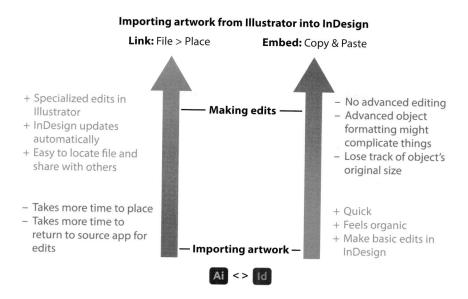

Importing artwork from Illustrator into InDesign

Link: File > Place   **Embed:** Copy & Paste

——— **Making edits** ———

+ Specialized edits in
  Illustrator
+ InDesign updates
  automatically
+ Easy to locate file and
  share with others

– No advanced editing
– Advanced object
  formatting might
  complicate things
– Lose track of object's
  original size

– Takes more time to place
– Takes more time to
  return to source app for
  edits

+ Quick
+ Feels organic
+ Make basic edits in
  InDesign

— **Importing artwork** —

Ai < > Id

Clearly, each method comes with certain advantages and disadvantages; you'll learn more about both in Lesson 5, "Using Illustrator Artwork in InDesign." There is also a third method: saving the artwork into a Creative Cloud Library and then placing it in InDesign, which you'll learn in Lessons 8, "Working with Creative Cloud Libraries," and 9, "Integration Through Collaboration."

Interoperability between teams

More and more organizations across different design industries are relying on remote workers, either by having their teams work from home or by hiring freelancers. This has increased the need for collaboration and for more complex workflows among teams, for which a solution is needed. This is because, as you'll discover in Lessons 8 and 9, traditional collaboration tools are not suited to handling industry-specific design workflows using complex assets. But as the need for collaboration increases, so does the frequency with which interoperability issues arise. This is why it's important that organizations realize that if entire teams are already relying on the Creative Cloud ecosystem almost every day of the week, the solution to these problems lies not in a third-party collaborative system, but in the one provided by Adobe.

Let's explore an everyday scenario. You're part of the in-house design department of a sportswear company. You're using the product image of a particular tennis shoe in Photoshop. You've applied layer masks, adjustment layers, and other nondestructive effects. The tennis shoe image is buried deep within your Photoshop composition. You've saved the composition on the company server, which allows others to access it and use it in their work.

Scope: You're not the only one who needs to use the graphic you've created. At least four other designers need access to it, and so do two external freelancers and one marketing manager (who doesn't have a Creative Cloud membership). Everyone needs access to the latest version.

Complication: The product manager responsible for all tennis products emails you a new version of the tennis shoe image. It's your job to update the Photoshop composition you created earlier and make sure everyone uses the latest version of the campaign image once you've finished your work.

Result: Once you update the tennis shoe image, you must inform everyone in the company that a new theme image needs to be used and where to find it. This means that all other projects—catalogs, posters, social media graphics, and so on—need to be manually updated by importing the new image from the server. This process is very time consuming and prone to error.

Solution: If the main Photoshop composition had been saved and shared via a Creative Cloud Library instead of hosting it on the server, others would have been able to place the library item directly into their own projects. A link to the original would have been created between the library and everyone's projects. When you altered the main tennis shoe image, everyone would have immediately seen the update to the latest version of the asset, updating all their projects. And sharing the Creative Cloud Library with freelancers would have been easy, without having to grant them access to the company server or sending them a few gigabytes of files via a file transfer system. Even the marketing manager would have been able to use the Photoshop assets in Microsoft solutions, thanks to an available add-on.

The return

Knowing how, when, and where to place these integrations gives you more freedom—freedom to create and iterate because you'll know how the components of your project connect and interact. What if you could save 15 minutes on a design, for example, by using Creative Cloud Libraries for saving and placing content in a design app instead of saving and importing the same asset from your server (over VPN)? That would mean you'd have 15 minutes to spare to do other things, like create an alternate-color version of your design for your customer to choose from. It's little things like this that will give you the value you're looking for when you use multiple Adobe design apps. When we refer to *value*, we often mean getting the best result from the time invested. In the end, time is the most precious currency we have. We don't want to waste it on things like working on unexpected design changes—knowing full well you can't bill the extra hours to your client, because it was you who didn't build the proper integrations into your design.

Another benefit is visual quality. If you know how to place and link certain files into other applications, you'll better understand how each step helps you safeguard the visual quality of your work. But when you copy and paste content across apps, you'll quickly notice that you've taken a one-way street—and that your beautifully crafted graphics are starting to show wear and tear.

Look at the resolution of the image in the following screenshot. It was copied in Photoshop and pasted into an InDesign document. After scaling it up and down a little bit, you notice the graphic doesn't look the way it should anymore in InDesign.

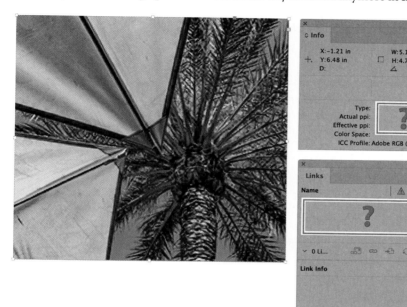

Inspecting the Info panel and Links panel, you see that InDesign has no information to show. No filename, file type, or any information on the effective resolution of the image. Not even the Preflight panel can find anything to display. In other words, it will be very difficult to verify whether your design meets the minimum print resolution requirements.

There are many more scenarios like this, where somewhere along the way you thought you could save a few minutes by taking a shortcut—but you might end up paying the price later by having to undo (or redo) everything.

Established file formats

Some projects in this book allow you to use Creative Cloud Libraries or cloud documents to store, use, and share branded assets. But most of the projects have you choose the appropriate file format when placing, linking, or embedding files from one project into another. This book focuses on the native Adobe file formats, which you'll learn more about later in this lesson. Before we dive into those, let's examine how native file formats compare to established file formats. By "established file formats" I mean file formats that are not native to Adobe applications, but are used by a wide range of applications from Adobe and from other developers. Established file formats are often used by designers out of habit—not because they offer a specific advantage.

Different formats for different needs

Let's start out by exploring the advantages and disadvantages of a few established file formats still used today by working graphic designers. However, it's possible that the potential disadvantages of these established file formats won't seem as important to all users because the term *graphic designer* is used very broadly today. Keep in mind that the job descriptions of graphic designers have evolved a great deal in the last 20 years. And modern design workflows depend on seamless integration among Adobe apps like Photoshop, Illustrator, and InDesign—integration that is difficult or impossible to achieve with established file formats.

Here are a couple of examples of design roles that rely on tight integration among Adobe apps and have become more common:

- Designers increasingly use Adobe software to create assets to include in PowerPoint presentations. PowerPoint designers are looking for better workflows that allow them to design and import both vector and rasterized graphics from apps like Illustrator and Photoshop into PowerPoint. Thus, their needs differ from print designers as they need only concern themselves with screen-resolution graphics.

- As the use of touch screen interfaces for digital devices increases, the demand has grown for UX/UI (user experience and user interface) designers who specialize in designing user experiences that resonate with specific audiences. To a UX designer, version control and the ability to quickly create multiple iterations of a design are important, and the interaction with other design apps like Photoshop and Illustrator is key.

The following discussion of the pros and cons of established file formats is not based on a specific job description of a graphic designer, but on the tools they use to deliver their work, i.e. Photoshop, Illustrator, and InDesign.

JPEG

JPEG (standing for Joint Photographic Experts Group and pronounced *JAY-peg*) is still the most commonly used file format. It was developed in 1992, and its adoption was tied to the rise of the internet in the 1990s, because it was the most efficient way of sending continuous-tone images over incredibly slow (by today's standards) networks and modems. But despite its age, JPEG is a very popular choice with many designers due to its small file size. That small file size is achieved by heavily compressing the image in a way that is (hopefully) invisible to the naked eye.

The value of JPEG for graphic designers

One advantage of JPEG is that it allows the user to decide the level of compression that is applied to the image. This gives the user control over the balance between image compression and visual quality.

Another reason that explains the popularity of JPEG is the fact that it's a widely supported file format. Any computer system or smart device is capable of reading and displaying JPEG files. Even the latest digital cameras allow you to shoot images and save them as JPEGs.

You can even create and save multiple paths in Photoshop when saving a JPEG image. This is a feature not many designers know or take advantage of.

The disadvantages of using JPEG

Although compression might be great for most people, it's not always so great for graphic designers or photographers. Design professionals are always looking for the best possible image quality. And as TVs, monitors, smartphones, and other devices evolve, so grows the need for higher resolutions and better image quality. This means that the need for better image quality is slowly becoming more important than saving a few megabytes per JPEG. This is particularly true now, as hard drives and cloud storage get cheaper every year and as broadband, 4G, and 5G get faster, allowing us to use less compression and instead prioritize image quality.

And here is the problem: when you apply certain adjustments to JPEGs in Photoshop or Lightroom, there is a good chance you will reveal compression artifacts. This JPEG compression is easily recognizable by its 8 by 8 pixel compression matrix. It's also very common to see JPEG artifacts when working with individual color channels in Photoshop. This makes it very difficult to use color channels in Photoshop for image retouching via channel blending or for creating complex selections. Notice the size of the selected artifact in the Info panel, as found in one of the color channels of this image:

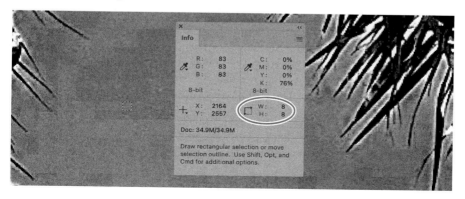

In spite of this problem, JPEG is still one of the best formats for saving and storing large numbers of high-quality images. Note that JPEG doesn't play a large role in this book because it doesn't allow you to set up workflows between Photoshop, Illustrator, and InDesign. Imagine placing a JPEG in InDesign or Illustrator, and then your client asks for a few Photoshop edits. You'd need to save the layered image as a PSD file, which would require you to have a second version of your image and, potentially, to relink your JPEG to a PSD file in InDesign or Illustrator. Again, more work you didn't count on.

Remember that this book is all about building integrations—and JPEG offers virtually none.

EPS

The Encapsulated PostScript format (EPS) was developed in 1987 by John Warnock and Chuck Geschke, the founders of Adobe. As its name implies, it's a file format that includes PostScript data—the same data that PDF files are built with. One of its unique properties is the fact it can include raster images, vector shapes, and live text. This made it the go-to file format for print output until PDF came along. But many designers still use it to save logos and other vector graphics—a habit this book will hopefully change.

The value of EPS for graphic designers

I can't really name any major advantages for this file format, which adds to the mystery of why certain organizations' file servers are filled with files in this format. Continuing to save vector artwork (or even images) as EPS files is something that is done out of habit; we're here to break people out of old habits.

The only advantage that EPS might have over other vector file formats is that it is still supported by many third-party solutions, including PowerPoint, CAD software, and other technical systems that might require vector content, such as those for developing satellite navigation software. This is because EPS offers universal compatibility in major systems and graphics applications. It is also used in older systems that don't support newer formats. However, even the industries that rely on those systems and graphic applications are starting to depend more on SVG files rather than EPS. SVG (Scalable Vector Graphics) is an XML-based vector file format that is primarily used for web applications. It has become a popular format for web and app developers because it is supported by most web browsers, because of its compression and scripting capabilities, and because it supports animations.

The disadvantages of using EPS

The best way to learn the disadvantages is by trying it out ourselves—let's save vector artwork as an EPS file.

You'll start by inspecting two Illustrator documents.

1   Start Illustrator, and choose Illustrator > Preferences > General (macOS) or Edit > Preferences > General (Windows).

2   In the Preferences dialog box, click Reset Preferences, then click OK in the Preferences dialog box. Click Restart Now in the dialog box that appears.

3   From the Lesson01 folder, open city.ai in Illustrator.

    Notice that the cloud objects are semitransparent, and that the sun object has a blur effect applied to it.

4   Click the Layers panel and note the two layers in the document.

5   Choose File > Save As and click Save On Your Computer. In the Save As dialog box, choose Illustrator EPS from the Format menu. Choose a folder on your desktop as the target folder, then click Save.

6   In the EPS Options dialog box, leave all settings at their defaults, click OK to save the file, and then close it.

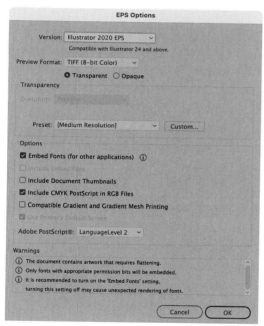

7   Start InDesign, and press Control+Option+Shift+Command (macOS) or Alt+Shift+Ctrl (Windows) to restore the default preferences.

8   When prompted, click Yes to delete the Adobe InDesign Settings file.

9   From the Lesson 01 folder, open 01-city-comp-start.indd. This document has one page with a blue background.

10 Use the Selection tool ▶ to select the blue frame. Then choose File > Place and place your saved EPS file on the page.

11 With the image still selected, choose Object > Fitting > Fill Frame Proportionally.

Notice that the clouds are no longer transparent in InDesign, and that the sun has a white square behind it. This is because EPS doesn't support transparency, which means that all transparent objects, transparent effects, and blending modes have been flattened and rasterized, turning them into images.

12 Use the Selection tool ▶ to select the placed EPS file, then try to choose Object > Object Layer Options. Notice the option is dimmed. This is because EPS doesn't support layers.

13 Close the InDesign document without saving.

To finish, notice the size of the saved EPS file in the Finder (macOS) or Explorer (Windows) window. It's nearly doubled compared to the original Illustrator document. Luckily for us, it is very easy to resave an EPS file as an AI file. When you do so, all the information in the original EPS file will be retained and the image will look exactly the same (though the file size will probably be smaller). If you still have a database of vector EPS images, it's time to convert them to AI.

Saving an image as EPS from Photoshop will give you similar results. There is no support for transparency or for layers or alpha channels. You'll also see an enormous increase in file size, as you can see in the following screenshot. A 9.3MB JPEG turned into a 49MB EPS monster. If EPS does this to a single file, imagine what that would mean for an entire database of images.

Just like JPEG, EPS doesn't provide any added value in the context of this book. In fact, it's very difficult to find any value at all for this dinosaur file format for graphic designers.

TIFF

Another classic is the Tagged Image File Format (TIFF). TIFF has always offered the best possible quality without any compression damage. It remains a popular format.

The value of TIFF for graphic designers

The main advantage of TIFF is that it's a lossless file format that is supported by most of today's digital devices and software. Additionally, it offers the possibility of saving Photoshop layers, alpha channels, spot channels, vector paths, and transparency. This makes TIFF an extremely versatile file format. In the world of digital cameras, TIFF is slowly being pushed out by formats like DNG, CR2, and others, as they offer the ability to edit raw image data, which you can't do with a TIFF file.

One way to make use of TIFF is to save a file from Photoshop and apply lossless compression (LZW or ZIP):

1 Start Photoshop, and choose Photoshop > Preferences > General (macOS) or Edit > Preferences > General (Windows).

2 In the Preferences dialog box, click Reset Preferences On Quit. Then restart Photoshop.

3 From the Lesson01 folder, open sydney.psd in Photoshop.

   This is a flattened image with no layers, alpha channels, or paths.

4 Choose File > Save As and choose TIFF from the Format menu.

5 Choose Lesson01 as the save location, and click Save.

6 In the TIFF Options dialog box, click LZW under Image Compression and click OK to confirm.

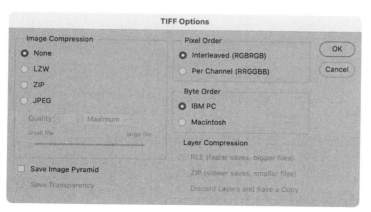

7 In the Finder (macOS) or Explorer (Windows), compare the file size of the original PSD file and the new TIFF version. The LZW TIFF is a lot smaller than the PSD file.

The disadvantages of using TIFF

Does this test prove you need to always save TIFF files instead of PSD (another lossless file format)? Not quite. This example showed a TIFF file that was significantly smaller than its PSD version, and that's great. However, once you start to add layers to your composition, you'll find that saving as TIFF might give you the opposite result, with the PSD file being the most compact version of your composition. And that is the integration we are looking for. So if you expect a TIFF image to have only a single layer throughout the entire course of a project, then nothing can go wrong with this workflow. However, the moment you start adding layers you might get into trouble.

Remember, this book is about integrations and the bidirectional movement of assets. Although layers are supported in the TIFF file format, when you place a layered TIFF in programs like InDesign and Illustrator you can't use any of the layer based features, such as layer comps or layer overrides.

This summary will help you understand when and how to use the three file formats just described.

Special file features

	JPEG	EPS	TIFF
Compression	Lossy (loss of quality)	None	Lossless (LZW or ZIP)
Asset type	Image	Vector + raster	Image
Clipping paths	Yes	Yes	Yes
Layers	No	No	Yes
Artboards	No	No	No
Live transparency	No	No	Yes
File size	Compact	Very large	Compact, unless saved with layers
Value to designers	• Mass storage of images for web or mobile • Can be useful outside Adobe ecosystem	• Can be useful outside Adobe ecosystem in limited contexts	• Store high-resolution images • Can be useful outside Adobe ecosystem

Native file formats

Adobe has always recommended the use of its native file formats for the purpose of cross-application integration—and that's exactly what you'll learn throughout this book. Be sure to leverage native file format capabilities as often as you can when you work within the Creative Cloud ecosystem. However, there might be one or two exceptions where you would still consider using a JPEG or TIFF version of a file:

- **Compatibility:** When you need to share a file with non-designers who don't have Adobe software and don't need access to your Photoshop layers or other special features. They only want the image without the original building blocks. Chances are that a simple, compact JPEG file will suffice.

- **File size:** When saving your file in a native file format would make it exceptionally large—for example, when designing graphics for large billboards and other large-format purposes. In these cases, it doesn't always makes sense to enlarge your original Photoshop composition with all its layers, masks, and other features, because the resulting PSD file would quickly become a dozen gigabytes or larger. This would very likely make it too bulky to comfortably use in InDesign or Illustrator. In this scenario, it makes more sense to save a flattened version of your file as a compressed TIFF that you enlarge afterward.

For your daily design projects, it is recommended to keep using the native Photoshop (PSD), InDesign (INDD), and Illustrator (AI) formats. The integration between the three apps is there, and it's a great way to keep your options open. Let's take a look at some of the details of these native file formats.

Photoshop (.psd)

The Photoshop Document (PSD) file format offers an extremely broad framework for storing a multitude of technical image information. This makes it an excellent file format for preparing and storing images for any output channel: print, web, or video. It includes support for image manipulation such as layers, masks, transparency, text, alpha channels, clipping paths, and a variety of other Photoshop-specific elements.

PSD offers print designers a way to convert images destined for print to color profiles or modes like CYMK, or to duotone or multichannel when using specialized spot channels.

Because it's possible to place native PSD files into InDesign and Illustrator layouts, no conversion to other file formats (like JPEG or TIFF) is required. This takes away the risk of inadvertently adjusting or manipulating the color or image quality data during saving. Instead, your image stays in its PSD specialized environment, and is placed directly into the InDesign or Illustrator layout. A Photoshop document supports transparency and layers at its core, which you can leverage when you place it into InDesign, Illustrator, or even other Photoshop documents. And with support for multiple artboards, it's even easier to create different iterations of the same design in a single PSD file.

For web designers, the RGB and Index color modes are supported by PSD, allowing you to use color lookup tables (CLUTs) of web-safe colors.

In addition, you can add as many alpha channels as you want to a PSD file as long as the total number of channels, including the color mode channels, doesn't exceed 56. And there is no limitation on the number of paths you can save in a document. To learn more about Photoshop paths and alpha channels, consult Lesson 4, "Using Photoshop Paths, Alpha Channels, and Grayscale Images in InDesign."

The PSD format does come with a few limitations. You can save no more than 2GB of data in a single PSD file, and the canvas may measure only 30,000 pixels in either width or height. If your design goes over these limitations, Photoshop will offer to save your document in Large Document Format (PSB) (with the .psb filename extension).

A PSB file offers the same features as a PSD file, but allows you to save canvases measuring up to 300,000 pixels in width or height and store up to 4 exabytes (over 4.2 billion gigabytes) of data in a single file. A PSB file cannot be placed in InDesign, but Illustrator does support it.

PSD integration matrix

The following matrix provides an overview of the integration capabilities of the PSD file format when a PSD is placed into InDesign, Illustrator, or another Photoshop document. Know that more integrations are possible when combined with Adobe apps such as XD, Premiere Pro, After Effects, and others, which is beyond the scope of this book. The matrix keys the features to lessons in this book.

	Ps PSD to Id InDesign	Ps PSD to Ai Illustrator	Ps PSD to Ps Photoshop
Override layers	Override layer visibilty, directly from InDesign (see Lesson 3)	Convert layers to Illustrator objects when placing (see Lesson 2)	No
Apply Photoshop paths	Apply any path saved within the PSD (see Lesson 4)	Apply clipping path when placing	No
Paste vector paths from PSD	No (go through AI first)	Yes (see Lesson 2)	Yes
Export vector paths	No	Yes (see Lesson 2)	No
Apply alpha channel	Apply alpha channel when placing (see Lesson 4)	No	No
Switch layer comps	Change layer comp from InDesign (see Lesson 3)	Apply layer comp when placing	Change layer comp from Photoshop (see Lesson 7)
Live transparency	Yes	Yes	Yes
Creative Cloud Libraries	Share colors, graphics, character styles (see Lessons 8 & 9)	Share colors, graphics, character styles (see Lessons 8 & 9)	Share colors, graphics, layer styles, gradients, character styles (see Lessons 8 & 9)

InDesign (.indd)

The InDesign Document (INDD) file format was introduced in 1999, when InDesign was released as the official successor to PageMaker. Adobe acquired this early page layout application in 1994, and it served as the basis for the first InDesign build.

INDD is a vector file format that is able to store all the ingredients needed for multi-page design layout projects, including styles, text, native vector artwork, swatches, and images. However, despite its impressive capabilities, it's a file format that is pretty isolated, as it's not possible to place or embed INDD files in other applications, like Photoshop or Illustrator. In fact, you are able to open an INDD file only in InDesign or Adobe InCopy, InDesign's little sibling for setting up copyediting workflows. But this shouldn't be a problem, because 99.9% of the time designers need to place assets from other applications into InDesign, not the other way around. And if you do feel like taking InDesign content into other Adobe apps, you can use Creative Cloud Libraries to do so (see Lesson 8).

INDD integration matrix

The following matrix offers you a quick overview of all the integration capabilities of the INDD file format with Photoshop and Illustrator. You'll immediately notice that this matrix is a lot smaller than the one for Photoshop. As mentioned, InDesign documents are typically on the receiving end when it comes to exchanging assets. Because of this, not a lot of integrations are available with Photoshop or Illustrator. However, a few interesting techniques are possible when you place one INDD file into another, or when you use Creative Cloud Libraries to repurpose InDesign assets in other Adobe apps.

	to InDesign	to Illustrator	to Photoshop
Place one or multiple pages	During placing (see Lesson 7)	Not possible	Not possible
Include bleed or slug while placing pages	During placing (see Lesson 7)	Not possible	Not possible
Paste vector paths from InDesign	Yes	Yes	As embedded Smart Object
Creative Cloud Libraries	Share colors, character styles, paragraph styles, text, graphics (see Lesson 8)	Share colors, character styles, paragraph styles, text, graphics (see Lesson 8)	Share colors, character styles, graphics (see Lesson 8)

Illustrator (.ai)

The Adobe Illustrator (AI) format has been Illustrator's native file format since 2000, when Illustrator 9 was introduced. Before Illustrator 9, EPS was the default file format when saving files from Illustrator. But as technology evolved over the years, it became clear that the EPS file format was becoming outdated. And to use multiple artboards, live transparency, and more complex tools and capabilities, a new home for native Illustrator documents needed to be found. For the most part, EPS been replaced by PDF when saving Illustrator files for print.

Illustrator private data

When saving an Illustrator file using the default settings, Illustrator uses PDF as a container to store all document information, with a special section inside the PDF that holds unique Illustrator data (which we call *private data*). This private data is needed in order to correctly read the file in Illustrator while preserving Illustrator's unique capabilities, and it is never read when opening an AI file using a PDF viewer such as Adobe Acrobat Reader. That private data is the only data Illustrator needs in order to display your document and allow you to edit it. However, consider the Illustrator Options dialog box, which opens when you save an Illustrator file:

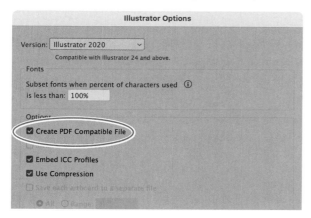

The Create PDF Compatible File option (which is selected by default) will embed a PDF version of the Illustrator private data into the AI file during saving. It's this PDF file that is read and used when placing or opening native Illustrator files in other applications. When you save a file with this option unselected, you will be greeted by the following result when trying to place the AI file in InDesign:

If you place an Illustrator document in InDesign, and that document was not saved with the Create PDF Compatible File option selected, you will see this error message instead of a file preview.

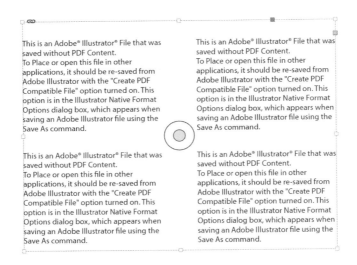

You will see the same message when trying to place the same file in Photoshop or when opening it in Acrobat Reader. Deselecting this option when saving makes it impossible to place or open native Illustrator documents in any other application (not just ones from Adobe), because these applications would normally place the PDF container information and not the private data. The fact that the PDF information is used during import into other Adobe apps is also made clear via not-so-subtle hints in the apps (as shown in the preceding figure). Pay attention to the highlighted areas of the following screenshots, where an Illustrator file is placed into Photoshop and InDesign, respectively:

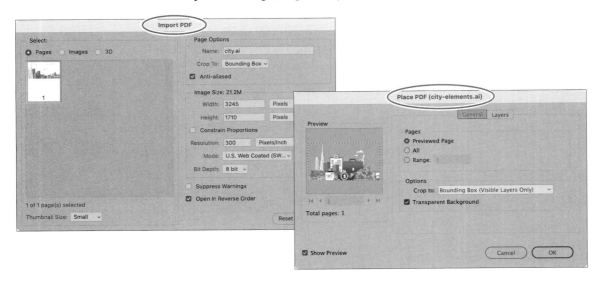

PDF versus AI

Now that we've established the fact that PDF data within an Illustrator document is what enables other apps to use the AI file, it's important to understand that this PDF data, which encapsulates the Illustrator private data in the file, is not the same data you get when you save a file to PDF for print output.

When you use the Save As command in Illustrator to save as a PDF file, note the Preserve Illustrator Editing Capabilities checkbox.

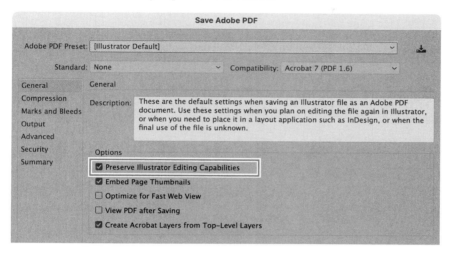

Selecting this option includes Illustrator's private data in the PDF, making it backward compatible with Illustrator. However, when you want to create a print-ready PDF according to ISO standards, it's impossible (and unnecessary) to include the private data.

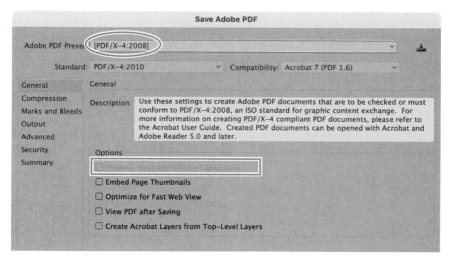

Because of this, I recommend that when you save an Illustrator document, save it as an AI file with Create PDF Compatible File selected in order to use the AI file in other applications. And if your client needs a PDF for print purposes, save a copy of your document as a PDF following the recommended ISO standard. If you start to interchange the formats by sending an AI file rather than a PDF to clients (for opening with a PDF viewer), and use a PDF as your Illustrator work document, there is always the risk that:

- Certain data in the file won't display correctly, depending on the PDF viewer.
- Edits made using PDF viewers will be applied only to the embedded PDF rather than to the Illustrator private data.

One of the reasons things can go wrong is that the PDF embedded in the AI file is created using an automated process, where you have no control over the various PDF options. But saving a file as a PDF does give you control over things like PDF version, layers, color management, and fonts.

AI integration matrix

Illustrator offers many compatibility and integration possibilities, mainly because the application in which we place the AI file picks up only the embedded PDF. Because of this, you can even place native Illustrator documents in Microsoft Office products like Word or PowerPoint while retaining live transparency.

	Ai to **Id** InDesign	**Ai** to **Ai** Illustrator	**Ai** to **Ps** Photoshop
Override layers	Override layer visibility, directly from InDesign (see Lesson 5)	No	No
Paste vector paths from AI	Yes (see Lesson 5)	Yes	Yes, as layers, paths, shapes or Smart Objects (see Lesson 6)
Live transparency	Yes	Yes	Yes
Place one or multiple artboards	During placing (see Lesson 5)	During placing (see Lesson 7)	During placing (see Lesson 6)
Crop placed AI to art or page box	During placing (see Lesson 5)	During placing (see Lesson 7)	During placing (see Lesson 6)
Place/open AI cloud documents	No	Yes, linked or embedded (see Lesson 9)	Yes, embedded (see Lesson 2)
Creative Cloud Libraries	Share colors, character styles, paragraph styles, text, graphics (see Lessons 8 & 9)	Share colors, character styles, paragraph styles, text, graphics (see Lessons 8 & 9)	Share colors, graphics, character styles (see Lessons 8 & 9)

Review questions

1 What is the primary advantage to using JPEG files?

2 What is the lossless compression called when saving a TIFF image?

3 Name two reasons why an AI file is better than an EPS file for saving vector artwork.

4 Name three capabilities of the PSD file format when placing in InDesign or Illustrator.

5 Why is it important to leave the Create PDF Compatible File option selected when saving a native Illustrator document?

Review answers

1 JPEG files excel at compressing image files while maintaining high image quality and giving you full control over the degree of compression. This makes it an excellent choice when saving large quantities of images.

2 TIFF offers two lossless compression algorithms that allow you to save images with no loss of quality. These are ZIP and LZW compression, both available from the TIFF dialog box when saving from Photoshop.

3 AI files support live transparency, multiple artboards, and layers. They also offer the most compact way of saving vector graphics, as EPS files can be two to three times as large as AI files.

4 Photoshop files offer many different capabilities, including support for alpha channels, paths, layers, and live transparency.

5 Selecting Create PDF Compatible File enables you to place the AI file in other applications, including InDesign, Photoshop, and third-party apps such as Microsoft Office.

2 ENRICHING ILLUSTRATOR ARTWORK WITH PHOTOSHOP CONTENT

Lesson overview

In this lesson, you'll learn how to do the following:

- Understand the different layer types in Adobe Photoshop.
- Place and embed Photoshop documents into Adobe Illustrator.
- Place and link local Photoshop documents into Illustrator.
- Place and link Photoshop cloud documents into Illustrator.
- Update linked Photoshop documents.
- Bring Photoshop paths into Illustrator.
- Apply a 3D effect to text.

 This lesson will take about 1 hour to complete. Please log in to your account at adobepress.com/DesignCIB to download the files for this lesson, or go to the "Getting Started" section at the beginning of this book and follow the instructions under "Accessing the Lesson Files and Web Edition." Store the files on your computer in a convenient location.

Your Account page is also where you'll find any updates to the lesson files. Look on the Lesson & Update Files tab to access the most current content.

The ability to place Adobe Photoshop content into Illustrator offers you a tremendous amount of flexibility and creative freedom.

Placing and managing Photoshop artwork in Illustrator

Creating documents that combine Photoshop and Illustrator artwork is a common workflow for designers. And the options available when bringing Photoshop content into your Illustrator document assure you a great deal of flexibility when going back and forth between applications.

Embedding versus linking when placing

Note: Once you create a link to a document, be careful about renaming or deleting the document or moving it to a different location. Doing so will break the link and Illustrator will prompt you to fix the link the next time you open the file.

Throughout this book, when you *place* content from one application into a document in another application you will often be presented with a choice between *embedding* it and *linking* it. Each method comes with its advantages and disadvantages, and it is up to you to decide which path to take. By the time you have finished the exercises in this book you'll be better able to make that choice.

- Linking inserts a reference to an external file. The linked file remains completely independent.

- Embedding inserts a copy of the entire document into the Illustrator document at full resolution.

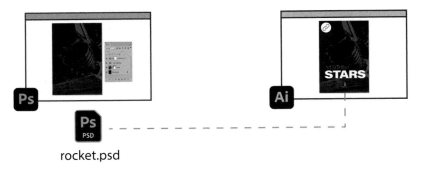

rocket.psd

Workflow criteria

Let's go over a few of the criteria that will help you make better workflow decisions. When in doubt, ask yourself the following questions.

Will the placed file be changed?

This is probably the most important question to ask yourself. How often might you need to update your placed document? Hypothetically speaking, what creative or technical impact would your project suffer if it were impossible for you to update the placed artwork in your document? If this question makes you nervous, it would be best to link the document instead of embedding it, to ensure easy future updates. Also remember that others might ask you to update your work later, since artwork often needs to go through an approval process when, for example, working for a client. So try to anticipate this as you build your projects.

Is the placed file a "heavy" file?

Another good argument for choosing to link the placed artwork instead of embedding it is the amount of data that you are bringing into Illustrator. Embedding means adding all data to the Illustrator document. This means that the entire file size of all placed Photoshop documents will increase your Illustrator document's size by potentially dozens or hundreds of megabytes (or even gigabytes) of data. This is not always problematic, but given the potential complexity of the placed Photoshop artwork, the complexity of the Illustrator document, your computer hardware specifications, and the available hard drive disk space and network bandwidth, you might want to consider linking versus embedding the Photoshop document in order to avoid slowdowns in your workflow.

Will I need to share the placed Photoshop document across teams or projects?

Also consider the possibility of needing to collaborate on your project with other stakeholders or team members by means of sharing the document—for example, via a server or online drive. Embedding Photoshop artwork (instead of linking) would take away the ability for them to access the same version you're working on. Additionally, you would no longer have the ability to place and link the same document in other Adobe applications, like InDesign, Illustrator, and others.

If this is the case, then the probability of needing to update multiple instances of the same Photoshop file at the same time is very high. This is a clear argument in favor of linking instead of embedding, since it allows us to link multiple documents to a single source of truth that can be easily updated for all projects at the same time.

It is also possible that others might need to use the same artwork in their design, especially when you work in a large team. If you choose to embed artwork, it might take some time to dissect and extract the embedded artwork from the Illustrator document before your teammates can use it.

When is it appropriate to embed Photoshop artwork in Illustrator?

The answer to this question is based entirely on the answers in the previous paragraphs. If the answer to all three questions is no, then embedding Photoshop artwork can be a good practice. Embedding Photoshop documents in Illustrator gives you the following advantages:

▶ **Tip:** Illustrator allows you to convert linked files into embedded files, and vice versa, using the Properties panel.

- You have the option of converting Photoshop layers into Illustrator objects while placing, giving you the ability to modify these objects directly in Illustrator.

- Embedding artwork in Illustrator enables you to apply the full range of filters and effects available in the app to the placed artwork.

- Embedding artwork makes it easier to manage your file.

Linking a Photoshop document in Illustrator

In the following exercise you'll learn how to place and link a Photoshop document into an Illustrator document and update its contents.

Getting started

You'll start the lesson by viewing an image of the final composition and placed artwork.

1 Start Photoshop, and choose Photoshop > Preferences > General (Mac) or Edit > Preferences > General (Win).

2 In the Preferences dialog box, click Reset Preferences On Quit. Then restart Photoshop.

3 From the Lesson02/Imports folder, open rocket-end.psd.

The image of a rocket has been recolored in Photoshop using adjustment layers. The final image will be used to create a poster in Illustrator.

4 Close rocket-end.psd.

5 Start Illustrator, and choose Illustrator > Preferences > General (Mac) or Edit > Preferences > General (Win).

6 In the Preferences dialog box, click Reset Preferences, then click OK.

7 In the dialog box that opens, click Restart Now.

8 From the Lesson02 folder, open L02-poster-end.ai.

Here you can see how the placed Photoshop document is used in Illustrator to create a poster.

9 Close the file.

Inspecting the Photoshop and Illustrator documents

1 Launch Photoshop and open rocket-start.psd from the Lesson02/Imports folder.

2 Choose File > Save As. Photoshop will prompt you to choose between saving the file as a local document and saving it as a cloud document. Select Don't Show Again, and click Save On Your Computer.

3 Save the file as **rocketWorking.psd**.

4 Inspect the Layers panel and notice that the design consists of three layers:

- A regular background layer.

- A layer named "rocket" with a vector mask attached.

- A fill layer called "color mapping."

⬤ **Note:** If you can't find the Layers panel, remember that it might be hidden. Choose Window > Layers to open it.

5 Choose Image > Image Size.

Notice that the document measures 24.25 in. x 36.25 in.

● **Note:** Despite its large dimensions, this document is too low in resolution for a printed poster. But since this exercise is about the importance of file linking, this is a problem we can ignore.

6 Click OK to close the dialog box.

7 Leave the file open.

8 Launch Illustrator.

9 From the Lesson02 folder, open L02-poster-start.ai.

10 Choose File > Save As. Illustrator will prompt you to choose between saving the file as a local document and saving it as a cloud document. Select Don't Show Again, and click Save On Your Computer.

11 Save the file as **L02-posterWorking.ai**.

● **Note:** The transparency grid has been turned on to make the white elements on the artboard easier to see.

12 Open the Layers panel and notice there are two layers:

- *text* holds all the text layers, which are currently the only visible elements in the document.

- *background*, which is currently empty.

13 In the Tools panel, select the Artboard tool ▣.

14 In the Properties panel, look at the Transform controls at the top right of the screen and notice that the artboard measures 24 x 36 in.

15 Choose File > Document Setup.

16 Notice that there is a bleed of 0.125 in. applied around the artboard.

17 Click OK to close the dialog box.

Placing and linking

1 In Illustrator, on the Layers panel select the layer named *background*.

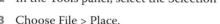

2 In the Tools panel, select the Selection tool ▶.

3 Choose File > Place.

4 Navigate to the folder containing rocketWorking.psd and select the file.

5 Make sure the Link option is selected and that the Template and Show Import Options options are unselected.

6 Click Place.

7 With the loaded cursor, click once on the artboard to place the Photoshop document.

Next, you'll position the linked file on the artboard. Recall that the artboard is 24 x 36, the linked file is 24.25 x 36.25, and the difference is equal to the bleed we defined in the Document Setup dialog box (0.125 on all sides).

With those values in mind, you'll set the upper-left corner of the file to be 0.125 to the left of the edge of the artboard and 0.125 above it; the linked file will be exactly centered over the artboard.

8 In the Properties panel, under Transform, click the top left Reference Point.

9 In the Properties panel, change both the X and Y values to **−0.125** in. to fit the image on the artboard.

The sum of the project artboard and bleed values equals the size of the Photoshop document, resulting in a perfect fit.

10 Looking at the Properties panel, notice that the graphic is labeled Linked File.

11 Click the Linked File label at the top left of the screen to temporarily open the Links panel.

Notice the link icon next to the artwork filename.

12 Double-click the placed filename to expand its properties.

The Location metadata provides the path to the linked source folder.

▶ **Tip:** Clicking the path to the placed link reveals the folder in which it resides.

Updating the Photoshop document

1 Return to Photoshop.

2 At the bottom of the Layers panel, click the New Adjustment Layer button and choose Hue/Saturation to create a new adjustment layer.

The Properties panel now shows Hue/Saturation options.

● **Note:** If you can't find the Proper- ties panel, choose Window > Properties.

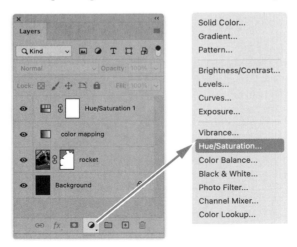

3 In the Properties panel, drag the Hue slider to the right until you reach a value of roughly **+140**. The rocket now turns bright green and the background receives a warm tint.

4 Choose File > Save to save your work.

5 Return to Illustrator.

6 Illustrator informs you that a linked file has been modified. Click Yes to update the file.

● **Note:** If you accidentally clicked No when you were prompted to update the linked file, you can always update the file in the Links panel (choose Window > Links).

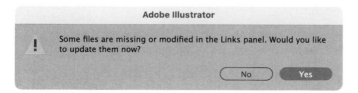

7 Save your work.

8 Close the file but leave Illustrator open.

Embedding a Photoshop document in Illustrator

The following exercise will present you with a good example of when to embed a Photoshop document into Illustrator.

● **Note:** This book assumes that Photoshop and Illustrator are using their default settings. If you are unsure of how to return to the default settings, review the steps in "Linking a Photoshop document in Illustrator."

Getting started

You'll start the lesson by viewing an image of the final composition and placed artwork.

1   From the Lesson02/Imports folder, open dish-start.psd in Photoshop.

2   Make sure Photoshop is using the Essentials workspace by choosing Window > Workspace > Essentials. Then choose Window > Workspace > Reset Essentials.

This Photoshop document will be embedded in Illustrator as part of an ad campaign.

3   Leave the document open, and from the Lesson02 folder, open L02-menu-end.ai in Illustrator.

4   Reset the Illustrator workspace by choosing Window > Workspace > Essentials and then choosing Window > Workspace > Reset Essentials.

This document is the finished menu ad. Notice that Illustrator was able to reuse vector shapes from Photoshop (situated around the dish) when it was placed.

5   Close the document but leave Illustrator open.

Inspecting the project files

1 Return to dish-start.psd in Photoshop.

2 Inspect the Layers panel and note that the design consists of seven layers:

- A regular background layer

- Three adjustment layers for changing the background's sharpness, color vibrancy, and contrast

- Three consecutively named shape layers

3 Return to Illustrator.

4 From the Lesson02 folder, open L02-menu-start.ai.

5 Choose File > Save As, and save the file as **L02-menuWorking.psd**.

6 Click the Layers panel and note that there are two layers:

- *text* holds all the text and shape layers, which are currently the only visible elements in the document.

- *background*, which is currently empty.

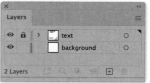

Placing and embedding

1 In Illustrator, click the background layer in order to add items to it.

2 Choose File > Place.

3 Navigate to the Lesson02/Imports folder and click to select dish-start.psd.

4 Deselect the Link option to embed the placed document.

5 Verify that the Template option is unselected.

6 Select Show Import Options.

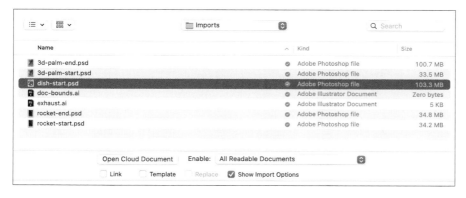

7 Click Place.

8 In the Photoshop Import Options dialog box, select Convert Layers To Objects. This option will keep Photoshop shape and type layers editable in Illustrator.

● **Note:** The message at the bottom of the dialog box warns us that because the Photoshop and Illustrator documents use different color modes, different transparency effects will result. This is not a concern in this exercise, because no transparent effects are used in the Photoshop document.

● **Note:** Photoshop shape or type layers affected by layer blending modes or adjustment layers will be flattened when placed into Illustrator. This prevents unexpected results. Because of this it will not be possible to manipulate these objects once they are imported into Illustrator.

9 Click OK to close the dialog box.

10 With the loaded cursor, start dragging from the upper-left corner of the red rectangle surrounding the document (the bleed) to the lower-right corner to place the graphic. The design will overflow the document a little bit, which is fine.

Editing converted objects

1   Use the Selection tool ![pointer] to select the placed image. The Properties panel identifies this object as a *group*.

2   Choose Object > Ungroup, or press Shift+Cmd+G/Shift+Ctrl+G.

3   Deselect all objects by clicking the gray zone surrounding the artboard.

4   In the Layers panel, twirl open the background layer by clicking the arrow icon. Note that the three Photoshop shape layers have been retained and are available for editing in Illustrator.

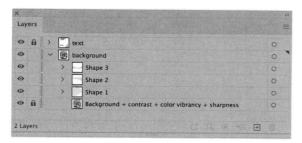

Now that this Photoshop file has been placed in Illustrator, the bottom layer in the background group is the product of merging the Photoshop background layer with the adjustment layers above it. This layer has also been locked because it was locked in the original Photoshop document.

5   Select the object named Shape 1 by clicking in the selection column at the far right side of the layer. A color box appears in the column to indicate that the layer is selected.

6   Hold down the Shift key and use the same method to add Shape 2 and Shape 3 to your selection.

7   Choose Window > Pathfinder to open the Pathfinder panel.

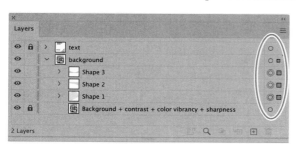

> **Tip:** When you embed Photoshop documents in Illustrator documents, shape layers will be converted into compound shapes, meaning they consist of more than one object. To avoid unexpected results, it is good practice to convert these compound shapes into regular objects first.

8   With the current active selection, click the Expand button in the Pathfinder panel to convert all compound shapes into regular objects.

The currently selected object type has changed from Compound Shape to Path.

9 Double-click the Fill color icon in the Tools panel to open the Color Picker, and change the color values of the selected objects as follows: C: **91%** M: **85%** Y: **38%** K: **30%**.

10 Click OK to close the Color Picker.

● **Note:** Because we chose to embed the Photoshop document in an Illustrator document, no edits made in the original Photoshop file will be reflected in the Illustrator composition.

11 In the Properties panel, lower the Opacity value to 50%.

12 Deselect all objects.

13 Save your work.

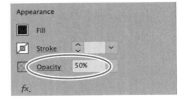

Copying and pasting graphics

In addition to using the Place command in Illustrator, it's also possible to copy and paste layers directly from Photoshop into Illustrator. If the Copy Merged command was used in Photoshop to copy information from multiple layers, all data will be merged and pasted as a single embedded image in Illustrator. There are two potential disadvantages to pasting from Photoshop:

First, if there is more data selected than your computer clipboard memory can store you will get an error that reads "Could Not Export The Clipboard Because It Is Too Big To Export." This means that there was more data selected than Photoshop can export, making it impossible to paste into Illustrator (or any other app for that matter).

Second, pasting from Photoshop doesn't offer you any import options for converting layers to objects.

Unembedding a placed file

Embedding a placed Photoshop file in Illustrator means that some or all Photoshop layers were merged during the import process. The Links panel in Illustrator will display all of the placed files in the current document, both linked and embedded. You can use commands on the Links panel menu to embed linked files and even to unembed embedded files. The Links panel identifies linked files using a link icon while embedded files have no additional icon. Selecting any link in the Links panel and clicking the Link Info button (the downward pointing triangle) will allow you to see additional information about the selected link. However, it is very important to realize that Illustrator can't recreate the original Photoshop layers during the unembedding process, which means the embedded file will be converted to a linked flattened Photoshop document.

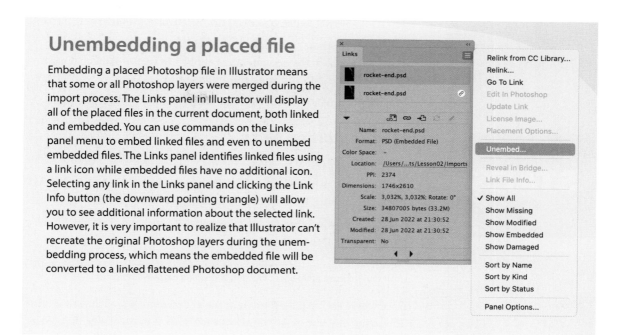

Using Photoshop paths in Illustrator

Adobe Illustrator is a vector drawing program. But other applications, such as Photoshop, also include the ability to draw vector paths. Photoshop's vector drawing tools, like the Pen or shape tools, allow you to accurately create shapes, masks, or selections. In the following exercise you'll learn how to recycle Photoshop vector paths by bringing them into Illustrator.

● **Note:** This book assumes that Photoshop and Illustrator are using their default settings. If you are unsure of how to return to the default settings, review the steps in " Linking a Photoshop document in Illustrator."

Getting started

You'll start the lesson by viewing an image of the final composition and placed artwork.

1   Return to Photoshop.

2   Reset the Photoshop Workspace by choosing Window > Workspace > Essentials and then choosing Window > Workspace > Reset Essentials.

3   Return to Illustrator.

4   Reset the Illustrator Workspace by choosing Window > Workspace > Essentials and then choosing Window > Workspace > Reset Essentials.

5 From the Lesson02 folder, open L02-advanced-poster-end.ai in Illustrator.

This project continues the rocket poster we worked on earlier. The line and grid patterns in the document are applied to vector paths that were created in Photoshop and copied into Illustrator.

6 Close the document without saving changes, but leave Illustrator open.

Viewing Photoshop paths

1 From Photoshop, open rocket-start.psd from the Lesson02/Imports folder.

2 Open the Paths panel, which is by default located in the same panel group as the Layers panel. If you can't find it, choose Window > Paths.

Note the five paths saved in the Paths panel. These were created with the Pen tool and Ellipse tool.

● **Note:** Read Lesson 4, "Using Photoshop Paths, Alpha Channels, and Grayscale Images in InDesign," to learn more about creating and saving paths in Photoshop.

3 To see where each path is located in the document, click each path in the Paths panel to select it. As you select each path, it becomes highlighted in the document.

Keep the file open.

Copying and pasting paths

In the next part of the exercise you'll learn how to reuse a Photoshop path in Illustrator by means of copying and pasting. We'll then apply a pattern fill to the paths in Illustrator.

1 In rocket-start.psd, in the Paths panel, click the path named rocket.

The rocket path becomes highlighted on the canvas.

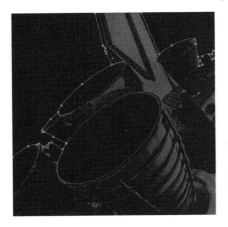

2 In the Tools panel, select the Path Selection tool ▶ (not to be confused with the Move tool ✛).

3 Click the path on the canvas to select it; note that its anchor points become highlighted.

4 Press Cmd+C/Ctrl+C to copy the path to the clipboard.

5 In Illustrator, open L02-advanced-poster-start.ai from the Lesson02 folder.

6 Choose File > Save As and save the file as **L02-advanced-posterWorking.ai**.

7 In the Layers panel, click to select the layer named pattern.

8 Press Cmd+V/Ctrl+V to paste the path.

9 In the Paste Options dialog box, select Compound Shape, then click OK.

10 With the active selection, double-click the Fill color in the Tools panel and apply a random color to the path in order to see it better.

11 Choose View > Smart Guides to activate Smart Guides (if there is a checkmark next to the menu item, that means it was already active).

▶ **Tip:** Since the pasted path doesn't include any overlapping shapes, it doesn't really matter which option you choose. But if you are pasting several overlapping shapes at once it is recommended to select Compound Shape, as it gives you more flexibility over how the individual shapes interact with each other. You can then use the Pathfinder panel in Illustrator to choose to add, subtract, or exclude individual pairs of objects.

12 Use the Selection tool 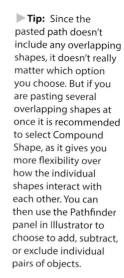 to align the rocket path with the lower-right corner of the bleed area. It should snap automatically to the edge thanks to the Smart Guides. When it's in position, deselect it.

We now have an object shaped like a rocket. But what we want to create is a shape that covers the entire artboard except for the rocket. In other words, we need a way to invert the shape we have. We'll use a large rectangle and the Pathfinder panel to achieve this.

13 In the Tools panel, select the Rectangle tool.

14 Using the Rectangle tool, draw a large rectangle from the upper-left corner of the bleed to the lower-right corner, completely overlapping our design. The Smart Guides should help you to perfectly align the rectangle to the corners of the bleed.

15 In the Layers panel, the pattern layer should now show you two objects named <Rectangle> and <Compound Path>. With the active selection of the rectangle, hold down the Shift key and click the same area next to the <Compound Path> layer to add it to the selection.

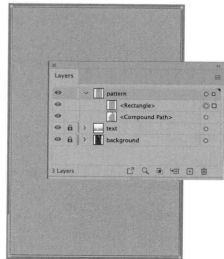

● **Note:** If needed, choose Window > Pathfinder to open the Pathfinder panel.

16 In the Pathfinder area in the Properties panel, click the Exclude button to make a rocket-shaped hole in the selection.

17 Open the Swatches panel and click the 6 lpi 40% pattern swatch to apply a purple line pattern to the fill of the shape.

18 Deselect the shape.

Exporting paths

In the next step we'll need to import the paths around the rocket exhausts into Illustrator. While doing so, we want to keep their relative positioning and move all four paths in unison. Because of this we'll choose the Export command as an alternative method for transferring Photoshop paths into Illustrator. There are two main advantages to this technique:

- Exporting paths creates a separate Illustrator.ai document, which you can store for future reference or easily share with others. Whereas copying and pasting a path should be considered a quick, one-off technique.

- The exported document will retain the canvas size and absolute position of all paths in the document.

1 Launch Photoshop and open rocket-start.psd from the Lesson02/Imports folder (if it's not already open).

2 Choose File > Export > Paths To Illustrator.

3. In the Export Paths To File dialog box, choose All Paths from the Paths menu. Click OK to confirm.

4. Name the file **exhaust.ai** and save it.

5. Return to Illustrator and open the newly created exhaust.ai.

   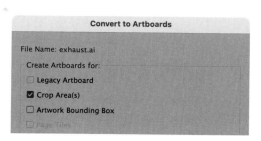

   It's important we choose the correct options when opening the document, as the wrong choice will disregard Photoshop's original canvas size and absolute path positioning.

6. In the Convert To Artboards dialog box, make sure only Crop Area(s) is selected.

7. Click OK to confirm.

   When Illustrator opens the document, it will append [Converted] to the filename. This is because the Export Paths To File dialog box in Photoshop creates documents in legacy Illustrator formats, which Illustrator first needs to convert to its newer file system.

8. Press Cmd+0/Ctrl+0 to to zoom out and fit the entire artboard onscreen.

9. Press Cmd+Y/Ctrl+Y to turn on Outline mode. This shows you the outlines of the exported paths.

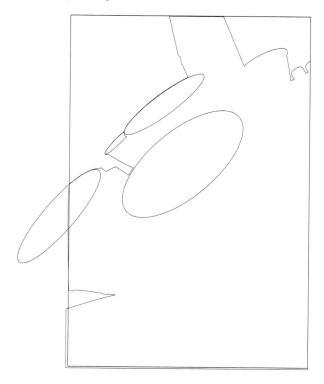

10 Using the Selection tool 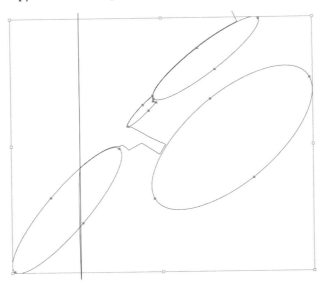, Shift-click to select the four exhaust objects and copy them to the clipboard. Don't select the rocket itself this time.

11 Return to L02-advanced-posterWorking.ai.

12 Make sure the pattern layer is still highlighted in the Layers panel.

13 Choose Edit > Paste In Front to paste the artwork in place at the top of the layer stack.

14 With the current selection still active, click the Grid .5 Inch Lines swatch in the Swatches panel to apply a green grid pattern. Keep the selection active.

15 Choose Effect > Distort & Transform > Transform.

16 In the Transform Effect dialog box, deselect Transform Objects and select Transform Patterns.

17 Now change the Angle value to **45°**.

18 Choose OK to close the dialog box, and then deselect all objects.

19 Save your work.

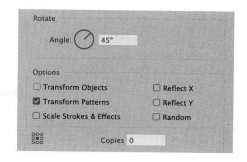

Photoshop cloud documents in Illustrator

Multiple applications in Adobe Creative Cloud offer the ability to save documents as cloud documents. This includes Adobe Photoshop, Illustrator, XD, Fresco, and InDesign. Saving a document as a cloud document unlocks specific features that you can use to your advantage. This exercise will demonstrate the basic linking functionality when working with a cloud document. The main thing to understand for now is that a cloud document is a regular document that is saved in Creative Cloud's online infrastructure instead of your desktop or server. This means the cloud document is available to you from any location (as long as you have an active internet connection).

▶**Tip:** To learn more about cloud documents, check out Lesson 9, "Collaborating using Creative Cloud Libraries and Cloud Documents."

Getting started

You'll start the lesson by viewing an image of the final composition and placed artwork.

1 Return to Photoshop.

2 Reset the Photoshop Workspace by choosing Window > Workspace > Essentials and then choosing Window > Workspace > Reset Essentials.

3 Return to Illustrator.

4 From the Lesson02 folder, open L02-holiday-end.ai in Illustrator.

The background in this image is a linked Photoshop cloud document. You'll soon learn how to place a Photoshop cloud document in Illustrator yourself. Additionally, you'll use Illustrator's 3D features to add 3D text to the design.

5 Reset the Illustrator Workspace by choosing Window > Workspace > Essentials and then choosing Window > Workspace > Reset Essentials.

6 Close the document but leave Illustrator open.

●**Note:** This book assumes that Photoshop and Illustrator are using their default settings. If you are unsure of how to return to the default settings, review the steps in "Linking a Photoshop document in Illustrator."

Saving a Photoshop cloud document

1   Launch Photoshop and open 3d-palm-start.psd from the Lesson02/Imports folder.

    This document is a local Photoshop file. We'll now save a copy of the document in the cloud.

2   Choose File > Save As.

3   In the Save As dialog box, select Save To Cloud Documents.

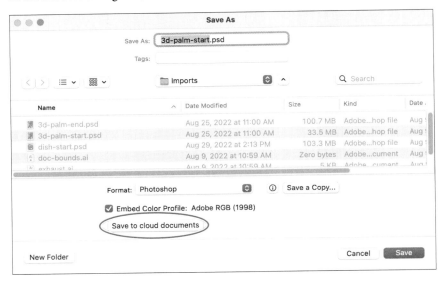

4   In the Save To Creative Cloud dialog box, name the file **3d-palm** and click Save to save the document as a Photoshop cloud document.

    The filename in the document tab changes to **3d-palm.psdc** and a cloud icon appears next to it. Leave the file open.

● **Note:** Photoshop cloud documents use the PSDC file format; the C stands for "cloud."

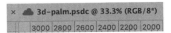

Placing a Photoshop cloud document in Illustrator

1   In Illustrator, open L02-holiday-start.ai from the Lesson02 folder.

2   Choose File > Save As and save the file as **L02-holidayWorking.ai**.

3. Inspect the Layers panel and notice that the design consists of three layers:

- *top frame* holds a white frame.
- *text* holds all text elements.
- *background* is an empty layer.

4. Click the background layer.

5. Choose File > Place.

6. In the dialog box that appears, click Open Cloud Document.

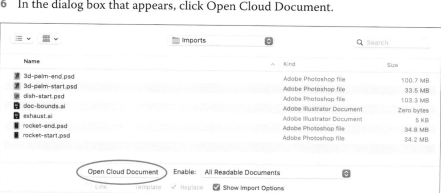

The Place From Creative Cloud dialog box opens, displaying all the cloud documents that are available for placing. This includes Photoshop cloud documents and documents from Adobe Fresco.

7. Click to select 3d-palm. Next, make sure Linked is selected at the bottom of the dialog box.

8. Click Place.

9. With the loaded cursor, drag from the upper-left corner of the artboard to the lower-right corner to place and fit the graphic to the artboard.

10. While the image is still selected, click the Linked File label at the top of the Properties panel to temporarily view the Links panel. Notice the cloud and link icons.

11 In the temporary Links panel, double-click the placed filename to expand its properties. Notice that the Location metadata clearly mentions the cloud source.

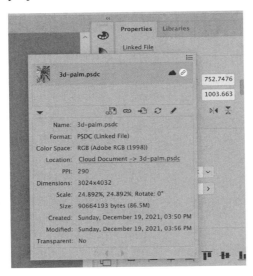

12 Click away from the Links panel to make it disappear.

Updating a Photoshop cloud document

1 Return to Photoshop, where 3d-palm.psdc should still be open.

2 In the Layers panel, select the Background layer.

3 Press Cmd+J/Ctrl+J to duplicate the layer.

4 Double-click the name of the duplicated layer and rename it **3d**.

In the next few steps we'll create a 3D effect by displacing the red channel of the layer.

5 Double-click the 3d layer thumbnail to open the Layer Style dialog box.

6 In the Advanced Blending section of the Blending Options panel you'll find three Channels options: R (red), G (green), and B (blue). Deselect G and B, leaving only the red channel active.

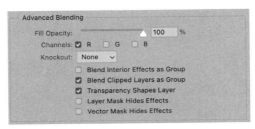

7 Click OK to close the dialog box.

8 Select the Move tool ⊹ from the Tools panel.

9 With the 3d layer still selected, hold down the Shift key and then press the Left Arrow key a few times to nudge the image to the left 10 pixels at a time. Nudge the layer about 10 times until you get a 3D effect.

10 Choose File > Save to update the cloud document.

11 Return to Illustrator and L02-holidayWorking.ai.

Illustrator presents you with a message that linked files are missing or have been modified.

12 Select the Background layer, then click Linked File in the Properties panel to display the Links panel.

The Update Available icon next to the cloud icon indicates the document needs to be refreshed.

13 Click the Update Link button to update the graphic.

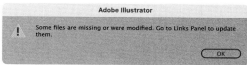

● **Note:** Because this is a cloud document, updating the link might take a few seconds after you click the button. Be patient.

Update Link button   Update Available icon

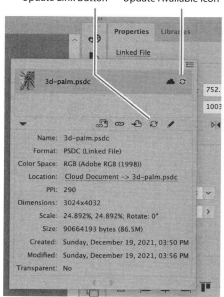

● **Note:** Because it's not possible to link your exercise to the author's cloud document, a local version was used to create L02-holiday-end.ai to illustrate the result of the project.

14 Keep the document open.

Adding 3D text

1 Using the Selection tool , select the "3D" object. This object consists of a pair of text characters that have been converted into outlines (shapes) with a white fill and a red and blue stroke, respectively.

● **Note:** At the time of writing, the 3D And Materials panel is still considered a Technology Preview by Adobe. This means it may not be completely production-ready yet. Exercise discretion while using it.

2 Choose Effect > 3D And Materials > Extrude & Bevel. The 3D And Materials panel appears.

3 In the 3D And Materials panel, change the Depth value to 100 px.

4 Change the Rotation values to 10°, 10°, and 0°.

5 Click the Lighting tab at the top of the panel.

   • Set Intensity to 100%.

   • Set Rotation to 84°.

   • Set Height to 44°.

   • Set Softness to 45%.

   • Deselect Ambient Light.

6 Close the 3D And Materials panel.

7 Save your work, and keep the file open.

Packaging the project

Every time you place and link files into Adobe Illustrator, a relationship is created between the two documents. This principle is the same regardless of the location of the linked document—that is, your hard drive, your server, or the cloud. When you ultimately finish your project, it is recommended that you package all the linked assets together.

The main advantage of packaging your work is that it creates a standalone version of your project with its own version of the linked files. This means that accidental changes to linked artwork—for example, changes made by someone who has access to the artwork but was unaware it was linked to your project—will not affect your main project.

When you create a package, a folder is created that holds the following:

- A duplicate of your project file.

- A subfolder that holds copies of all linked content.

- A subfolder that has copies of all the local fonts used in the document. Note that because of licensing restrictions, fonts synchronized via Adobe Fonts are never included in a package, only local fonts.

Note: Because embedded graphics are included in the Illustrator document, you will not find them in a separate folder. Only linked content is collected.

Then, all links in the duplicate project (in this case, the Illustrator document) are relinked to the duplicated linked files in the newly created subfolder.

1 Choose File > Package.

2 Choose a location to store the packaged folder.

3 Name the folder **L02-holiday-end_Folder**.

   Leave all options selected.

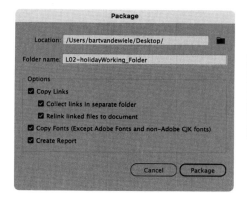 

4 Click Package.

   If a prompt with legal information regarding fonts appears, click OK.

Once your package is created, it is ready to be sent to others (your printer, client, or coworker) or to be archived on a server as a backup.

Note: Because all fonts in this project were converted to outlines, no fonts will be packaged. Also, when this is written, cloud documents will not be included in an Illustrator package.

Review questions

1 Name two advantages of linking a Photoshop document in Illustrator, compared to embedding.

2 You are viewing Import Options of an embedded Photoshop document in Illustrator and select Convert Layers To Objects. What will happen to any adjustment layers that exist in the placed Photoshop document?

3 Name one advantage of using the Export > Paths To Illustrator command in Photoshop, compared to pasting paths from Photoshop to Illustrator.

4 What might prevent you from copying and pasting graphics from Photoshop into Illustrator?

5 After you've embedded a layered Photoshop document in Illustrator, is there still a way to recover the original document?

Review answers

1 Linking a Photoshop document in Illustrator allows the user to update the original file in Photoshop. It can also prevent the Illustrator file from becoming "heavy," since the Photoshop document is not embedded in the Illustrator document.

2 Illustrator can't convert Photoshop adjustment layers to Illustrator objects. Because of this, all adjustment layers will be merged down into the first image layer in the Photoshop layer stack.

3 Using the Paths To Illustrator command in Photoshop will allow you to export all paths in the Photoshop document at once. Additionally, the exported file will match the original Photoshop canvas size.

4 When you have more data selected in Photoshop than your computer clipboard can store, an error message will appear that tells you the clipboard can't be exported.

5 Embedding a Photoshop document in Illustrator will flatten the document permanently. It is possible to convert the embedded file to a linked file by choosing the Unembed command from the Links panel menu, however this will result in a flattened linked file being created.

3 USING LAYERED PHOTOSHOP FILES IN INDESIGN

Lesson overview

In this lesson, you'll learn how to do the following:

- Change the layer visibility of placed Adobe Photoshop documents in Adobe InDesign to achieve various effects.

- Learn techniques for discovering layer overrides in a document.

- Build layer comps in Photoshop.

- Update layer comps.

- Use Layer comps for creating multiple versions of the same document in InDesign.

 This lesson will take about 45 minutes to complete. Please log in to your account on adobepress.com/DesignCIB to download the files for this lesson, or go to the "Getting Started" section at the beginning of this book and follow the instructions under "Accessing the lesson files and Web Edition." Store the files on your computer in a convenient location.

Your Account page is also where you'll find any updates to the lesson files. Look on the Lesson & Update Files tab to access the most current content.

Photoshop layer comps let you create variations of an image within a single Photoshop document. This feature gains extra power when you place these documents in InDesign. The ability to control the visibility of Photoshop layers in InDesign lets you create layouts that incorporate the variants you set up in Photoshop.

Managing Photoshop layer visibility in InDesign

In the previous lesson you learned that layers play an essential role in Adobe Photoshop documents and are part of the DNA of that document. Showing or hiding a single layer in the layer stack can dramatically change the look and feel of a design. While the ability to show and hide layers in Photoshop adds flexibility when designing a document, it can also work to your disadvantage in some situations.

Version control

I'm sure we've all been there before. You are working on a design in Photoshop that needs to be placed in InDesign and you can't decide which version of your design you like best. Do you go for a version full of special effects and extra detail, or for an alternate version in which all those special layers are hidden? Although it's easy to quickly show or hide the special effects layers while working in Photoshop, it can be challenging to make that switch within InDesign.

So how do we solve this? One method would be to duplicate the Photoshop document and save both versions as separate documents. That way, your client can choose to place version A or version B in InDesign. And there is nothing wrong with that. However, this comes with a few disadvantages:

- Duplicating your Photoshop document means you must manage two files for a single design.

- Photoshop documents can take up a lot of storage space, so this scenario would double the amount of space needed to store the project.

- Because both versions also have layers in common with one another, it can be challenging to update both Photoshop designs when a change is required to one of these shared layers.

- Replacing version A with version B from within InDesign can require multiple steps, depending on the complexity of your InDesign document.

The InDesign approach

The solution to this problem lies within Adobe InDesign, which gives you the unique ability to decide which layers of a placed document should remain visible or hidden, without altering the original document. This is what we call a *local layer override*. And InDesign allows you to apply layer overrides when placing Photoshop documents, Illustrator documents, PDF documents, or other InDesign documents. The latter is what we sometimes refer to as *document nesting*, and you can learn more about it in Lesson 7, "Nesting Documents."

The advantage of creating layer overrides is that it allows you to create different versions of your placed document by showing or hiding specific layers from that document without altering the original.

While all this seems amazing, there are a few risks you need to look out for. We'll discuss them in depth throughout this lesson.

Tip: When you override layers in InDesign, you'll notice that the original Photoshop document looks unaltered when it's opened in Photoshop.

Creating different versions using adjustment layers

In this first exercise you'll learn how to radically change the look and feel of a Photoshop document in InDesign by showing or hiding adjustment layers. This technique allows us to create alternative versions of the same design using only a single Photoshop document.

Inspecting the Photoshop document

1 Start Photoshop, and choose Photoshop > Preferences > General (macOS) or Edit > Preferences > General (Windows).

   The Preferences dialog box opens.

2 Click Reset Preferences On Quit and click OK in the confirmation dialog box. Then restart Photoshop.

3 Open pier.psd from the Lesson03/Imports folder.

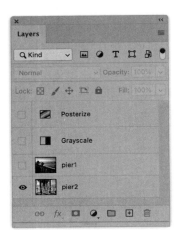

4 Inspect the Layers panel and notice there are four layers in total:

- An image layer named pier1

- An image layer named pier2

- An adjustment layer named Grayscale that converts all layers underneath it to black and white

- An adjustment layer named Posterize that applies the Posterize effect to all layers underneath it

● **Note:** Both adjustment layers are currently hidden (or deactivated). This lets us choose which adjustment layer we want to use with which image layer after the document is placed into InDesign.

Placing the Photoshop document and overriding layers

1 Start InDesign, and then press Control+Option+Shift+Command/ Alt+Shift+Ctrl to restore the default preferences.

2 When prompted, click Yes to delete the Adobe InDesign Settings file.

3 From the Lesson03 folder, open L03-postcard-start.indd.

4 Choose File > Save As, and save the file as **L03-postcardWorking.indd**.

5 Using the Selection tool ▶, select the gray graphics frame on the page.

6 Choose File > Place, and navigate to the Imports subfolder within the Lesson03 folder. Select the file pier.psd and, if necessary, deselect Show Import Options at the bottom of the dialog box. Click Open to place the file.

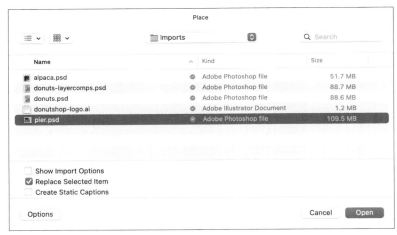

7 Using the Selection tool ▶, select the Ventura Pier text object. Note that the text has been converted to a graphics frame containing the text converted to outlines.

8 With the selection active, Choose File > Place.

9 Select pier.psd again, but this time, select Show Import Options before clicking Open.

▶ **Tip:** Text that has been converted to outlines is converted to vector shapes and will no longer be editable as live text.

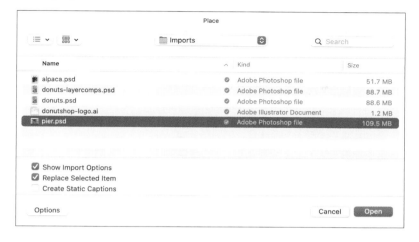

10 Click Open to display the Image Import Options dialog box.

11 In the Image Import Options dialog box, click the Layers tab to display the document layers.

▶ **Tip:** You can also temporarily activate the Import Options by holding down the Shift key while choosing Open.

12 Click the empty area to the left of the Grayscale layer to make it visible. An eye icon appears and the preview window updates accordingly, showing a grayscale version of the image.

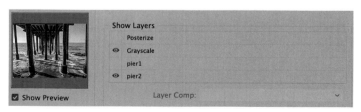

13 Click OK to place the alternate version of the photo in the text object. Keep the file open.

Overriding Photoshop layers after placing

1 Continue with the previous exercise and navigate to page two of L03-postcardWorking.indd.

2 Select the gray graphics frame.

3 Choose File > Place.

4 Deselect Show Import Options.

5 Select pier.psd and click Open to place the file into the selected frame.

6 With the placed image selected, choose Object > Object Layer Options.

⬤ Note: Make sure Preview is selected.

7 Click the empty column to the left of the pier1 layer to make it visible. Notice that the composition updates by showing an alternative image.

8 Click the empty column to the left of the Posterize layer to activate it.

The Posterize adjustment layer changes the appearance of the file.

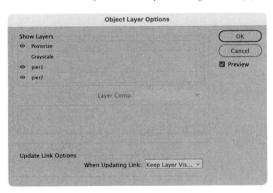

9 Click OK to close the Object Layer Options dialog box, and keep the document open.

> **⬤ Note:** What is quite remarkable is that this specific combination of active and inactive layers is unique to this InDesign composition. And InDesign will properly render any layer, adjustment layer, or blending mode combination directly on the page. If you like, experiment by activating and deactivating specific layer combinations.

How can overriding layers go wrong?

As you've learned from this example (and as you'll see in the examples still to come in this and future lessons), overriding layers adds a lot of flexibility to your workflow. And it provides great value when placing native Photoshop documents in InDesign. But there is one big caveat that you need to be aware of: InDesign might undo all your layer overrides if you're not careful.

When you place a Photoshop document in InDesign, InDesign will take notice of the current layer structure of the placed file. This means it will inspect and remember:

- The total number of layers in the source application (in this case, Photoshop)
- The order of the layers
- The layer names

Because of this, it is of paramount importance that we keep the original layer structure intact in the source document when working with layer overrides. This means we need to avoid:

- Adding or removing layers
- Renaming layers
- Changing the order of existing layers
- Changing the visibility of existing layers

Doing any of these things means that the updated Photoshop document will have a different layer structure compared to the version you placed originally in InDesign. This will confuse InDesign and cause it to *reset all layer overrides* and revert to the most recently saved version of your placed document. There is no way to avoid this behavior for Photoshop documents, and if you want to recover your work, you'd need to reapply the layer overrides in InDesign.

▶ **Tip:** There is a way to partially avoid this behavior when overriding layers from placed Illustrator documents, PDFs, and InDesign documents. Learn more about it in Lesson 5, "Using Illustrator Artwork in InDesign."

A few tips to help you get organized

There is a workaround that will help you avoid unwelcome layer override resets in InDesign. One of the main reasons why InDesign's reset behavior is a problem is because we often want to add additional layers to our Photoshop composition after we've placed (and overridden) the document in InDesign.

It is important to understand that while InDesign is sensitive to the layer structure itself—that is, layer name, order, visibility, and so on—it is not looking at the contents or types of layers in the stack. This means you can still go ahead and make updates to existing layers by:

- Changing layer transparency
- Changing blending modes

continues on next page

- Adding, removing, or updating layer styles of existing layers
- Changing adjustment layer settings, masks, fill layers, and other types of layers

This means that anything goes as long as you keep the original layer structure intact. So you can make your Photoshop composition future-proof by adding empty placeholder layers in your document to anticipate potential layer additions. For example, if you believe you might add a layer or three to your composition in the future, you can add three empty (or hidden) layers to your current composition and give them generic names like Layer 1, Layer 2, and Layer 3. Then you can later use these "placeholder layers" to add your additional content. For example, you could import an image into Layer 1, add a fill layer that you then name Layer 2, and add an adjustment layer that you rename Layer 3.

Again, InDesign doesn't care about the contents of the layer or the layer type. As long as you have a Layer 1, Layer 2, and Layer 3, InDesign will not reset your overrides, because the original layer structure never changed. It's not a perfect workaround, but it does allow for a degree of flexibility.

How to detect layer overrides in a document

To better prepare you for unpleasant surprises in InDesign when updating placed Photoshop documents, we need to have some sort of early warning system that tells us when layers of a placed file have been overridden. This isn't a problem for the previous exercise because we clearly set the layer overrides ourselves. But we might be confronted with documents created by teammates, freelancers, or ourselves a long time ago. And in those cases, we might not know (or remember) the history or build-up of those documents. So how can InDesign assist us in these situations?

Viewing layer overrides in the Links panel

The Links panel in InDesign is a highly configurable panel and offers the ability to present you with link information that is hidden by default. Let's set up the Links panel so it can show us which linked files have layer overrides in the document.

1   Choose Window > Links.

2   Open the panel menu and choose Panel Options.

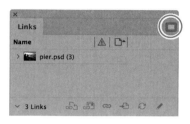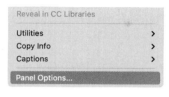

► **Tip:** If you hold down Option/Alt and click the link icon of a placed graphic (in the top left corner of the object), InDesign will automatically open the Links panel and select the link in the panel.

3   At the top of the Panel Options dialog box, choose Large Rows from the Row Size menu to see larger thumbnails in the Links panel.

4   In the Show Column list, select Layer Overrides.

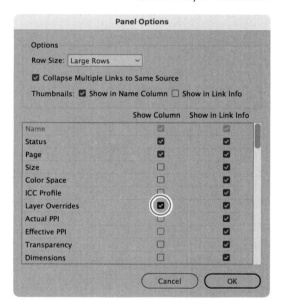

5   Click OK to close the dialog box.

6   If necessary, expand the Links panel to view the newly added Layer Overrides column.

The Layer Overrides column is represented by an eye icon. In this example we see the following information:

▶ **Tip:** Double-click the Yes or No in the Layer Overrides column to open the Object Layer Options dialog box for that image.

- If you look closely, you can see that the thumbnails of pier.psd all look different, because each one represents a different version of the placed image.

- Placed links that have overridden layers have a Yes in the column; ones whose visible layers match those of the linked document have a No in the column.

- The number in parentheses next to the word Yes represents the number of layers that have been overridden.

Using the Preflight panel for detecting layer overrides

The Preflight panel allows you to set up automatic alerts based on set criteria when using text, setting document properties, managing colors, or working with images. It's a sometimes overlooked feature within InDesign that can work to your advantage if you give it a little attention. In this scenario, we'll configure the Preflight panel to alert us when layer overrides have been detected in the document. Unfortunately, the Preflight panel was built for detecting errors in a document that might prevent us from going to print—for example, image resolution that is too low, fonts that are too small, missing document bleed, and so on. This means that detected layer overrides will be listed as an error, whereas we only want a "heads up" when viewing documents, especially when opening documents we didn't create ourselves. So take this "error message" in the Preflight panel with a grain of salt.

▶ **Tip:** Alternatively, you can open the Preflight panel by double-clicking the message at the bottom of your screen listing the number of preflight errors.

1 Choose Window > Output > Preflight.

2 Open the panel menu and choose Define Profiles.

Note the [Basic] profile in the left column, which is currently selected. This profile can't be edited, so we need to make a copy of it first.

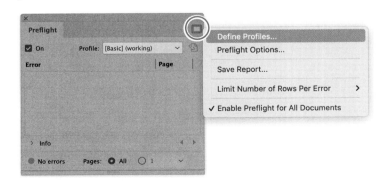

3 Click the plus icon at the bottom of the window to create a new profile, and name it **layer overrides**.

4 Click the arrowhead to the left of the IMAGES And OBJECTS category to display the available settings. Select Layer Visibility Overrides from the list.

You can set additional options, but doing so is beyond the scope of this book.

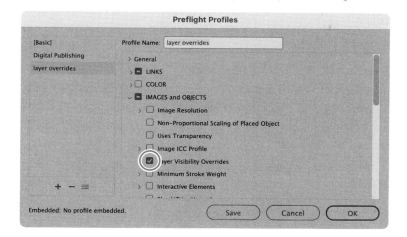

5 Click OK to close the dialog box.

6 Activate the newly created profile by choosing it from the Profile menu. Notice it has found two errors.

7 In the Error list, double-click the IMAGES And OBJECTS category and double-click Layer Visibility Override (2) to open the results of the search.

● **Note:** The Preflight panel will make live updates while you work in InDesign. This means that it will automatically add or remove errors as you work.

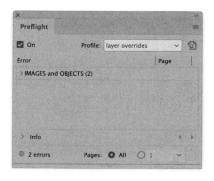
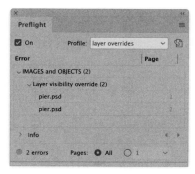

8 Double-click the first pier.psd item in the list of errors to navigate to the image in the document. Repeat this process for the second listing of pier.psd.

▶ **Tip:** It is good practice to create a preflight profile that helps you quickly analyze, and build a report on, documents that you receive from other InDesign users—for example, a profile that detects small font sizes, low resolution graphics, overset text, spot colors, layer overrides, and so on. Afterward, you can always switch to a proper prepress profile or deactivate the Preflight panel altogether.

Using layer transparency to your advantage

In this exercise you'll learn how to create a classic magazine cover on which the top of the main subject overlaps with the title and text of the magazine. Achieving this requires a simple layer override in InDesign.

Inspecting the Photoshop document

1 Launch Photoshop and open alpaca.psd from the Lesson03/Imports folder.

2 Inspect the Layers panel and notice there are two layers in total:

- The Background layer
- A layer containing an alpaca on a transparent background

Placing and overriding the document in InDesign

1 Switch to InDesign and open L03-alpaca-cover-start.indd from the Lesson03 folder.

2 Choose File > Save As, and save the file as **L03-alpaca-coverWorking.indd**.

3 Notice the document has a total of three layers: text, logo, and background.

● **Note:** If you can't see the Layers panel, choose Window > Layers.

4 Select the background frame.

5 Choose File > Place.

6 Navigate to the Imports folder and select alpaca.psd. There is no need to view the Import Options at this time.

7 Click Open to place the file.

The alpaca image has now filled the graphics frame on the background layer. In the next few steps you'll place a copy of the background image on the logo layer, making it overlap with the logo. And you'll finish off by hiding the alpaca's background using InDesign layer options.

8 With the image selection still active, press Command+C/Ctrl+C to copy the image.

9 In the Layers panel, select the logo layer.

10 Choose Edit > Paste In Place to paste a copy of the alpaca image on the logo layer. This copy of the image will hide the magazine's logo but not the rest of the text on the cover (because that text is placed on a different layer).

11 While the image is still selected, right-click the image and choose Object Layer Options.

12 In the Object Layer Options dialog box, make sure that Preview is selected and hide the Background layer by clicking its eye icon.

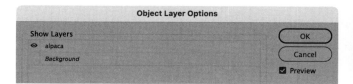

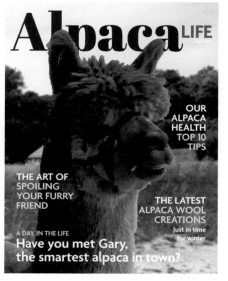

13 Click OK to close the dialog box.

Placing a duplicate of the alpaca (on its otherwise transparent layer) above the logo at exactly the same location as the original image gives the impression of depth and creates an easy and popular effect.

Photoshop layer comps

In the previous exercises you learned that layer overrides are nothing more than showing or hiding Photoshop layers from InDesign. And while this does create opportunities, we are often hungry for more control and creativity. And that is exactly where Photoshop layer comps come in.

What is the purpose of a layer comp?

Layer comps (short for "compositions") allow you to build preset combinations of Photoshop layers that go beyond basic layer visibility. You can use layer comps when placing Photoshop documents in InDesign or Illustrator or when nesting other Photoshop documents.

Layer comps are an ideal solution when:

- You want to save a layer in different positions on the canvas—for example, a version in which a layer is positioned in the upper-left corner and another version in which that layer is in the lower-right corner—without having to duplicate the layer.

- You want to experiment using different layer styles to create various effects.

- You want to avoid confusion and errors when you need to manage the visibility of many layers at the same time for various versions of the image.

● **Note:** If you want to learn more about nesting, consult Lesson 7, "Nesting Documents."

- You want to switch to a different nested Smart Object when using nested Photoshop documents.

Using Photoshop layer comps in InDesign

In this exercise you will learn how to create and save a layer comp in Photoshop and how to take advantage of it in InDesign.

Inspecting the Photoshop document

1   Launch Photoshop and open donuts.psd from the Lesson03/Imports folder.

    This is a fairly complex Photoshop document that holds a combination of different layers. The design will be used in InDesign to create multiple versions of a poster campaign promoting different flavors of donuts.

    The current combination of layers shows the blueberry-flavored donut with colored sprinkles. Depending on the combination of layers used we can create a chocolate version with white sprinkles, a strawberry version, or an apple version. All of this will be achieved using layer comps.

2   Choose Window > Layer Comps.

    The Layer Comps panel shows only a layer comp named Last Document State. This is the default setting when no custom layer comps are created. We'll start out by creating the apple version first.

Creating the first two layer comps

1 In the Layers panel in Photoshop, hide the blueberry layer and make the apple layer visible.

2 In the Layer Comps panel, click the plus icon in the lower-right corner to create a new layer comp.

3 Name the new layer comp **apple**.

Next, we need to choose which layer features we want to capture or ignore in the layer comp for this specific combination of layers.

The layer comp captures the status of all layers in the document, not just the currently selected layer.

4 In the New Layer Comp dialog box, make sure that Visibility and Appearance (Layer Style) are selected and that Position and Layer Comp Selection For Smart Objects are unselected.

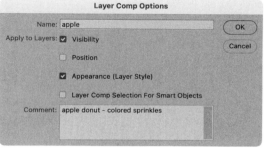

5 In the Comment field, enter **apple donut - colored sprinkles**.

6 Click OK to save the layer comp.

7 In the Layers panel, hide the apple layer to reveal the strawberry layer underneath.

8 Create another layer comp by clicking the plus icon in the Layer Comps panel.

9 Name the new layer comp **strawberry**.

10 In the dialog box, make sure that Visibility and Appearance (Layer Style) are selected and that Position and Layer Comp Selection For Smart Objects are unselected, and enter **strawberry donut - colored sprinkles** in the Comment field. Then click OK to save the second layer comp, and leave the document open.

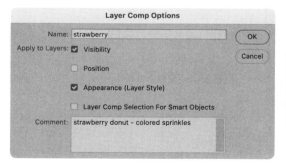

Creating the last layer comp

1 In the Layers panel in Photoshop, show the chocolate topping layer.

2 Show the brown bg layer to change the background.

3 Hide the mixed sprinkles layer, and view the white sprinkles layer.

Note that the drop shadow of the donuts doesn't look right on some parts of the brown background. This is because the drop shadow—which is applied to the strawberry layer (which acts as the base layer)—is set to a blending mode that worked better on a colored background. We need to update the layer style applied to that layer.

4 Click the arrow to the right of the *fx* icon to display the layer effects on the layer style applied to the strawberry layer.

5 Double-click the name of the Drop Shadow effect to open the Layer Style dialog box.

6 In the Layer Style dialog box, change the Blend Mode setting from Overlay to Multiply to better blend the shadow with the background. Click OK to close the dialog box.

7 Create a new layer comp by clicking the plus icon in the Layer Comps panel.

8 Name the new layer comp **chocolate**. Make sure Visibility and Appearance (Layer Style) are selected (since we altered their settings, we need to make sure they will be recorded into the layer comp). Position and Layer Comp Selection For Smart Objects should remain unselected.

9 In the Comment field, enter **chocolate donut - white sprinkles - brown background** and click OK to close the dialog box.

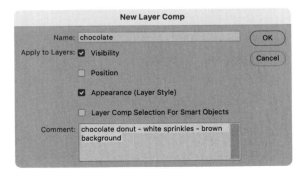

10 Try out your three different layer comps by clicking the box to the left of the name of each layer comp, very similar to the eye icon of regular layers.

11 Choose File > Save As, and save your document as **donuts-layercomps.psd**.

12 Keep the file open.

Note: It doesn't matter which layer comp is active when you save the document in Photoshop.

Using Photoshop layer comps in InDesign

1 Launch InDesign and open L03-poster-start.indd from the Lesson03 folder.

2 Choose File > Save As, and save the file as **L03-posterWorking.indd**.

3 Select the gray graphics frame using the Selection tool 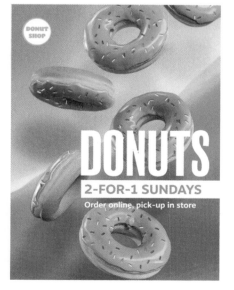.

4 Choose File > Place.

5 Navigate to your newly saved donuts-layercomps.psd and select it.

6 Select Show Import Options at the bottom of the dialog box.

7 Click Open.

8 In the Image Import Options dialog box, click the Layers tab.

9 From the Layer Comp menu, choose apple. Notice that the comments we entered in Photoshop are also shown in InDesign to help us identify the chosen version.

Note: Your version of the dialog box might look slightly different depending on the layer comp that was active when you saved the PSD file.

10 Click OK to place the file.

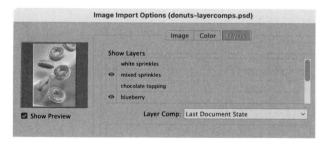

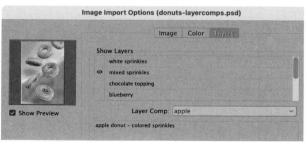

Switching to a different layer comp in InDesign

Next, we'll create an alternative version for the poster design.

1 In InDesign, choose Window > Pages to view the Pages panel.

2 Click the page 1 thumbnail to select it, then right-click the thumbnail and choose Duplicate Spread to create a copy of it. This second page will hold the alternative poster design.

3 Navigate to page 2 by double-clicking its thumbnail in the Pages panel.

4 Select the donut image, then right-click and choose Object Layer Options.

5 From the Layer Comp menu, choose chocolate and click OK.

● **Note:** When choosing a layer comp in the Object Layer Options dialog box, it is still possible to manually show or hide specific Photoshop layers from the list. That lets you use layer comps as starting points for other versions.

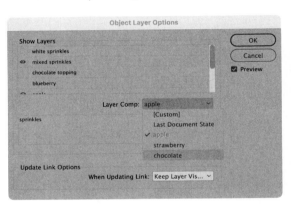
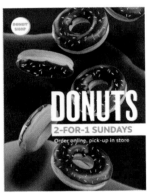

Updating a layer comp in Photoshop

The following steps explain how to update an existing layer comp in Photoshop. In this scenario we want to update the existing apple donut to a blueberry version.

1 Return to Photoshop and open donuts-layercomps.psd.

2 In the Layer Comps panel, apply the apple layer comp.

3 In the Layers panel, hide the apple layer and show the blueberry layer.

   Notice that making changes to an active layer comp will make that layer comp icon jump to the Last Document State position, because the layer combination no longer matches what was originally saved.

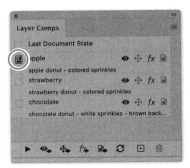

4 In the Layer Comps panel, double-click the apple layer comp to see its options.

5 In the Layer Comp Options dialog box change the name of the layer comp to **blueberry**. In the Comment field, replace the word "apple" with **blueberry**.

6 Click OK to close the Layer Comp Options dialog box.

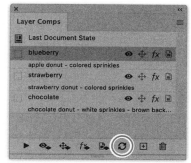

7 In the Layer Comps panel, click the Update Layer Comp button at the bottom of the panel to refresh the currently selected layer comp with the current layer settings. Note that the active layer comp icon moves to the blueberry layer comp.

8 Save your document.

9 Return to InDesign.

Updating a layer comp within a placed PSD file in InDesign might update your InDesign document, depending on which layer comp is visible within the InDesign document.

10 Update the links of all placed images by Option-clicking/Alt-clicking the Update Link button in the Links panel.

▶ **Tip:** If you want to practice a bit more, create additional layer comps by combining different donuts with different sprinkles, creating additional flavors, or changing the position of the layers.

Converting layer comps to Photoshop documents

When you find that a specific layer comp is satisfactory, it's likely that you'll want to export that version in a separate Photoshop document.

1 In Photoshop, open donuts-layercomps.psd.

2 In the Layer Comps panel, select the layer comp(s) you want to export.

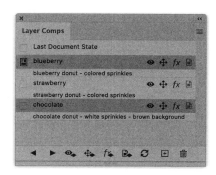

▶ **Tip:** You can select more than one layer comp by Shift- or Command/Ctrl-clicking.

3 Choose File > Export > Layer Comps To Files.

4   In the Layer Comps To Files dialog box, select Selected Layer Comps Only to export only your selected layer comps rather than all of them.

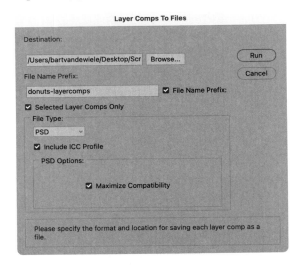

5   Choose a destination folder and click Run.

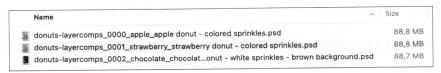

Embedding placed documents into InDesign

InDesign also supports the ability to embed placed images into a document, but this practice is usually not recommended since you risk bloating the InDesign file size, resulting in lowered performance. There are a few exceptions where embedding a link might be beneficial:

- When using placed images that have a relatively small file size.

- When you feel it's just not worth maintaining a link to the original file. Embedding the link could then simplify your document because everything would then be embedded.

- When you fear the link to the placed file might be broken by someone else moving, renaming, or deleting the original document.

Keep in mind that when you embed a Photoshop document, *it will no longer be possible to access its layers from InDesign.* This means that it will no longer be possible to apply layer overrides or change layer comps.

▶ **Tip:** When you embed a Photoshop document that has layer overrides or is using a layer comp, the document will be embedded using that configuration.

How to embed a placed graphic

To embed a placed (linked) graphic, follow these steps.

1 In InDesign, choose Window > Links to display the Links panel.

2 Select donutshop-logo in the Links panel.

3 Click the panel menu and choose Embed Link.

   The Links panel adds an Embedded icon next to the name of the link, signifying it is now included in the InDesign document.

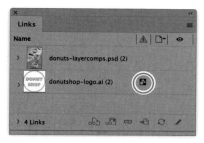

Note: If the link you want to embed has multiple instances, the command will read Embed All Instances Of [your link].

How to unembed a placed graphic

It is possible to unembed a file from an InDesign document. This action extracts the embedded document, places it in a specified location, and then creates a link between the file and the InDesign document.

1 Select donutshop-logo.ai again in the Links panel.

2 Open the Links panel menu and choose Unembed Link.

   Note: If the link you want to unembed has multiple instances, the command will read Unembed All Instances Of [your link].

   InDesign asks whether you want to link to the original file or to a file that it extracts from the InDesign document and places in a folder.

3 Let's pretend we don't have the original available; click No.

4 Use the dialog box to navigate to a location where you want to place the extracted link, and click Choose.

Packaging the project

When you place content in InDesign, a relationship is created between InDesign and the placed Photoshop document. When you finish your project, it is recommended that you package all the linked assets together to create a project backup or archive. When you create a package, the following actions are performed:

- A folder is created that holds:
    - A duplicate of your project file
    - A subfolder that holds a copy of all linked content
    - A subfolder that has a copy of all the local fonts used in the document
- All links in the duplicate project (in this case, the InDesign document) are relinked to the copied links in the newly created subfolder.

The main advantage of packaging your work is that it creates a standalone version of your project with its own version of the linked files. This means that accidental changes to linked artwork will not affect your main project.

1   From the Lesson03 folder open L03-poster-end.indd.

2   Choose File > Package.

3   Optionally, review all information to verify what will be included in the package.

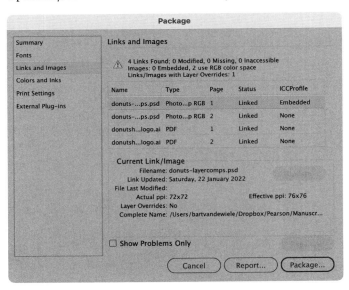

4   Click Package. If a dialog box opens asking you to save your file, click Save.

5   In the Create Package Folder dialog box, name the folder **poster-package**.

Note: For legal reasons, fonts synchronized via Adobe Fonts are never included in a package, only local fonts are.

Note: Since embedded graphics are already included in the InDesign document, you will not find them in a separate folder. Only linked content is collected.

6 If you want, add a PDF version of the document and/or an IDML version by selecting the appropriate options. IDML documents can be opened by those who are using an older version of InDesign.

7 Click Package to create the package.

Review questions

1 After you've placed a Photoshop document in InDesign, what can go wrong when overriding the visibility of Photoshop layers, and which actions might trigger this?

2 Which two methods can you use in InDesign to detect overridden layers of a placed document?

3 Which two layer comp properties did we use while creating a Photoshop layer comp?

4 How can you convert a Photoshop layer comp into a separate Photoshop document?

5 Why is it not recommended to embed placed images into an InDesign document?

Review answers

1 Adding or deleting layers in Photoshop, renaming layers, changing the layer stacking order, or changing the layer visibility of a placed Photoshop document in InDesign that has its layers overridden can unintentionally revert all Photoshop layers to their original visibility.

2 You can either create a custom preflight profile using the Preflight panel or activate the Layer Overrides option from the Links panel options.

3 The layer comp properties used in the exercise included the Visibility and Appearance (Layer Style). Additionally, you can choose Position and Layer Comp Selection For Smart Objects.

4 Choose File > Export > Layer Comps To Files.

5 Embedding placed images into an InDesign document makes the InDesign file heavier, makes it impossible to edit the original file in Photoshop or Illustrator, and makes it more difficult to share the placed image with others.

4 USING PHOTOSHOP PATHS, ALPHA CHANNELS, AND GRAYSCALE IMAGES IN INDESIGN

Lesson overview

In this lesson, you'll learn how to do the following:

- Understand the differences between a path and a clipping path in Photoshop.
- Reuse Photoshop paths in InDesign.
- Identify different use cases when choosing between paths and an alpha channel in Photoshop.
- Reuse a Photoshop alpha channel in InDesign.
- Prepare grayscale images in Photoshop and recolor them in InDesign.

 This lesson will take about 45 minutes to complete. Please log in to your account at adobepress.com/DesignCIB to download the files for this lesson, or go to the "Getting Started" section at the beginning of this book and follow the instructions under "Accessing the lesson files and Web Edition." Store the files on your computer in a convenient location.

Your Account page is also where you'll find any updates to the lesson files. Look on the Lesson & Update Files tab to access the most current content.

Capital of the island of Crete

Abore dolento cus illam quiae none vellab iuntota tibero maion cupta peri cumentus in consent vel mollatempor aut quia volum voloratio. Ut labo. Tem et posandam, sunto que modio. Nequi dem volorit iumqui sitatent omnis esecess imporro volessin res acepudi aquatet alitaque ne velles sus esto modit hillupt aectas corerspit fuga. Ori con ne culpa namus min consed es ma vellitassint autatqui ditatibus, acipicidebis que officiust doluptur, cusdam, sunda con rehenis re voloreribus venti dignimi llabor autas moloriberit, ipsam earum digni ommolore, sum quam, arum ut autas autes sam qui untiatiae. Evelictatum aut labori doluptatum non rerovid erferiatis dolores evel il intisquas dis magnissere officia pedi berum et eosaess inveles ciusdae. Mus mossus nis cum dolupta testiosaes alignam, serionse dolum repudio nemperi onecte dendiae. Vid quam archicit hicipsum eum doluptatem nonsequi ipsapidenda ipic to quaectatio et autatumquo et perumquis eiciat essim hit ea nossinctat re, quunt prRo quibus moles rehenecescil in culluptas accae num enes aut labo. Nempores velest, tent, officil ex expliqui dolecus qui qui corpore prorion senimolorem qui ut molore nonsequi alis eatiur aut quo tem libusdaepta pratium repudanis solorro omnihillam is dolende vellique vendi omnihil iur, ut omnisquo qui de ped ut peribusciisi aligenihici con et que deserum quuntusda nam dolorestiam coreperatum ius essi aut adiantiatio molorepedit deles as di ut fugia que pellectem. Et arumquo ommolestiam ratam nam venim faccus dellorae erum quam, odiam quas dollatem iusam sitio. Nam que qui aute símila borepta cus ex eumquid ionetur moditia ate volore

This lesson will teach you how to recolor grayscale images in InDesign and isolate parts of an image using clipping paths and alpha channels.

Photoshop paths

As discussed in Lesson 2, "Enriching Illustrator Artwork with Photoshop Content," Photoshop supports the use and creation of vector paths within a document. The purpose of a Photoshop path can vary, depending on your design. You can draw paths in Photoshop by using a combination of the Pen tool and shape tools like the Rectangle tool, Ellipse tool, and so on. Common examples include:

- Drawing paths to create simple or complex geometry as shape layers.

- Using path tools to trace images, allowing you to later convert the path into a selection.

- Converting paths into a vector mask.

In all of these examples, paths contribute to the overall design, whether in the form of special layers or defining selections. But it is also possible to simply use the Paths panel to store paths inside a Photoshop document in case you ever need them later. And what's even better is that Adobe InDesign can also access these stored paths when the Photoshop document is placed in InDesign.

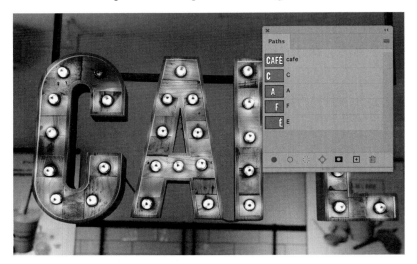

Paths versus clipping paths

Every time you use a path-creation tool in Photoshop, you'll create a work path that you can save in the Paths panel. Saving a regular path in the Paths panel is often done as a means of backing up the path for future use—for example, to load it as a selection, copy it to other documents, or use it as a vector shape.

You can also choose to set one of the document paths as a clipping path. The benefit of a clipping path is that it allows you to define transparent and opaque areas for your entire Photoshop document when placing the document in other applications, like InDesign or Illustrator. But keep in mind that a clipping path only allows for an area to be either visible or invisible. Semitransparent areas are not possible. A typical example of using a clipping path is to isolate an object from its background—for example, when creating a product catalog.

Using clipping paths in InDesign

In the following exercise, you'll learn how to convert a path to a clipping path in Photoshop. You'll then reuse the clipping path when placing the document in InDesign.

Converting a path to a clipping path

1 Start Photoshop, and choose Photoshop > Preferences > General (macOS) or Edit > Preferences > General (Windows).

The Preferences dialog box opens.

2 Click Reset Preferences On Quit and click OK in the confirmation dialog box. Then restart Photoshop.

3 Open plane.psd from the Lesson04/Imports folder.

4 Choose Window > Paths to open the Paths panel. Notice there is already a saved path available within the document.

5 Click the path name in the Paths panel. The selected path is highlighted in blue on the canvas.

The path around the airplane will allow it to be extracted from the background, which can then be made transparent.

6 With the current path selected, open the Paths panel menu and choose Clipping Path.

7 In the Clipping Path dialog box, Path 1 is already chosen from the Path menu.

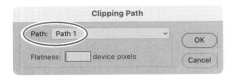

●**Note:** You can have only one clipping path per Photoshop document. If you try to convert a second path to a clipping path, it will replace the first one.

8 Leave the Flatness option blank so that when you print the image, your printer's default value will be used (this determines how many straight lines are used to draw the curve of the path). Click OK to close the dialog box and convert Path 1 into a clipping path.

The path name now appears in bold, signifying that this path is a clipping path.

9 Double-click the path name and rename it **plane-clipping**.

10 Choose File > Save As and save the document as **plane-clipping.psd**.

Applying a clipping path in InDesign

In this part of the exercise you'll learn how to use the clipping path in a Photoshop document that's been placed in InDesign. Additionally, we'll adjust text wrap options to wrap the document text around the clipped image.

1 Start InDesign, and then press Control+Option+Shift+Command/ Alt+Shift+Ctrl to restore the default preferences.

2   When prompted, click Yes to delete the Adobe InDesign Settings file.

3   From the Lesson04 folder, open L04-magazine-start.indd.

4   Save the file as **L04-magazineWorking.indd**.

5   Without selecting anything, choose File > Place.

6   Navigate to the folder where you saved plane-clipping.psd, and select the file.

7   Make sure Show Import Options is selected, then click Open.

The Image Import Options dialog box opens. The image preview already shows the plane as an isolated image. This is because the clipping path is already applied by default.

8   Click the Image tab in the Image Import Options dialog box.

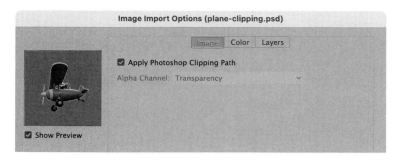

● **Note:** If your image preview doesn't look like this figure, you can use the copy of plane-clipping.psd provided in Lesson04/Imports.

9   As an experiment, deselect Apply Photoshop Clipping Path and watch the preview image update. This is what would happen if you were to choose to place the document without applying the clipping path.

10 Select Apply Photoshop Clipping Path and click OK to place the image.

11 Start dragging from the middle of the top margin of page 2 to define the size
of the image (don't release the mouse button yet!). Notice that the tool tip displays the scale of the image as you move the mouse. Release the mouse button
to place the image at roughly 12% of its size.

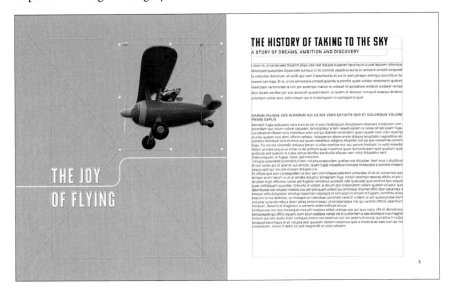

12 Use the Selection tool ▶ to move the image to the right edge of the facing page,
with the wing overlapping the article introduction.

The image appears behind the text because the text is on a layer that sits above
the image layer.

Leave the document open.

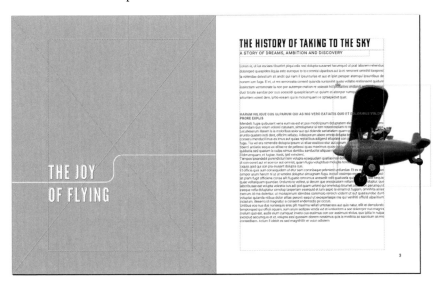

Wrapping text around an image

1 Select the placed plane image.

2 Choose Window > Text Wrap.

3 Select the Wrap Around Object Shape option, which allows you to wrap text around a nonrectangular shape (which we'll define next).

4 In the Wrap Options area, choose Largest Area from the Wrap To menu.

5 In the Contour Options area, choose Same As Clipping from the Type menu in order to use the embedded clipping path as the text wrap bounding box.

6 Change the Top Offset value to **0.25 in.**

7 Save your file.

Using a Photoshop alpha channel

Alpha channels in Photoshop are the pixel equivalent of paths in that they give you a way to control transparency. The main difference between the two is that alpha channels are always rasterized (that is, resolution dependent) and allow for 256 levels of transparency, but paths are vectors and don't support partial transparency. The applications are also similar within Photoshop:

• You can save complex selections as alpha channels.

• Some filters can use alpha channels to help define the areas of an image that they affect.

• Alpha channels can be reused in other applications, such as InDesign and even Microsoft Office apps like PowerPoint or Word.

Viewing and saving an alpha channel

1   From the Lesson04/Imports folder, open window-seat.psd in Photoshop.

2   Open the Layers panel and notice these layers:

* A layer group that holds an image layer, two adjustment layers, and a layer mask that is disabled

* A gradient fill layer at the bottom of the stack

3   Enable the layer mask of the layer group by Shift-clicking its thumbnail. The mask covers the airplane window, so when it is enabled it renders the window area transparent, showing the gradient fill layer underneath.

Note: The layer mask includes soft edges, which results in semitransparent pixels in the file. This would be impossible to achieve using a vector mask or clipping path.

4   Option/Alt-click the layer mask thumbnail in the Layers panel. Photoshop now displays only the mask.

5 Option/Alt-click the layer mask thumbnail again to view the layers normally.

6 Deselect the layer group by clicking in the empty area underneath the gradient fill layer on the Layers panel. The layer is no longer highlighted in the panel.

7 Command/Ctrl-click the layer mask thumbnail to load it as a selection.

8 Choose Window > Channels to display the Channels panel.

9 At the bottom of the Channels panel, click the Save Selection As Channel button to convert the active selection to an alpha channel.

10 Choose Select > Deselect.

> ● **Note:** The normal channels in the Channels panel represent the basic color channels that make up an image, but an alpha channel is basically a mask that represents not a color but only a selected area.

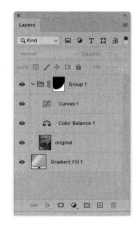

11 Double-click the alpha channel name, rename it window, and press Return/Enter to confirm.

12 Click the RGB channel to display the normal color channels.

13 Choose File > Save As and save your file as **window-seat-alpha.psd**.

> ● **Note:** Since the alpha channel will determine the document visibility when placing in InDesign, it doesn't matter whether the layer mask was left active or inactive.

Applying an alpha channel in InDesign

1 Return to InDesign, where L04-magazineWorking.indd should still be open.

2 Focus on the left page of the document and notice the gray graphics frame.

3 Select the graphics frame and choose File > Place.

4 From the Lesson04/Imports folder, choose plane-approach.jpg and deselect Show Import Options.

5 Click Open to place the image in the frame.

6 In the Tools panel, select the Rectangle Frame tool ⊠.

7 Drag out a graphics frame that covers the entire left page, dragging from the upper-left corner of the page to the lower-right corner.

8 Choose File > Place.

9 Navigate to the folder where you saved window-seat-alpha.psd.

10 Select window-seat-alpha.psd and make sure Show Import Options is selected this time. Click Open.

11 In the Image Import Options dialog box, click the Image tab.

By default, Transparency is chosen from the Alpha Channel menu, rather than the alpha channel that we created.

12 From the Alpha Channel menu, choose window (our newly saved alpha channel).

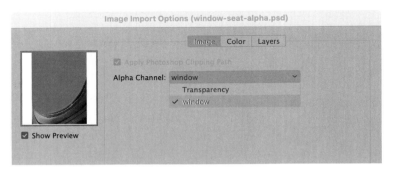

13 Click OK to confirm.

14 With the current selection active, choose Object > Fitting > Fill Frame Proportionally. Keep the frame selected.

15 Choose Window > Layers to display the Layers panel.

16 Click the lock icon next to the text elements layer to unlock it.

17 Drag the blue square at the right side of the images layer upward and drop it onto the text elements layer. This moves the placed image on top of everything else.

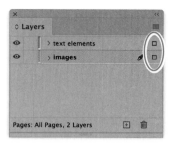

The alpha channel has allowed us to have a blurry edge at the bottom of the window image. This would not have been possible using a regular path, which allows only hard edges.

18 Save your file.

Why didn't we use regular layer overrides?

The previous exercise might remind you of a similar exercise we conducted in Lesson 3, "Using Layered Photoshop Files in InDesign" in which we used layer overrides to place a transparent image of a llama at the top of the stack. So how is this approach different from what we did before?

• Alpha channels in InDesign act as a type of mask that is applied to the entire Photoshop document upon placing; individual layer overrides simply show or hide specific layers in InDesign. So layer overrides manipulate the content of a placed Photoshop document, whereas an alpha channel is a type of "wrapper" that applies to the entire document, without manipulating the content layers at all.

• Alpha channels aren't as sensitive as layer overrides when used in InDesign. This means that it's impossible for an alpha channel to reset itself if we ever change the layers in the Photoshop document. This makes it a safer choice in some scenarios, and it means we could go back to the original Photoshop document and add, change, or remove as many layers as we like.

● **Note:** You can still combine alpha channels with layer overrides in InDesign if needed.

▶ **Tip:** You can use your alpha channel to simulate a clipping path in InDesign. To achieve this, select the placed Photoshop document and choose Object > Clipping Path > Options. From there, change the Type option to alpha channel.

Using multiple Photoshop paths

The next exercise shows you how to reuse multiple paths from the same Photoshop document in InDesign.

Inspecting all documents

1 From the Lesson04/Imports folder, open A.psd in Photoshop.

2 Open the Paths panel and notice that there is a path named Path 1. Select the path to highlight it on the canvas. It traces the outline of the letter *A*.

3 Close the document.

4 From the Lesson04/Imports folder, open B.psd in Photoshop.

5 Perform step 2 for this file; notice that the path traces the outline of the letter *B*.

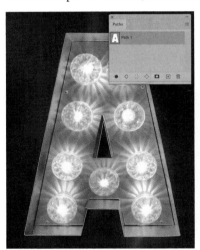 

6 Close the document.

7 From the Lesson04/Imports folder, open cafe-letters.psd in Photoshop.

8 Inspect the Paths panel and notice that there are multiple paths saved in the document: one path that holds all the letters, and separate paths for each individual letter.

9 Close the document.

Reusing paths in InDesign

1   From the Lesson04 folder, open L04-flyer-start.indd in InDesign.

2   Save the file as **L04-flyerWorking.indd**.

3   Choose File > Place.

4   Navigate to the Lesson04/Imports folder and select A.psd. Make sure Show Import Options is unselected.

The reason we can't use the Image Import Options dialog box here is that there is no way to make a regular path act as a clipping path during placing.

5   Choose Open to place the file.

6   Drag to place the image at roughly 5% of its original size.

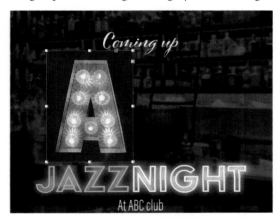

7   While the image is still selected, choose Object > Clipping Path > Options.

8   From the Type menu in the dialog box, choose Photoshop Path. InDesign will choose the only available path in the document by default—in this case, Path 1.

9   Click OK.

Unlike when using a clipping path, which changes the size of the graphics frame when applied, the graphics frame in InDesign remains the same size after applying Path 1. But since Path 1 is smaller than the graphics frame, it results in a gap between the clipped image and the graphics frame. The next few steps help you update the graphics frame size by making it fit the clipped image.

10 Using the Selection tool , click the placed image to select it.

11 Choose Object > Clipping Path > Convert Clipping Path To Frame to make the Photoshop path act as the graphics frame.

This makes it easier to select and manipulate the letter *A*, as it's no longer "hovering" inside a larger empty frame. Additionally, it is now easier to set the absolute size and positioning in InDesign using coordinates.

12 Place the image B.psd the same way you did before, and place it next to the letter *A*.

13 Keep the document open.

Changing paths in InDesign

1 Place cafe-letters.psd the same way you placed the other images.

2 Choose Object > Clipping Path > Options.

3 From the Type menu in the dialog, choose Photoshop Path. Then choose path C from the list of available paths and click OK.

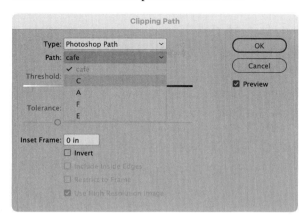

4 Choose Object > Clipping Path > Convert Clipping Path To Frame.

5 Position the letters *A*, *B*, and *C* closer together so they spell out ABC.

▶ **Tip:** It is possible to combine this technique with the text wrap options we used in the previous exercise.

Keep the file open.

In the next steps, you'll learn how to change to different paths in case of a multipath Photoshop document.

6 Using the Selection tool ▶, select the letter *C* image.

7 Choose Object > Clipping Path > Options.

8 Choose Photoshop Path from the Type menu if necessary, but this time choose the letter F from the Path menu.

ADOBE PHOTOSHOP, ILLUSTRATOR, AND INDESIGN COLLABORATION AND WORKFLOW CLASSROOM IN A BOOK **103**

9 Click OK to close the dialog box.

The newly chosen path doesn't match the updated shape of the graphics frame, which is still shaped as a letter *C*. Don't deselect the image.

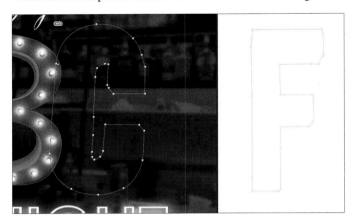

10 Choose Object > Clipping Path > Convert Clipping Path To Frame to update the graphics frame.

11 Deselect the image, then use the Selection tool to select and rearrange the individual letters until they spell the word *FAB*.

▶ **Tip:** This technique allows you to use the same image in multiple ways, without having to first extract and save separate Photoshop documents. Additionally, any adjustment layers added to the original Photoshop document will apply to all letters and update all versions at the same time.

12 Save your document.

Recoloring Photoshop grayscale images in InDesign

The next technique you'll learn allows you to take grayscale Photoshop documents and dynamically recolor them in InDesign. Traditionally, this technique is often used to prepare images for specialized print output—for example, using Pantone colors to create monotone or duotone images. But you can even apply CMYK, RGB, or spot colors from InDesign to achieve more creative effects.

Isn't this something you can achieve using Photoshop instead? In short, yes. But the answer is more complex than that. With documents destined for traditional print output, it is imperative that you keep full control over the document's colors. And this technique is perfect when you:

- Want to apply the same InDesign swatches to text, native vector artwork, and placed images at the same time.

- Want to create monotone or duotone images using spot colors.

- Need to recolor multiple images with the same InDesign swatch, or want an easy way to update the chosen color of these images all at once.

Despite Photoshop's impressive array of options for recoloring images and its various adjustment layers, it doesn't always offer the smoothest experience:

- Creating spot channels in Photoshop can be challenging for some users.

- Using spot channels can create duplicate spot color swatches when placed in InDesign, causing confusion.

- Photoshop and InDesign (and Illustrator) use different color management settings, which may result in visual differences when using the same Pantone colors across multiple apps. It's possible to configure your apps to overcome this, but it requires expert knowledge of color management.

- Changing multiple recolored images at the same time can be time consuming.

Preparing grayscale images in Photoshop

Preparing images for this recoloring technique is very easy. The only thing you need to do is convert your images to the grayscale color mode in Photoshop. But it's important not to be hasty! Even though simply choosing Image > Mode > Grayscale in Photoshop works, it will often result in a grayscale image that lacks contrast. And contrast is very important for this technique.

When you recolor an image in InDesign by applying a swatch, InDesign will replace every pixel that is black (or a shade of gray) with the chosen color (or tint). This means that a pixel that is 100% black will be recolored with a tint that is 100% of the chosen color. A pixel that is 30% black will become 30% of the color, and so on.

When you create grayscale images, you need to make sure that you use the full range from black to white because (1) that lets you use the full tonal range of the color you've chosen to recolor the image, and (2) there is no other way to adjust the image contrast in InDesign.

1 From the Lesson04/Imports folder, open heraklion.psd in Photoshop.

2 At the bottom of the Layers panel, click the New Adjustment Layer button and choose Black & White to create a Black & White adjustment layer.

3 Use the Properties panel to view the available options.

> **Tip:** If you don't see the Properties panel, choose Window > Properties.

Next, we'll increase the contrast of the generated grayscale image.

4 Click the On-Image Adjustment tool in the Properties panel.

5 Drag on the sky toward the right in order to convert it completely to white. This changes the value of the Blue slider in the Properties panel to 300.

6 Drag left on a wall to darken all walls. The Yellow slider moves to the left.

7 Drag left on the roof tiles, which will manipulate the Red slider in the Properties panel.

● **Note:** Be careful not to overdo the adjustments, as extreme changes can emphasize compression artifacts if the image had previously been saved as a JPEG file.

8 Choose Window > Info to open the Info panel.

9 Click one of the eyedropper icons in the Info panel and choose Grayscale from the menu to switch to that color space.

10 Move your cursor over the image while keeping an eye on the Grayscale values in the Info panel. It now shows the grayscale tint percentage, which gives us a way of predicting the intensity of the color we will apply in InDesign.

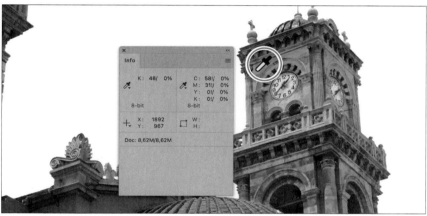

The Info panel displays two grayscale values. The value on the left represents the original grayscale tint percentage; the one on the right represents the updated tint percentage.

Now that we've created an image that is rich in contrast, it's time to convert the document to grayscale.

11 Choose Image > Mode > Grayscale.

The Black & White adjustment layer we just created can't live in a grayscale composition, only in an RGB. This is why we need to merge the layers during conversion.

12 When prompted, click Flatten to merge the Black & White adjustment layer with the background.

13 When Photoshop asks whether you're sure you want to discard all color information, click Discard.

14 Choose File > Save As and save the file as **heraklion-blackwhite.psd**.

● **Note:** The technique of recoloring a grayscale image using InDesign also works when the image has been saved from Photoshop as a JPEG or TIFF. But only a PSD offers the flexibility of adding layers and building a grayscale composition without bloating the file (as a TIFF does). However, it's important to understand that PSD files with transparency can't be recolored using InDesign.

15 Close the file.

Recoloring the cover image in InDesign

1　From the Lesson04 folder, open L04-book-cover-start.indd in InDesign.

2　Open the Swatches panel by choosing Window > Color > Swatches.

3　Note that the Swatches panel holds five swatches that were added to this file, in addition to four defaults. The five added swatches are:

- Two Pantone swatches with numbers 7451 and 561

- Two tint swatches of Pantone 561, with tints of 20% and 30%

- One gradient swatch that transitions between the Pantone 561 20% swatch and the Pantone 7451 swatch

4　Using the Selection tool ▶, select the main graphics frame on the front cover of the book.

5　Choose File > Place.

6　Navigate to the folder where you saved heraklion-blackwhite.psd. Select that file, and deselect Import Options.

7　Click Open to place the image, but don't deselect it yet.

8　With the current selection active, click the PANTONE 561 C 20% swatch to apply the color to the image fill. This recolors each white pixel in proportion to the amount of white it contained.

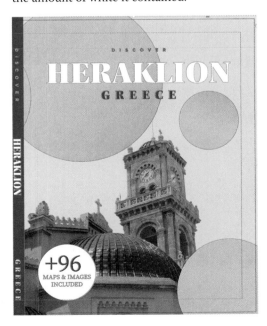

9 Using the Selection tool , double-click the image to select its contents. A brown selection frame appears around the image itself.

The Swatches panel shows that a black swatch is applied to the contents of the image. This is because we saved the image as a grayscale image from Photoshop.

10 Apply the PANTONE 561 C swatch to the selected image.

The first step of our recoloring process was to apply a swatch to the fill of a placed grayscale image. This recolored all pixels in proportion to the amount of white they contained. This resulted in an image that looked like it used a combination of color for the highlights and grayscale and black for the shadows. The second step applied a second swatch to recolor all shadows in the image.

Recoloring the back cover image in InDesign

1 From the Lesson04/Imports folder, open heraklion-alt.psd in Photoshop.

2 Repeat the previous Photoshop steps for properly converting the image to grayscale and improving the overall contrast.

3 Save the image as **heraklion-alt-blackwhite.psd**.

4 Return to InDesign.

5 Select the blue background frame on the back cover of the project.

6 Choose File > Place.

7 Navigate to the folder where you saved heraklion-alt-blackwhite.psd. Select the file, then click Open.

8 With the selection active, choose Object > Fitting > Fill Frame Proportionally to fill the entire frame.

9 Deselect the image.

10 In the Swatches panel, select the PANTONE 7451 C swatch.

11 Open the Swatches panel menu and choose New Tint Swatch.

12 Set a value of **30%**, and click OK to add the swatch to the Swatches panel and close the window.

13 Apply the newly created 30% swatch to the background of the back cover image.

14 Select the image itself by double-clicking it, and apply the PANTONE 7451 C swatch.

15 Keep the file open.

Updating existing colors

One of the main advantages of using InDesign swatches and tint swatches is that it allows you to dynamically update all colors in the document by changing the base swatch color values.

1 Continue with the previous file and make sure nothing is selected. In the Swatches panel, double-click the PANTONE 561 C swatch.

The Swatch Options dialog box opens.

2 Make sure that PANTONE+ Solid Coated is chosen from the Color Mode menu. In the text input field, enter the Pantone number **683**. This is a purple color. Click OK to close the dialog box.

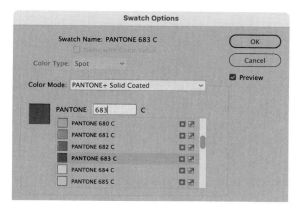

All swatches that were based on the original PANTONE 561 C swatch have now updated with the new color. This includes the tint swatches and the gradient swatch.

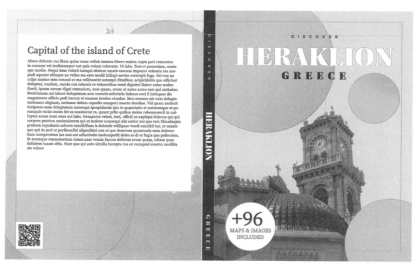

3 Use the Selection tool ▶ to select the QR code on the back cover.

The top of the Properties panel should say "Object (QR Code)."

4 Choose Object > Edit QR Code.

5 In the Edit QR Code dialog box, click the Color tab.

6 Select the newly created PANTONE 683 swatch.

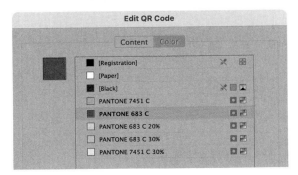

● **Note:** You can update the current Pantone swatches with any color swatch you want, including process CMYK or RGB swatches. This is a great aid to creativity.

7 Choose OK to close the dialog box.

Viewing spot colors more accurately

Because this project uses only Pantone colors, it's important to view the used spot colors as realistically as possible before creating a PDF for print. And to achieve proper duotone output, we need to verify that no process colors have been used. To do so, we need to activate the Separations Preview feature in InDesign. This will allow us to inspect individual color separations and will force InDesign to view the used Pantone colors using its LAB values, which offer a more realistic representation of the colors in the document.

1 Choose Window > Output > Separations Preview.

2 Choose Separations from the View menu on the panel.

3 Expand the height of the Separations Preview panel to view all separations in the list. Hide all except the Pantone separations by clicking the CMYK visibility icon.

● **Note:** By default, if only one color separation is visible, it is displayed in black and white.

4 Once you are done inspecting all color separations, close the Separations Preview panel.

5 Save your document and close it.

6 Optionally, create a package of your document using the steps described in Lesson 3.

Review questions

1   What is the difference between a path and a clipping path when placing a Photoshop document in InDesign?

2   What is the difference between applying a clipping path and applying an alpha channel to a placed Photoshop document in InDesign?

3   Which color mode do you need to use in Photoshop to prepare an image for recoloring in InDesign?

4   What is the benefit of recoloring images using InDesign, as opposed to using Photoshop, for a print project?

5   How can you verify the color separations of an InDesign document?

Review answers

1   By default, a clipping path will be automatically applied to the imported document dur-
    ing placing, and the resulting graphics frame in InDesign will have the same dimensions
    as the clipping path itself. Also, you can save only one clipping path in a Photoshop
    document. When you use regular paths, you can save as many as you like in the
    Photoshop document and choose which one to apply to the document in InDesign after
    it has been placed. Additionally, you might need to use the Convert Clipping Path To
    Frame command to make the graphics frame fit the size of the path.

2   A clipping path can only show or hide parts of an image, always resulting in a hard frame
    edge. Alpha channels allow for 256 levels of transparency to hide or reveal an image
    when placed in InDesign, which can create smooth edges and semitransparent regions.

3   InDesign can recolor placed PSD, TIFF, and JPEG images that use the grayscale
    color mode.

4   InDesign offers the ability of globally updating all colors in a document by updating
    a single swatch. Recoloring multiple images in Photoshop, on the other hand, would
    require you to recolor every image one by one.

5   To view a document's color separations in InDesign, choose Window > Output >
    Separations Preview.

5 USING ILLUSTRATOR ARTWORK IN INDESIGN

Lesson overview

In this lesson, you'll learn how to do the following:

- Correctly set up Illustrator layers and artboards for placing into InDesign.
- Override Illustrator layers from InDesign.
- Place one or more Illustrator artboards in InDesign.
- Choose between layers or artboards in Illustrator.
- Paste Illustrator artwork into InDesign.

 This lesson will take about 75 minutes to complete. Please log in to your account on adobepress.com/DesignCIB to download the files for this lesson, or go to the "Getting Started" section at the beginning of this book and follow the instructions under "Accessing the lesson files and Web Edition." Store the files on your computer in a convenient location.

Your Account page is also where you'll find any updates to the lesson files. Look on the Lesson & Update Files tab to access the most current content.

This lesson teaches you how to master the process of bringing vector artwork from Illustrator into InDesign. You'll learn the differences between placing and pasting artwork, and the importance of artboards and layers.

Using Illustrator layers in InDesign

In the following exercise you'll learn how to override Illustrator layers in InDesign. You'll notice that this workflow is similar to the one you learned in Lesson 3, "Using layered Photoshop files in InDesign," but there are important differences.

Getting started

You'll start the lesson by viewing an image of the final composition and placed artwork.

1 Start Photoshop, and choose Photoshop > Preferences > General (macOS) or Edit > Preferences > General (Windows).

The Photoshop Preferences dialog box opens.

2 Click Reset Preferences On Quit and click OK in the confirmation dialog box. Then restart Photoshop.

3 From the Lesson05/Imports folder, open trex.psd.

Note that all the layers that make up the T-rex are grouped separately from the Background layer.

4 Close the file without saving.

5 Start Illustrator, and choose Illustrator > Preferences > General (macOS) or Edit > Preferences > General (Windows).

The Preferences dialog box opens.

6 Click Reset Preferences, then click OK to close the dialog box.

7 Click Restart Now in the confirmation dialog box to restart Illustrator and reset preferences.

8 From the Lesson05/Imports folder, open dino-logo.ai.

9 Choose Window > Layers to display the Layers panel.

Notice that there is a hidden layer, which we'll use to display an alternative version of the logo in InDesign.

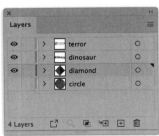

10 Close the file without saving.

11 Start InDesign, and then press Control+Option+Shift+Command (macOS) or Alt+Shift+Ctrl (Windows) to restore the default preferences.

12 When prompted, click Yes to delete the Adobe InDesign Settings file.

13 From the Lesson05 folder, open L05-dino-ad-end.indd.

This dinosaur ad features the placed trex.psd document and the dino-logo.ai Illustrator logo. Note that the dinosaur partially overlaps the logo. To achieve this, we'll use the same technique as in Lesson 3 (the alpaca magazine cover project), which uses layer overrides.

14 Close L05-dino-ad-end.indd without saving.

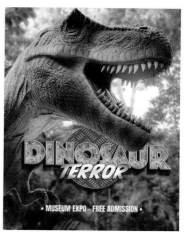

About Illustrator layers

Adobe Illustrator's layer system works differently from that of Photoshop. In a nutshell, Illustrator uses a hierarchy that consists of three "levels." And it's important to understand how this works in order to properly override Illustrator layers from within InDesign.

- **Top-level layer:** This is the highest level in the layer hierarchy in a document. Each layer comes with its own color and name, as well as other options, which can be set by double-clicking the layer name. A layer can be viewed as a sort of folder that can hold the elements you draw in Illustrator, and it can even hold other layers (sublayers) that each hold their respective objects.

- **Sublayer:** This is a layer that was dragged into an existing layer in order to create a second level. Using sublayers allows you to place a set of objects into another group of objects. This is not to be confused with the Group command in the Object menu. Because a sublayer is merely a normal layer that was dragged down one level (or created directly using the Layers panel), you can still double-click it in order to set specific layer options.

- **Object:** Every object you draw or place in Illustrator is listed in a layer or sublayer and is enclosed with < > characters by default.

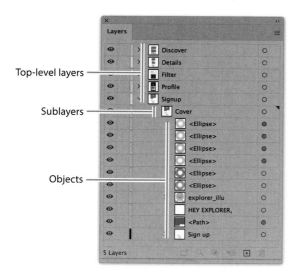

If you want to override Illustrator layers from within InDesign, make sure that all objects you want to show or hide are located on a top-level layer (not a sublayer), since sublayers can't be overridden in InDesign.

Placing the Illustrator logo

1 Return to InDesign and open L05-dino-ad-start.indd from the Lesson05 folder.

2 Choose File > Save As, and save the file as **L05-dino-adWorking.indd**.

3 Choose Window > Layers to view the Layers panel.

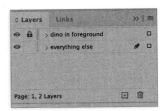

Notice there are two layers, one of which is locked. The locked layer (dino in foreground) holds a graphics frame that holds the T-rex Photoshop composition (trex.psd). If you look closely you can see the diagonal red frame edge running across the page. The bottom layer (everything else) holds the same dinosaur PSD file, plus an additional text frame.

4 Make sure the bottom layer (everything else) is selected in the Layers panel.

5 Choose File > Place.

6 Navigate to the Lessson05/Imports folder and select dino-logo.ai.

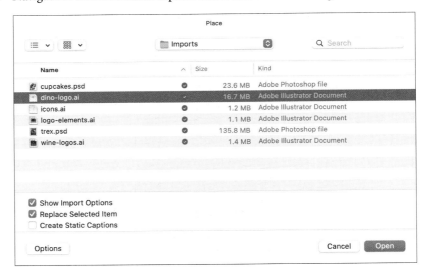

7 Make sure Show Import Options is selected at the bottom of the dialog box, and click Open.

8 In the Place PDF dialog box, make sure Transparent Background is selected. This will ensure no white background appears behind the artwork.

9 Click OK to continue placing the logo.

10 With the loaded cursor, drag to place the logo at approximately 140% of its original size onto the page.

The logo is partially overlapped by the duplicate T-rex composition, which is located in the locked layer. We now need to hide the background of that placed PSD file in order to have only the T-rex itself overlap with the logo. This will create a sense of depth, just like we did with the alpaca magazine cover in Lesson 3.

11 In the Layers panel, click the lock icon of the top-most layer to unlock it.

12 Use the Selection tool ▶ to select the overlapping T-rex image, and choose Object > Object Layer Options.

13 In the Object Layer Options dialog box, click the eye icon next to the layer named Background in order to hide it.

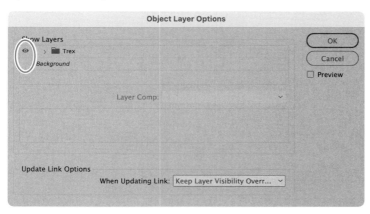

14 Click OK to close the dialog box.

15 Using the Layers panel, lock the top layer again.

With the background hidden, we can see that only the T-rex is left and is overlapping with the logo.

16 Use the Selection tool ▶ to move and center the logo on the page.

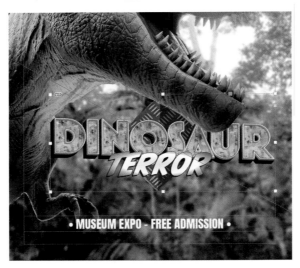

Overriding Illustrator layers

Now you'll change the look of the Illustrator logo by overriding the layers from InDesign.

1 Select the placed logo using the Selection tool ▶.

2 Choose Object > Object Layer Options.

3 From the Object Layer Options dialog box, deactivate the diamond layer and activate the circle layer.

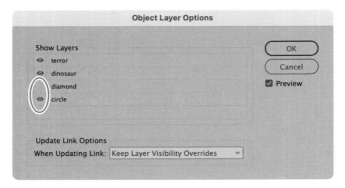

4   Click OK to close the dialog box.

We now have a different version of the logo in InDesign, while the original linked Illustrator document remains unaltered.

Changing InDesign File Handling preferences

As described in Lesson 3, there is a risk of InDesign undoing your layer overrides if you alter the layer structure of the Illustrator file after placing. The specific actions that we need to be careful of when altering the original file are:

* Adding or removing layers
* Renaming layers
* Changing the order of existing layers
* Changing the visibility of existing layers

Fortunately, an option in InDesign Preferences allows us to partially bypass InDesign's default behavior of resetting a placed file to its default layer visibility. To set this option:

In macOS: Choose InDesign > Preferences > File Handling.

In Windows: Choose Edit > Preferences > File Handling.

In the File Handling pane of the Preferences dialog box, select Hide New Layers When Updating Or Relinking and click OK to close the dialog box.

When this option is selected, adding new layers to an already placed and overridden Illustrator document will no longer result in an error that causes the overridden layers to be reset. But keep in mind that all other actions described above will still result in a layer reset in InDesign.

● **Note:** This preference applies to placed Illustrator, InDesign, and PDF documents. It doesn't apply to placed Photoshop documents.

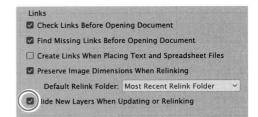

Creating an additional version

Now that we've changed InDesign's preferences, we can go ahead and add an additional layer to the Illustrator logo without accidentally resetting the layer visibility in InDesign.

1 In Illustrator, open dino-logo.ai from the Lesson05/Imports folder.

2 Choose Window > Layers to view the Layers panel.

3 Drag the terror layer onto the New Layer button in the Layers panel to duplicate it.

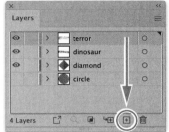

4 Click the eye icon of the original terror layer to hide it.

5 Double-click the newly duplicated layer name and rename it **island**; press Return/Enter to confirm.

6 Using the Selection tool ▶, double-click the text element to edit the text. Remove the word *TERROR* and replace it with *ISLAND*.

7 Save and close the file.

8 Return to InDesign.

9 In the Links panel, click the Update Link button to update the outdated Illustrator file.

The logo still displays TERROR, as it did before relinking, because InDesign will honor layer overrides and we haven't instructed InDesign to hide the terror layer yet.

▶ **Tip:** A quick alternative way of updating an out-of-date graphic is to use the Selection tool to click the triangle icon in the corner of the graphics frame on the page.

10 Select the logo in the layout.

11 Right-click the selected logo and choose Object Layer Options.

12 Notice that the newly created island layer is listed and hidden. Unhide the island layer and hide the terror layer.

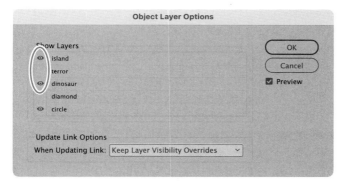

13 Click OK to close the dialog box.

Tip: See Lesson 3 to learn how to spot layer overrides in InDesign by using the Links panel or by creating a custom preflight profile.

14 Save your work and close the file.

Because we added an additional layer to the placed logo in Illustrator, we'd normally receive an error message in InDesign telling us all overridden layers will be reset to their defaults if we choose to update the file. But the new File Handling preference setting avoided this behavior. Also notice that the island layer was hidden when we accessed the Object Layer Options, while the layer was still visible in the original Illustrator file.

Using Illustrator artboards in InDesign

● **Note:** This book assumes that InDesign and Illustrator are using their default settings. If you are unsure of how to return to the default settings, review the steps in the section "Linking a Photoshop document in Illustrator" in Lesson 2, "Enriching Illustrator Artwork with Photoshop Content."

In this exercise you'll create a flyer by placing artwork from Illustrator artboards in InDesign, and you'll see that this can be a great alternative to overriding Illustrator layers.

Getting started

You'll start the lesson by viewing an image of the final composition and placed artwork.

1 From Illustrator, open wine-logos.ai from the Lesson05/Imports folder.

2 Reset the Illustrator workspace by choosing Window > Workspace > Essentials, followed by Window > Workspace > Reset Essentials.

3 Choose Window > Artboards to display the Artboards panel. Notice that all artboards have been uniquely named.

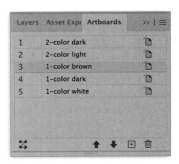

This Illustrator document contains five different versions of the same logo, each on a separate artboard. When you place this document in InDesign, you can choose which version of the logo to use depending on the situation.

4 Open icons.ai from the Lesson05/Imports folder.

This document has four artboards with white and black icons.

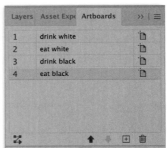

5 Close the file.

6 In InDesign, open L05-wine-food-end.indd from the Lesson05 folder.

7 Reset the InDesign Workspace by choosing Window > Workspace > Essentials and then choosing Window > Workspace > Reset Essentials.

The InDesign document uses one of the five logos from wine-logos.ai and the white icons from icons.ai.

8 Close the file.

Placing an artboard in InDesign

As you learned in Lesson 1, "Workflows and File Formats," when you place an AI file in InDesign you're placing a PDF version of that Illustrator document. That's why the title of the Import Options dialog box in InDesign reads *Place PDF* when you place an Illustrator file. This also means the options in the dialog box are PDF-specific; the options most relevant to an Illustrator file are:

- **Pages:** Use the Pages option to specify the artboard or artboards in the AI file that you want to place in the InDesign document.

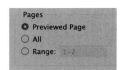

- **Cropping:** The Crop To option allows you to choose a PDF page box setting. This is a predefined zone within the file reserved for print-specific purposes. For example, *Bleed* refers to the PDF BleedBox, which defines the region of the entire page, including the bleed area. The more familiar you are with printing and prepress-specific options when working with PDF, the higher the chance that this sounds familiar to you.

Here is a quick rundown of how to use cropping options to your advantage when placing Illustrator documents: choosing Bounding Box will place the objects in visible (or all) layers, Trim will place the entire artboard, and Bleed will place the entire artboard—including the document bleed. The other crop options won't have a different effect when placing Illustrator documents, as the regions they refer to can't be set in Illustrator.

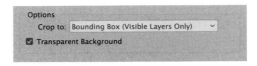

Now that we're familiar with the basics, let's take a look at how you can place or update artboards in InDesign.

1 From InDesign, open L05-wine-food-start.indd from the Lesson05 folder.

2 Choose File > Save As and save your file as **L05-wine-foodWorking.indd**.

3 Choose Window > Layers to display the Layers panel.

4 Click the top (red) layer to highlight it.

   We need to place the company logo on the flyer and have five different logo versions to choose from. We'll choose the brown version first and see if it's a good match with the design.

5 Choose File > Place, navigate to the Lesson05/Imports folder, and select wine-logos.ai.

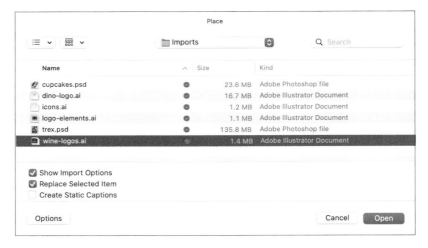

6 Make sure Show Import Options is selected, then click Open.

7 In the Place PDF dialog box, use the navigation arrows below the Preview window to navigate to page 3, which is the brown logo.

8 Make sure Show Preview is selected under the Pages option and that Transparent Background is also selected.

Because we want to place only the logo artwork without the artboard, it's important to leave the Crop To option at its default setting: Bounding Box (Visible Layers Only).

9 Click OK to confirm.

10 With the loaded cursor, drag to place the logo on the page at roughly 50% of its original size (the cursor preview will show its size during dragging).

11 Using the Selection tool ▶, move the logo to the right side of the vertical white line, aligning its left side with the word *PAIRING*. Then deselect.

Changing to a different artboard

Unfortunately, there is no menu, hidden panel, or other option in InDesign that will change to a different Illustrator artboard after its initial import. The only method available for switching between artboards is to relink the placed Illustrator file with itself while triggering the Import Options dialog box again. We could use the Place command again, but this time we'll use the Links panel instead.

As we continue the current exercise, notice that the brown logo isn't as legible against the dark background as we'd hoped. So we need to change the brown logo to the white logo.

1   Use the Selection tool ![selection tool] to select the placed logo.

2   Choose Window > Links to display the Links panel.

Note that the selected logo is highlighted in the Links panel, and its name reads *wine-logos.ai:3*. The number at the end of the filename represents the number of the placed artboard. Unfortunately, it's not possible to also display the name of the artboard.

3   In the Links panel, click the Relink button.

Note: If you can't see the Show Import Options checkbox, click the Options button.

4   Navigate to the Lesson05/Imports folder and select wine-logos.ai. Make sure Show Import Options is selected.

5   Click Open.

6   In the Place PDF dialog box, select the last page (that is, the last artboard) of the file and click OK to replace the brown logo with the white logo.

7   Deselect the logo and keep the file open.

Placing multiple artboards

Next we'll place multiple artboards at once—in this case, two icons from a different Illustrator document.

1   Choose File > Place.

2   In the Lesson05/Imports folder, select icons.ai.

3   Make sure Show Import Options is selected, then click Open.

4   In the Place PDF dialog box, cycle through the different pages using the Preview option.

Note that there are two white icons and two black icons. For this exercise we need to use the white icons, which are on pages 1 and 2.

5   In the Pages area, click Range and enter **1,2**.

Leave all other options at their default settings.

6   Click OK.

Pages
○ Previewed Page
○ All
● Range: 1,2

7   Drag in the InDesign document with the loaded cursor to place the first icon. Its size should not be larger than the height of the word *WINE* on the page.

8   Now do the same for the second icon, giving it approximately the same size.

9   Position the bottle icon to the left of the word *WINE* and position the food icon to the left of the word *FOOD*.

10 Select both icons, and click the Align Horizontal Centers button in the Properties panel to center both icons.

Note: When you package an InDesign document that holds a multi-artboard Illustrator file, the entire Illustrator file—not only the placed artboards—will be included in the package.

11 Revisit the Links panel and note that the two placed icons are listed under the same placed file, but each with different previews and artboard page references.

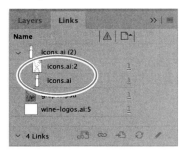

12 Save and close the file.

Converting artboards to files

There will be occasions when you need to step away from creating multiple artboards in a single Illustrator file and instead save every artboard in separate Illustrator files. For example, imagine you have a file that holds 15 different icons, all positioned on separate artboards. An external party requests that all the icons be delivered to them as separate Illustrator files for processing or distribution purposes.

We need to avoid having to manually select the icons one by one and paste them into 15 new Illustrator files. Luckily for us, Illustrator makes it easy for us to split artboards into separate files:

1 In Ilustrator, open Lesson05/Imports open wine-logos.ai if it isn't already open.

2 Choose File > Save As.

3 Navigate to your desktop and create a new folder called **Wine logos**.

4 Leave the file format as Adobe Illustrator AI, and click Save.

5 In the Illustrator Options dialog box, select Save Each Artboard To A Separate File.

6 Click OK.

Illustrator exports all artboards to separate AI files. Each file takes its name from the source file, with the artboard name appended to it.

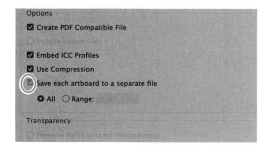

7 Close the file.

Should you use layer overrides or artboards?

Now that you've learned how to override Illustrator layers and place Illustrator artboards in InDesign it's time to evaluate some of the arguments for and against both techniques.

But before we get into that it's important to realize that it is not always necessary to make that choice, because the techniques are *not* mutually exclusive. This means that you can choose to place one of multiple Illustrator artboards that themselves contain artwork that consists of multiple layers, and these can also be overridden in InDesign.

To take one example, imagine you're working on an illustration of a world map in Illustrator for an international client. Your Illustrator file is quite complex, with many paths, map icons, and even a placed Photoshop file. Your design needs to be delivered to the prepress department, where it will be placed in InDesign as part of a larger poster campaign. And because of the international nature of the campaign, you have one Illustrator artboard that shows the North American continent and another that shows the European continent.

Because you chose to create both artboards in the same file, you were able to:

- Synchronize symbols, swatches, graphic styles, text styles, and effects across both artboards
- Share the same layer structure between both artboards
- See both designs next to each other to verify that their visual styles match
- Synchronize last-minute changes across both designs
- Deliver a single file to the prepress department

And because you built a proper layer structure and used separate artboards (instead of separate files), the prepress department is able to:

- Choose which artboard to place in InDesign (or Photoshop for, for example, creating web graphics)
- Override layers from InDesign for showing or hiding details like the map icons and other elements
- Package the entire campaign when the project is over

Ask yourself the following questions

It's not always easy choosing between the two techniques. In some cases it might be best to use layer overrides; in other cases it would be better to use artboards. Here are a few questions you can ask yourself to help you make up your mind.

How often are artwork updates required?

As explained in this book, overriding layers in InDesign comes with certain risks. This means that the more updates and design changes are required within Illustrator, the higher the risk of running into a layer reset in InDesign. Because of this, it's often a lot safer to place artboards instead of overriding layers when you will need heavy design changes later on. If you're expecting only small changes, you're free to choose the technique you like best.

Do I need to name my design to identify it?

One disadvantage of using placed artboards is the fact that we can't see the name of the artboard prior to placing it in InDesign, whereas it *is* possible to view the name of a layer in InDesign while overriding it. If it's difficult to visually distinguish one Illustrator artboard from another, it might be easier to instead use named layers when placing in InDesign. For example, imagine you have a file that has a Pantone version of a logo and a CMYK version of a logo, each on separate artboards. You might not be able to distinguish the Pantone version from the CMYK version during placing in InDesign, whereas placing the logos on named layers will offer you certainty because the layers would be named accordingly.

Do I need to link my file into Photoshop?

As you'll learn in Lesson 6, "Using Illustrator Artwork in Photoshop," it is also possible to place and link an Illustrator file in Photoshop. And while you do so, Photoshop will ask you which artboard you want to place (if multiple artboards are present in the AI file). This means you have control over the design or version you import (and link) into Photoshop. But unfortunately, Photoshop doesn't offer a way to override layers once they're placed, which means you can only rely on artboards for creating separate versions you want to have available in Photoshop. So if you also expect to use the same Illustrator file in InDesign, it's best to choose a solution that works for all applications in your workflow.

Will I need to save every version as a separate file?

As explained earlier in this lesson, Illustrator offers an easy way to save every artboard to a separate Illustrator file, which adds to the flexibility of artboards in Illustrator. But if the versions you created in Illustrator are based on layer visibility instead of on artboards, you'd need to manually copy and resave every file when someone requests separate file versions. This could be a heavy argument against using layer-based versions.

Conclusion

The above questions are merely guidelines, as there is no official wrong or right way of placing artwork. But taking this advice into consideration will result in flexibility and time gains.

Pasting Illustrator artwork into InDesign

The last exercise in this lesson focuses on copying and pasting artwork from Illustrator into InDesign. And although every computer user grew up with the concept of copy and paste, it's important to realize that many things can go wrong if you decide to paste rather than place Illustrator artwork into InDesign.

● **Note:** This book assumes that InDesign and Illustrator are using their default settings. If you are unsure of how to return to the default settings, review the steps in the "Getting started" section at the beginning of this lesson.

Things to know before you start

Before we start to copy and paste artwork from Illustrator into InDesign it's important to know more about the background process of it all. After all, Illustrator files can get very complex and can include effects, patterns, rasterized images, art brushes, masks, and many other things. This means that we're not even certain whether our artwork will survive the trip when pasting to InDesign and still look exactly the way it looked in Illustrator. Additionally, we need to make sure our actions don't have a negative effect on our InDesign document.

Setting Illustrator preferences

Illustrator offers us a variety of settings that determine how data is saved to the clipboard. Not knowing which options to choose before copying artwork into other applications might cause radically different results, depending on these settings. And these settings don't apply to InDesign alone, because we can copy artwork from Illustrator into many third-party apps as well. You might even find that some combinations of settings render a certain result in InDesign while rendering different results when used in combination with third-party apps.

* In macOS: Choose Illustrator > Preferences > Clipboard Handling.

* In Windows: Choose Edit > Preferences > Clipboard Handling.

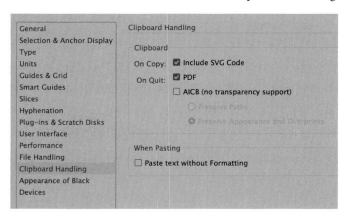

The main question you have to ask yourself is, "Are there any transparent objects in my document, or have I applied any transparent effects to my artwork?" If you haven't, then changing these settings will not make a difference. But if you do have transparent objects, it's important to pay attention.

It is impossible to copy Illustrator objects that use transparency and paste them into InDesign while retaining the live transparency *and* keeping the object editable.

For example, if you take a simple Illustrator shape with a 100% magenta color applied, lower its opacity to 50%, and then paste that object into InDesign, you will end up with a shape with 100% opacity and a 50% magenta tint applied to visually mimic the transparency effect. And what's even worse is that rasterized Illustrator effects—for example, a Drop Shadow effect—will be pasted as an opaque image that isn't listed in the Links panel.

A simple rule

There are a few recommendations when dealing with such a situation:

- If your artwork has no transparent objects or effects applied, copy and paste the artwork from Illustrator into InDesign using Illustrator's default settings. However, be on the lookout for other complications. (See "Other potential problems" later in this lesson.)

- If your artwork has transparency options applied to objects, verify that the same transparency options are also available in InDesign (for example, opacity and blending modes). That way, you can reapply the same effects in InDesign once the artwork is pasted. To achieve this, ensure that the Include SVG Code and PDF options are unselected in Illustrator Preferences and that AICB Preserve Paths is selected.

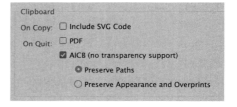

Alternatively, you can select the last option, Preserve Appearance And Overprints, which will replicate the transparent effects by altering the original shapes and adding additional ones if needed.

Note: Be sure to change the preferences before you use the Copy command. After you change the preferences, you will need to choose the Copy command again for the changes to take effect in the clipboard.

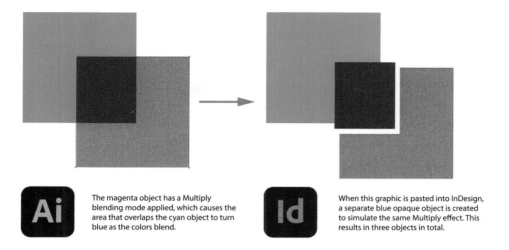

The magenta object has a Multiply blending mode applied, which causes the area that overlaps the cyan object to turn blue as the colors blend.

When this graphic is pasted into InDesign, a separate blue opaque object is created to simulate the same Multiply effect. This results in three objects in total.

- If your artwork has transparency options applied that are *not* available in InDesign, or if you are using any effects, then you can choose to paste the artwork into InDesign as a transparent PDF. To achieve this, you need to first set an additional preference in InDesign before pasting:

- In macOS: Choose InDesign > Preferences > Clipboard Handling.

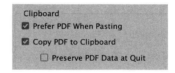

- In Windows: Choose Edit > Preferences > Clipboard Handling.

Select Prefer PDF When Pasting to paste all artwork while keeping transparency intact, but without the ability to change the vectors in InDesign.

Other potential problems

Unfortunately, we're not out of the woods yet. When copying artwork from Illustrator, keep an eye out for the following dangers:

- If your Illustrator and InDesign documents use different color modes or profiles, you might see unexpected color shifts in your design. Pay special attention to black because RGB black can cause problems when converted to CMYK and vice versa. There is also the risk of accidentally bringing in spot colors.

- Pasted radial and linear gradients from Illustrator are supported in InDesign, but other gradient types—for example, freeform gradients or gradient mesh—will be rasterized at low resolution when pasted into InDesign and will not be listed in the Links panel.

- Depending on their complexity, pasting Illustrator patterns can cause a mess in InDesign because it can potentially import hundreds of vector objects, grouped and clipped within one another.

- Pasted text from Illustrator will be converted to outlines in InDesign and will no longer be editable. To keep the text editable in InDesign, it needs to be copied using the Type tool in Illustrator and pasted into a text frame in InDesign. However, keep in mind that none of your original Illustrator text formatting will be preserved after pasting in InDesign.

- Rasterized images from Illustrator—for example, pasted JPEG files and other placed content—will not be listed in the InDesign Links panel.

- When pasting artwork into InDesign you run the risk of accidentally recoloring the artwork when you update an InDesign swatch. And there is a chance you might scale it nonproportionally without any way of verifying its original scale and proportions. It is recommended that you not paste certain artwork, such as logos, into InDesign at all; use the Place command instead.

- Illustrator features like masks, brushes, graphic styles, and others can lead to unexpected results. Thoroughly inspect the artwork in InDesign.

If you think you might run into any of the problems described in this lesson, it is highly recommended that you place the Illustrator file into InDesign instead of copying and pasting. A placed Illustrator document in InDesign supports transparency, layers, and artboards; is listed in the Links panel; and allows you to update the original document and see its changes reflected in InDesign.

When to paste

Despite all the warnings in this lesson, there are still many use cases for which pasting artwork from Illustrator offers a clear advantage. Overall, it is safe to paste into InDesign objects that are not too complex and that don't use transparency. A few examples are:

- Pasting a decorative element that you want to use as a text frame or graphics frame in InDesign

- Using an Illustrator graphic as a bullet character in InDesign

- Using an Illustrator vector shape to wrap text around in InDesign

- Pasting a die-cut or other technical outline into InDesign

- Pasting special arrows, or other difficult-to-create objects, for which you need to change the stroke or fill color in InDesign

Putting it into practice

The following exercise will provide you with a good example of importing Illustrator artwork into InDesign by pasting. Before you start, make sure the Clipboard Handling preferences are still at their default settings.

Getting started

This project explains the basics of copying and pasting artwork from Illustrator into InDesign. You'll start the lesson by viewing an image of the final composition and pasted artwork.

1   In Illustrator, open logo-elements.ai from the Lesson05/Imports folder.

2   Reset the Illustrator Workspace by choosing Window > Workspace > Essentials, followed by Window > Workspace > Reset Essentials.

This document has two artboards, each containing vector shapes that we'll copy from Illustrator and paste into InDesign.

3   Leave the file open.

4   In InDesign, open L05-baking-end.indd from the Lesson05 folder.

5   Reset the InDesign Workspace by choosing Window > Workspace > Essentials, followed by Window > Workspace > Reset Essentials.

This document represents the finished version of a sticker design to advertise baking classes. Notice how the Illustrator shapes have been used in various ways. The frame has several InDesign effects applied, and there is even an image placed into the Illustrator artwork. All other illustrations have their colors slightly altered and are used as decoration.

6   Close the file.

Importing the main frame

1   Go to Illustrator and open logo-elements.ai from the Lesson05/Imports folder.

2   In the first artboard, use the Selection tool 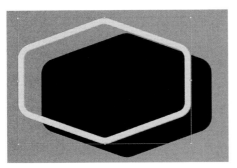 to select the light gray frame.

3   Choose Edit > Copy.

4   Go to InDesign and open L05-baking-start.indd from the Lesson05 folder.

5   Choose File > Save As and save your file as **L05-bakingWorking.indd**.

Before we continue, we need to change one of InDesign's default preferences so that we can select locked objects and change their Fill and Stroke properties.

6   In macOS, choose InDesign > Preferences > General.

In Windows, choose Edit > Preferences > General.

7   Deselect Prevent Selection Of Locked Objects, and click OK to close.

8   Choose Edit > Paste.

9   In the Properties panel, make sure the W and H properties are linked by clicking the Constrain Proportions button (if necessary). This will ensure that the shape scales proportionally.

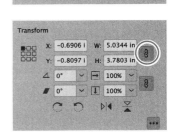

10   In the Properties panel, change the width to **3.5 in** and press Return/Enter.

11   In the Properties panel, click the first icon in the Align options to change the alignment from To Selection to To Page. Then click the Align Horizontal Centers button to center the shape horizontally.

12 Make sure the reference point is set to the top left. Then enter **0.04 in** in the Y field.

13 Deselect the shape.

14 Select the Direct Selection tool  from the Tools panel, and marquee-drag over the bottom half of the shape to select the anchor points in the bottom half of the shape.

15 Hold down the Shift key and press the Up Arrow key four times to shrink the height of the shape. Then deselect the shape.

16 Choose Window > Layers to display the Layers panel. Then click the arrow next to the layer name (Layer 1) to expand the layer structure.

Notice there is only one object in the stack that is not locked: <compound path>, the object we just pasted from Illustrator. We need to rename the shape in order to make it easily identifiable.

17 Click the name of the <compound path> object in the Layers panel to highlight it. Click once again to select it and change its name to **frame**, and then press Return/Enter to confirm the change.

18 With the frame selected, open the Swatches panel and apply the [Paper] swatch to the object's fill.

19 In the Layers panel, click the square area to the left of the object name to lock it. Then save your file.

20 Return to Illustrator.

21 Copy the black shape from Illustrator and paste it into InDesign.

22 Scale the object down and move it on top of the white frame until its top, left, and right edges overlap with the frame edges.

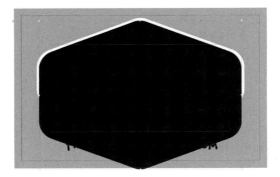

23 In the Layers panel, rename the object **image placeholder**.

24 Drag the object below the frame object in the layer stack.

25 Use the Direct Selection tool 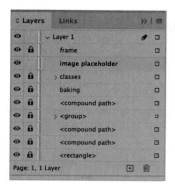 to select the bottom portion of the frame and move the points up until it disappears behind the white frame.

26 Deselect the object.

27 In the Layers panel, lock the image placeholder object.

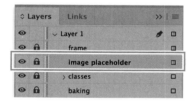

Importing the banners

1 Continuing to work in Illustrator and in logo-elements.ai, select the left banner object at the bottom of the artboard and copy it.

2 Return to InDesign and paste the banner object.

3 Using the Layers panel, name the object **left banner**.

4 Use the Direct Selection tool  to select the two points on the right side of the shape.

5 Drag the two corner points to the left to shrink the shape until the object width is approximately 0.25 in.

6 Use the Selection tool 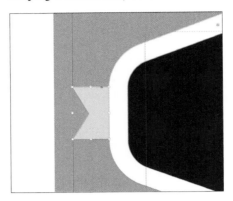 to move the banner to the left side of the frame object, keeping it horizontally centered with the frame.

7 Apply the [Paper] swatch to the object's fill.

8 Choose Edit > Duplicate to duplicate the banner.

9 Use the Layers panel to rename the duplicate **right banner**.

10 Choose Object > Transform > Flip Horizontal to make the banner face the opposite direction.

11 Position the banner on the right side of the frame, horizontally centered with the left banner.

12 Deselect all objects.

13 Use the Layers panel to lock the left and right banners.

Adding effects

Now we'll add a bit of depth to the pasted vector shapes by adding effects.

1 Use the Selection tool ▶ to select the frame object.

2 Choose Window > Effects to display the Effects panel.

3 In the Effects panel, double-click the text Object: Normal 100% to open the Effects dialog box.

4 Select Preview in the bottom left of the dialog box.

5 Click the words Bevel And Emboss (not the checkbox beside them) to apply the effect and display its options.

6 Change the Technique setting to Chisel Hard.

7 Set the Size to **0.125 in**.

8 Enter **90** for Angle and **45** for Altitude.

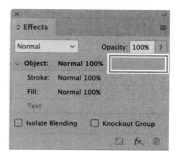

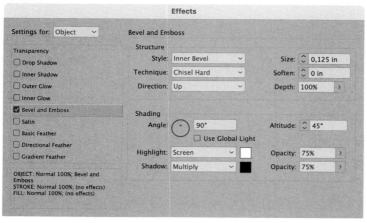

We chose an angle of 90° so that the effect highlight will be applied vertically to the object. Next, we'll finish the effect by changing the shadow color and adding a drop shadow at the same angle.

9 Set the Opacity for Shadow to **100%**.

10 Click the Shadow color box, click to select the darker pink swatch in the Effect Color dialog box, and then click OK.

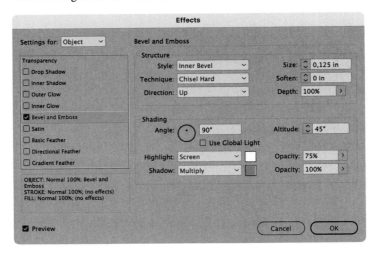

11 Click the Drop Shadow effect to apply it and view its options.

● **Note:** The applied effects might seem as if they are low resolution, but they will be rendered at high resolution once exported.

12 Click the Set Shadow Color button (next to the Blending Mode menu) to change the shadow's color in the Effect Color dialog box. Select the darker pink swatch. Click OK to close.

13 For Angle, enter **90** (the same value we used for the Bevel And Emboss effect).

14 Change Y Offset value to **0.0625 in**, and notice that this also changes the Distance value.

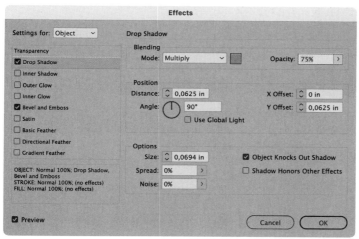

15 Click OK to close the Effects dialog box. Keep the object selected.

Duplicating effects and adding an image

Now we'll take the effects we just created and duplicate them on the left and right banner objects.

1 With the frame object selected, look at the Effects panel and note the *fx* icon next to Object: Normal 100% in the panel. This icon represents all effects currently applied to the object.

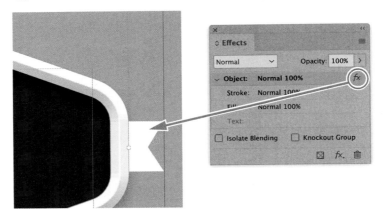

2 Drag the *fx* icon from the Effects panel onto the right banner object in the layout (not in the Layers panel).

This duplicates all effects and applies them to the banner object.

3 Do the same for the left banner object.

4 In the Layers panel, drag the frame object to the top of the stack.

Next, we'll place an image in the image placeholder frame.

5 Using the Selection tool ▶, select the image placeholder object.

6 Choose File > Place.

7 Navigate to the Lesson05/Imports folder and select cupcakes.psd. Make sure Show Import Options is unselected.

8 Click Open to place the image.

9 With the active selection, click the first button in the Frame Fitting category of the Properties panel (Fill Frame Proportionally) to fit the image in the frame. Notice there is still an empty area on the right side of the image.

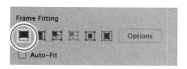

10 Click the center of the image to select the Content Grabber. This will select the image within the graphics frame.

11 Shift-drag the lower-right corner outward to scale the image up. Do this until the cupcakes fill the empty area on the right.

● **Note:** You might need to zoom out a little bit in order to see the corner.

12 Deselect the image.

13 In the Layers panel, drag the baking and classes objects to the top of the stack.

Importing the illustrations

To finish the design we need to bring in the cooking illustrations from Illustrator one by one.

1 Return to Illustrator and choose 2 baking illustrations from the Artboard Navigator menu, located at the bottom of the Illustrator window. This artboard holds all illustrations.

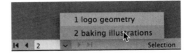

2 Use the Selection tool ▶ to select the strawberry. Then choose Edit > Copy.

3 Return to InDesign and choose Edit > Paste to paste it on the design.

4 Scale the object down a little bit and place it in the upper-left corner of the page.

5 Return to Illustrator and do the same with the cupcake object, but place it in the upper-right corner of the page in InDesign.

6 Repeat the process for the apron, placing it in the lower-left corner in InDesign.

7 Do the same with the oven mitt and whisk, copying them individually and placing them on the bottom right in InDesign.

Scaling and positioning these illustrations is not an exact science. So feel free to play around with the object position, scale, and rotation until you find a composition you like. Alternatively, you can use the Layers panel to change the stacking order of the objects, making some illustrations appear behind the frame and image.

8 Return to Illustrator and copy the rolling pin; paste it into the InDesign document.

9 Scale the rolling pin down until it's just large enough to fit between the baking text and the bottom edge of the frame. Don't deselect it.

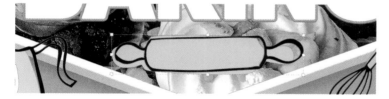

10 Look at the Layers panel and notice that the rolling pin is the top-most object in the stack. Now drag it down the stack until it is just under the object named classes.

To make it seem as if the word *classes* is written on the rolling pin, use the arrow keys on the keyboard to nudge the text around the rolling pin until the text is nicely centered.

Updating swatches

Let's take a look at how the pasted objects changed our list of swatches in InDesign.

1   Open the Swatches panel.

Notice that various swatches were added to the Swatches panel. All these colors were brought into InDesign by pasting objects from Illustrator. Also notice there is no additional black or white swatch added to the Swatches panel, despite many objects using these colors in Illustrator. This is because InDesign is automatically applying its own black and white swatch to these objects.

2   In the Swatches panel, double-click the light blue swatch, named c25m0y16k0, to edit it.

3   In the Swatch Options dialog box, increase the Cyan value to **50%**, and then click OK to close the dialog box.

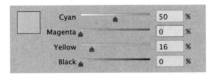

4   Make sure nothing is selected. Then from the Swatches panel, double-click the light green swatch, named c27m0y59k0, to edit it.

5   Increase Cyan to **50%** and Yellow to **100%**, and then click OK to close the dialog box.

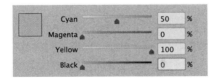

We've just updated the blue and green colors in the illustrations by simply editing their imported swatches in InDesign.

6   Make sure nothing is selected. Then, in the Swatches panel, click the swatch named c13m10y10k0 to highlight it.

7   Shift-click the last swatch in the list to select all the imported colors.

8   Double-click any of the selected swatch color thumbnails to open the Swatch Options dialog box.

9 Select the Name With Color Value checkbox, then click OK to close the dialog box.

The color values in the original swatch names no longer represent their actual color values; selecting Name With Color Value ensures that all swatch names will update accordingly when you change their values in the future.

10 Use the Selection tool ▶ to select the word *fresh*, and apply the light blue swatch.

11 Select the text *from the* and apply the [Paper] swatch.

12 Select the text *oven* and apply the yellow swatch.

13 Select the text *.com* and apply the light blue swatch again.

14 Deselect everything and save your work.

15 Close the file.

Review questions

1 When placing an Illustrator file in InDesign, which layer types can be overridden?

2 What does the option Hide New Layers When Updating Or Relinking, found in the File Handling section of InDesign Preferences, do?

3 How can you save multiple artboards within a single Illustrator file as separate Illustrator files?

4 After placing an Illustrator artboard in InDesign, how can you change the placed artboard to a different artboard within the same file from InDesign?

5 Name three potential problems when pasting Illustrator artwork into InDesign.

Review answers

1 It is only possible to override top-level layers from placed Illustrator documents in InDesign. Sublayers are not accessible.

2 When an Illustrator or PDF file has overridden layers in InDesign, selecting Hide New Layers When Updating Or Relinking avoids a layer override reset when adding new layers to the placed file.

3 To save Illustrator artboards as separate Illustrator files, choose File > Save As, click Save, and select Save Each Artboard To A Separate File in the Illustrator Options dialog box.

4 First select the placed file using the Selection tool. Then choose File > Place and reselect the same Illustrator document. Select Show Import Options and click Place. From the Place PDF dialog box, choose the artboard you want and click OK to confirm.

5 First, not all Illustrator objects and effects are supported by InDesign. Examples include freeform gradients, art brushes, transparent effects, and many others. Second, unexpected color conversions might occur when Illustrator and InDesign use different color modes. Third, because pasted artwork is converted into native InDesign artwork, you might accidentally transform artwork nonproportionally. If you don't need to directly edit the pasted artwork in InDesign, it is recommended to import the Illustrator artwork using the Place command.

6 USING ILLUSTRATOR ARTWORK IN PHOTOSHOP

Lesson overview

In this lesson, you'll learn how to do the following:

- Choose among the various methods of bringing Illustrator artwork into Photoshop.

- Understand the embedding process when placing Illustrator files into Photoshop documents.

- Understand the importance of linking to original documents.

- Use the bounding box to your advantage during placing.

- Choose the correct options when pasting artwork from Illustrator.

This lesson will take about 40 minutes to complete. Please log in to your account at adobepress.com/DesignCIB to download the files for this lesson, or go to the "Getting Started" section at the beginning of this book and follow the instructions under "Accessing the lesson files and Web Edition." Store the files on your computer in a convenient location.

Your Account page is also where you'll find any updates to the lesson files. Look on the Lesson & Update Files tab to access the most current content.

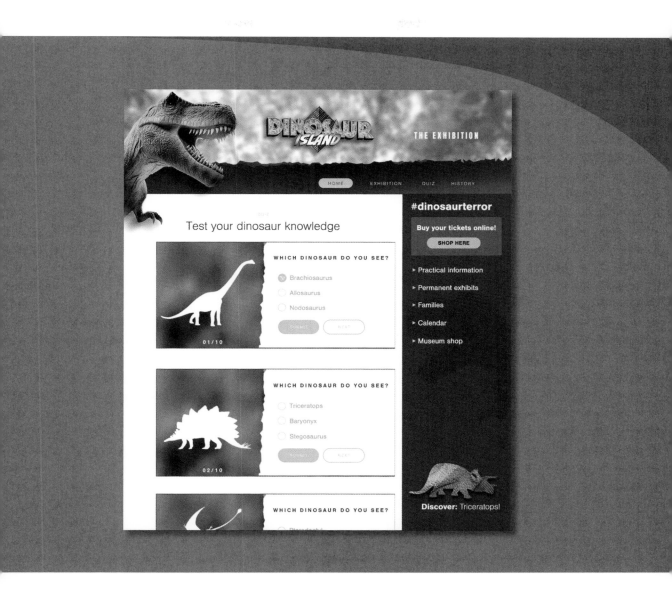

Knowing how to properly import Illustrator content into Photoshop will drastically speed up your workflow, help reduce the total number of Photoshop layers in your images, and make round-tripping to Illustrator easy.

Combining Illustrator and Photoshop

This lesson provides you with a deep dive into how Illustrator and Photoshop interact with each other. Lesson 2, "Enriching Illustrator Artwork with Photoshop Content," provided you with an overview of the importing and linking functions going from Photoshop into Illustrator. In this lesson we'll explore the opposite direction. And while exploring this subject, you'll learn that there are several considerations when choosing an import method:

- Do you want to keep the imported Illustrator text editable in Photoshop?

- Do you want to keep the vector shapes editable in Photoshop?

- Do you need to retain a link to the original AI file?

- Do you want to include a selection of your artwork in Photoshop? A single artboard? Or the entire document? And should that document be the original AI file or an embedded copy?

By the time you reach the end of this lesson you'll be able to answer these questions and pick the method that is best suited for your own workflows.

Embedding Illustrator artwork in Photoshop

The first exercise looks at how you can place and embed an Illustrator artboard or an entire Illustrator file in a Photoshop composition. The principle you learned in Lesson 2 of embedding a PSD file in Illustrator is not entirely the same when reversing the direction of the workflow:

- After you embed a Photoshop document in Illustrator and need to edit the document again in Photoshop, you need to first unembed the file. Unembedding means extracting the file and saving it as an external document. When you then edit the file back in Photoshop, you need to replace the version previously placed into Illustrator. This can be a very painful process.

- When you embed an Illustrator document in Photoshop and need to edit the document again in Illustrator, all you need to do is double-click the Smart Object that represents the placed artwork. Photoshop will then take you to Illustrator, where you can immediately edit the file; once it's saved, the Photoshop document will update. In other words, there is always a straight line toward Illustrator.

Let's take a look at how this works in practice.

Getting started

You'll start this lesson by viewing an image of the final composition and placed artwork.

1 Start Photoshop, and choose Photoshop > Preferences > General (macOS) or Edit > Preferences > General (Windows).

   The Preferences dialog box opens.

2 Click Reset Preferences On Quit and click OK in the confirmation dialog box. Then restart Photoshop.

3 From the Lesson06 folder, open L06-exhibition-end.psd.

   This document is part of a web design project in which multiple icons from Illustrator were placed and embedded. Additionally, the icons were recolored by applying a layer style.

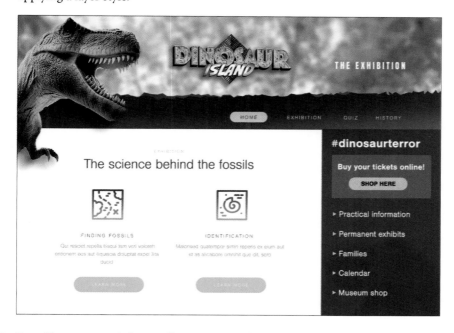

● **Note:** The first time you open a Photoshop document with linked Smart Objects, choose Layer > Smart Objects > Update All Modified Content to resolve the issue and remove the yellow warning triangles.

4 Start Illustrator, and choose Illustrator > Preferences > General (macOS) or Edit > Preferences > General (Windows).

   The Preferences dialog box opens.

5 Click Reset Preferences, then click OK to close the dialog box.

6 Click Restart Now in the confirmation dialog box to restart Illustrator and reset preferences.

7　From the Lesson06/Imports folder, open paleontology-icons.ai in Illustrator.

This Illustrator document contains the icons used on the exhibition web page. Notice there are more icons available than the ones used in Photoshop.

8　In Photoshop, close L06-exhibition-end.psd without saving, but leave paleontology-icons.ai open in Illustrator.

Placing the Illustrator file

Before you place the file, it's important to do a proper inspection of the artwork you're bringing into Photoshop. Is the artwork on a separate artboard, or is it part of a larger design, of which you need to use only a specific part? Here are your two options when you want to embed the artwork:

- If the artwork is located on its own artboard, using the Place Embedded command in Photoshop is recommended.

- If the artwork is not on its own separate artboard, you can copy the artwork from Illustrator and then paste it as embedded artwork (more on this subject later in this lesson).

1　In Illustrator, take a closer look at paleontology-icons.ai.

Note that all icons are on separate artboards. All artboards are the same size, and all icons have the same approximate size and are centered on the artboard. This is important because we can take advantage of the area surrounding the icon on the artboard.

Some artwork—for example, icons and logos—might require the designer to leave a certain amount of whitespace (or "padding") around the artwork. So let's imagine that the whitespace surrounding the icons in paleontology-icons.ai needs to be taken into account when placing in Photoshop.

2　Go to Photoshop and open L06-exhibition-start.psd.

The Layers panel shows that there are many layers in this document. To make it easier to navigate the document, we'll detach the Layers panel from the workspace and make it fit the height of our screen.

3 Choose File > Save As and save your file as **L06-exhibitionWorking.psd**.

4 Drag the Layers panel tab toward the center of the screen to detach it from the application frame. Then grab the bottom edge and drag to expand the panel downward as far as you can. This allows us to view all layers at once.

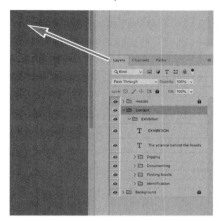

The three colors used in the Layers panel help identify the different parts of the Photoshop document. The red and blue groups are locked, and the green group is available for editing.

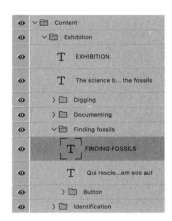

5 Expand the Content group in the Layers panel and expand the "Finding fossils" group within it.

6 Select the FINDING FOSSILS type layer.

7 Choose File > Place Embedded.

8 Navigate to Lesson06/Imports and double-click paleontology-icons.ai. The Open As Smart Object dialog box appears. Leave the dialog box open for the next exercise.

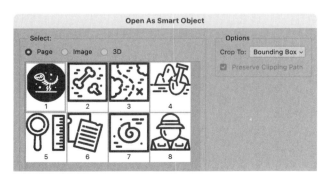

Choosing import options

In this screen we need to select the artwork (or artboard) we want to place and embed into Photoshop. Also note that there is the option to choose a different crop at the top right of the dialog box. These options are similar to those we used when placing Illustrator documents into InDesign in Lesson 5, "Using Illustrator Artwork in InDesign."

Placing artwork using the default settings, with Bounding Box chosen from the Crop To menu, would place the artwork from the selected artboard into Photoshop without including the artboard bounds—that is, it would lose the "padding" that surrounds the artwork. Let's take advantage of this padding in this exercise.

1 In the Open As Smart Object dialog box, change the Crop To option to Crop Box.

The preview updates and now includes the entire artboard.

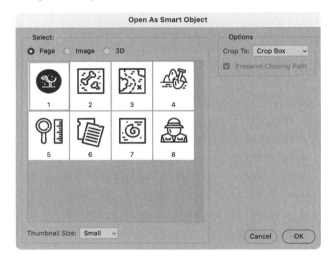

2 Select artboard 3 (which represents a map) and click OK.

Photoshop will place the artwork (including the artboard whitespace) but offers the option to transform it before we commit.

3 Enter **50%** for the width and height in the Options bar, but don't press Return/Enter yet.

4 Move the object so it sits above the *FINDING FOSSILS* text, and center it by positioning the center bounding box handles over the middle guide.

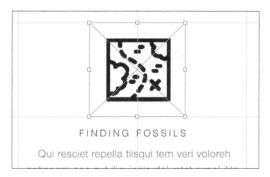

5 Press Return/Enter to confirm the size and placement.

6 Double-click the newly added paleontology-icons layer and rename it **fossils icon**.

The reason we waited to commit our edits (by pressing Return/Enter) until after we positioned the graphic is because committing the edits takes us out of Free Transform mode, and that would hide the bounding box around the object. This way, we are able to leverage the padding around the placed artwork to create the proper distance between the text and the icon.

Also, notice the special icon that was added to the layer thumbnail in the Layers panel. This icon allows us to recognize embedded Smart Objects, which is what the placed Illustrator file has now become.

▶ **Tip:** If you want to inspect the padding around the artwork again, choose Edit > Free Transform to temporarily display it. Press Return/Enter to complete the transformation, or press Esc to cancel.

Importing the remaining icons

Repeat the preceding steps, placing three more artboards from the paleontology-icons.ai file. Unfortunately, it's impossible to place multiple artboards at once, meaning we have to repeat this process three more times.

1 Place artboard 7 on the IDENTIFICATION type layer.

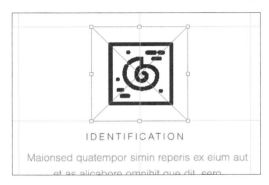

2 Place artboard 4 on the DIGGING type layer.

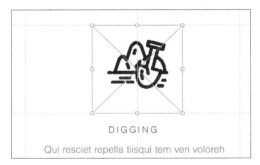

3 Lastly, place artboard 6 on the DOCUMENTING type layer.

In each case, rename the new Smart Object to match the name of its type layer.

Recoloring the icons

Now we'll recolor the icons to better match the look and feel of the website. We could double-click the icons to edit them in Illustrator and update the Photoshop document, but this time we'll use a slightly different approach. There is nothing wrong with the Illustrator method, but it's important to learn how to combine a placed Illustrator file with Photoshop's capabilities, so we'll recolor the icons using a layer style. The advantage of this is that it allows you to "manage" project colors locally, within the Photoshop document.

1   In the Documenting group, select the documenting icon layer we just added.

2   Double-click the blank area next to the layer name to open the Layer Style dialog box.

3   Click the words *Gradient Overlay* in the list of available effects (don't click the checkbox next to them).

4   Click the gradient ramp to open the Gradient Editor.

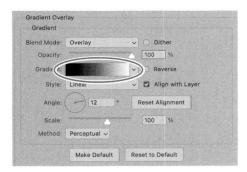

5   Click the left color stop and then click the color thumbnail to open the Color Picker.

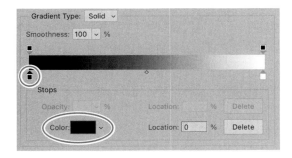

6   Move your cursor outside the Color Picker, turning it into the Eyedropper tool ![eyedropper]. Then click a green-yellowish color anywhere on the Photoshop canvas. (You may need to rearrange the open dialog boxes in order to see the color.)

7   Click OK to confirm.

8 Now do the same with the right color stop, but pick a darker color from the website interface.

Clicking different colors immediately changes the icon's look and feel. Feel free to experiment until you've found a combination you like.

9 When finished, click OK to close the Color Picker, click OK to close the Gradient Editor, and click OK to close the Layer Style dialog box.

Now that the Gradient Overlay effect is applied, you'll see it attached to the icon layer.

▶ **Tip:** Using the filter options in the Layers panel is an excellent way of quickly hiding elements you don't need to see during your design process. Feel free to experiment with the various options.

10 At the top of the Layers panel, click the Filter For Smart Objects button to view only the Smart Objects in the file. This shows you the four icons we've placed.

11 Option/Alt-drag the Gradient Overlay effect tag onto the other icons to duplicate the effect.

12 Click the Filter For Smart Objects button again to deselect it.

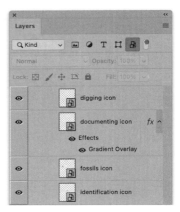
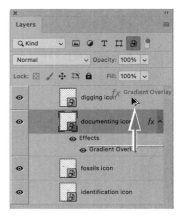

Editing artwork

Now you'll learn how to edit the embedded artwork in Illustrator and see it update in your Photoshop project.

1   In the Photoshop Layers panel, expand the Identification group.

2   In the Layers panel, click the identification icon layer to select it. Then click Edit Contents in the Properties panel to edit the icon in Illustrator. (You might need to scroll down in the Properties panel in order to see the Edit Contents button.) If a dialog box asks you to save changes, click OK.

In Illustrator, you'll receive a warning that says the file was edited outside Illustrator and you'll be presented with two options: Discard Changes or Keep Changes. You'll learn the difference in the next few steps.

3   Leave the default option, Discard Changes, selected. Click OK to continue.

4   Illustrator displays the icon onscreen. Choose View > Fit All In Window.

We suddenly have *all* artboards available in Illustrator instead of only the identification icon. Also notice the filename, which clearly shows which artboard was referenced in Photoshop during placing.

> ×   archeology-icons Page 7.ai @ 271.73 % (RGB/Preview)

If we had selected Keep Changes in step 3, we would see only one artboard in Illustrator instead of all of them. And that one artboard would be the one icon we placed in Photoshop.

5   Switch back to the identification icon in Illustrator. Use the Selection tool ![Selection tool] to select the icon; notice that it is a group of objects.

6   Double-click the object to enter Isolation mode. This allows you to edit all objects in this group without ungrouping them.

7   Select all five objects that make up the shell.

8   Rotate the selected art **−90°**.

9   Choose File > Save, then close the file.

10 Return to Photoshop and notice that the artwork has updated while retaining the recolor effect. Save your file.

> ▶ **Tip:** You can change the appearance of placed icons in Photoshop by simply moving artwork from one artboard to another in Illustrator. Look at the artboard number in the filename to know which artboard to move your artwork to.

Smart Object relationships

As you noticed, one powerful feature of placing an embedded file with artboards is that Photoshop always includes the entire Illustrator file. This can be helpful because it means the rest of the Illustrator file will travel with the Photoshop document and will never truly be lost. If we had selected and copied only one icon from that file in Illustrator and pasted it as a Smart Object into Photoshop (we'll discuss the various paste options later in this lesson), we would have brought in only that icon and nothing else.

However, be mindful that the four placed icons originate from the same Illustrator source but don't behave that way. In fact, despite their common origin, Photoshop created four different Smart Object layers. Let's run a quick test to make this clear.

▶ **Tip:** You can also double-click the layer thumbnail to invoke the Edit Contents command.

1   In Photoshop, edit one of the placed icons by selecting its layer in the Layers panel and clicking the Edit Contents button in the Properties panel. Select Discard Changes when prompted by Illustrator.

    The entire embedded file opens in Illustrator, focusing on the artboard that represents the icon you placed in Photoshop.

2   In the same file, edit a different icon that you know was also placed in Photoshop.

3   Save and close your file. Then return to Photoshop.

    Notice that Photoshop shows only the edits made to the icon you originally double-clicked.

    This is because every Place Embedded command creates a separate Smart Object that has no relationship with other Smart Objects, regardless of the fact that they all originate from the same Illustrator document.

    ● **Note:** If you duplicate one Smart Object and then edit it, all changes will affect both the original Smart Object and its duplicate. This is common Photoshop Smart Object behavior. If you want to duplicate a Smart Object in Photoshop that doesn't share the edits made to its contents, choose Layer > Smart Objects > New Smart Object Via Copy.

4   It is not required to save the changes you made to the exercise. Close the file.

The difference between placing and opening

There is one more method that allows you to bring in Illustrator artwork: simply open the original Illustrator document in Photoshop. To accomplish this, in Photoshop choose File > Open and double-click the Illustrator file.

Opening an Illustrator file (as opposed to placing it) will:

•   Allow you to import multiple artboards at once.

•   Force you to choose a resolution that will be used to rasterize all artwork. This means you will no longer be able to scale and transform the artwork nondestructively.

- Not allow you to double-click the layer and return to Illustrator for easy updates. All ties to Illustrator will be severed.

- Open each artboard as a separate Photoshop document instead of importing the artwork into the currently open document.

The price you pay when opening an Illustrator file in Photoshop is often too high, because the artwork will no longer be treated as vector artwork and you lose the ability to edit in Illustrator.

Linking Illustrator artwork in Photoshop

You could almost say that embedding an entire Illustrator document is the same as linking a file. After all, the entire file is embedded in Photoshop and you seem to retain a way of editing the original document in Illustrator. Well, not quite.

Be mindful of the fact that the file we embed into Photoshop will always be a duplicate, and not the original Illustrator document. Editing an embedded Illustrator document will update only that instance of the artwork. As you learned in the previous exercise, every Place Embedded command creates a Smart Object that is unlinked from the others, even if they all originate from the same Illustrator document.

Which file types can you link in Photoshop?

You learned the main principles of linking versus embedding, and their potential advantages, in Lesson 2. Photoshop gives us the ability to link not just Illustrator documents but also many other document types:

▶ **Tip:** You can embed these file types using the techniques you learned in the previous exercise.

- Vector files, like AI, EPS, SVG, and PDF

- Image files, like JPEG, TIFF, PNG, and many others

- Photoshop PSD files (more about this in Lesson 7, "Nesting Documents")

- Video files, like MOV and MP4

The next section teaches you how and why it's a good idea to link an Illustrator file as opposed to embedding it. In Lesson 7 you'll see a few examples of linking PSD files in Photoshop.

A linked file is still a Smart Object in Photoshop, just as an embedded file is. You can nondestructively apply filters and effects to it, and Photoshop's Smart Object options and commands can be applied.

● **Note:** This book assumes that Photoshop and Illustrator are using their default settings. If you are unsure of how to return to the default settings, review the steps in "Getting started" earlier in this lesson.

Getting started

To get started with linking Illustrator artwork in Photoshop, you'll view an image of the final composition and placed artwork.

1 From the Lesson06 folder, open L06-history-end.psd in Photoshop.

This document represents a different page of the dinosaur website we worked on earlier. The timeline holds beautiful illustrations of prehistoric animals and dinosaurs. There is also a logo in the header of the web page.

2 From the Lesson06/Imports folder, open geochronological.ai in Illustrator.

This Illustrator document contains all the illustrations you saw in the Photoshop composition. Notice that every animal is on its own artboard, and note how complex some of these illustrations are. Some of them consist of hundreds of individual objects.

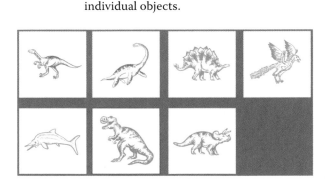

3 From the Lesson06/Imports folder, open dino-logo.ai in Illustrator.

You should be familiar with this logo from the exercises in Lesson 5.

4 Close all files.

Placing and linking the logo

The first step is to place the logo of the website in the header of the page. And more importantly, we also need to do this for the page in the previous exercise.

1 From the Lesson06 folder, open L06-history-start.psd in Photoshop.

2 Choose File > Save As and save the file as **L06-historyWorking.psd**.

3 In the Layers panel, select the Header group.

4 Choose File > Place Linked.

5 Navigate to the Lesson06/Imports folder and double-click dino-logo.ai.

Note that this Open As Smart Object dialog box is exactly the same as the Open As Smart dialog box you get when you use the Place Embedded command. Because we only need to place the artwork itself, ignoring the artboard dimension, we can place the logo using the default settings.

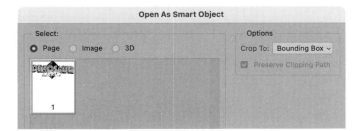

6 Click OK to start the place process.

7 While the logo is still in Free Transform mode, position it between the dinosaur and the text at the top of the screen.

8 Use the Options bar to increase the size of the logo to **110%**.

9 Press Return/Enter to confirm.

Identifying a linked file

Let's look at how you can recognize the difference between an embedded and a linked file in Photoshop.

Look at the layer of the placed logo and notice that the layer thumbnail differs from those of the Smart Objects in the previous exercise. The small chain icon in the thumbnail makes it clear that this is a linked file rather than an embedded file.

When a linked layer is selected in the Layers panel, you'll see additional options available in the Properties panel:

- The Properties panel will clearly identify the layer as a Linked Smart Object.

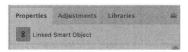

- It will also clearly display the path to the original Illustrator file, which is displayed only when using linked files.

- An additional button, named *Embed*, invites the user to convert the linked file into an embedded Smart Object. This button is only available when using linked files, and you might need to scroll down in the Properties panel to see it.

The Properties panel in Photoshop acts very similarly to the Links panel in InDesign and Illustrator, allowing you to view the link path, embed the link, relink the file, or update modified content.

▶ **Tip:** Click the file path in the Properties panel to display additional options.

Adding effects

Let's add effects and a filter. Remember that a linked file is still a Smart Object, meaning we can apply filters and effects nondestructively.

1   In Photoshop, the dino-logo layer should still be selected in the Layers panel.

2   Double-click the area next to the layer name in the Layers panel to open the Layer Style dialog box.

3   Click the name of the Drop Shadow effect (don't just click the checkbox), to apply the effect and display its options. Make sure Preview is selected.

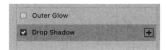

4   Enter the following values:

   • Opacity: **45%**

   • Angle: **90°**

   • Distance: **10px**

   • Spread: **26%**

   • Size: **16 px**

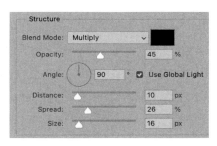

5   Click OK to close the dialog box.

Changing the size of the placed Illustrator logo in Photoshop might slightly reduce its sharpness. The next step adds a bit of sharpness by applying a filter.

6   With the logo layer still selected in the Layers panel, choose Filter > Sharpen > Unsharp Mask.

7   In the Unsharp Mask dialog box, change Amount to **80%**, Radius to **1.3px**, and Threshold to **0**, then click OK.

Both the layer style and the Smart Filter are now attached to the layer itself as non-destructive effects.

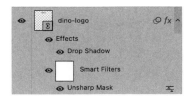

Duplicating the logo

The logo we just placed and optimized needs to be replicated on all the other web pages of the site. This means we need to duplicate the logo layer onto the exhibition page in the previous exercise, but also onto the page in the next exercise. We'll end up having a total of three instances of the same logo file across three different files. But unlike an embedded Illustrator document, all three instances will link to the original Illustrator document.

● **Note:** This is the file we built in the previous exercise. If you didn't save the previous exercise, open L06-exhibition-end.psd from the Lesson06 folder instead.

1 In Photoshop, open exhibitionWorking.psd.

2 In the Layers panel, select the Header group.

It's important to select the layer on top of which the logo layer will be duplicated in the next steps. Think of this step as setting the "destination" of the duplicate layer.

3 Return to historyWorking.psd.

4 With the dino-logo layer selected in the Layers panel, choose Layer > Duplicate Layer.

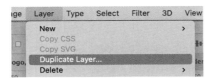

● **Note:** If you named your file differently in the previous exercise, you'll see a different file-name in the dialog box.

5 In the Duplicate Layer dialog box, choose exhibitionWorking.psd as the destination document.

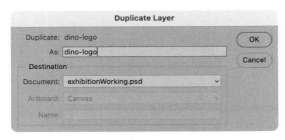

6 Remove the word *copy* from the duplicate layer file name so the layer name remains dino-logo, and click OK to duplicate the layer.

▶ **Tip:** The Duplicate Layer command places the duplicate layer in the same absolute position as the source document.

7 Return to exhibitionWorking.psd.

Look at the Layers panel and notice that the logo was added to the document.

8 Open L06-quiz-start.psd from the Lesson06 folder.

This document will be the starting point of the next exercise.

9 Repeat steps 4–6 to duplicate the logo into L06-quiz-start.psd.

Leave all three Photoshop documents open.

Editing the original logo

Because we're linking to the original Illustrator document, located in the Lesson06/Imports folder, we have a single "source of truth" for the three Photoshop documents in our exercise. Next, we'll make a small edit in Illustrator and see its changes reflected in Photoshop.

1   In Photoshop, in any of the three open files, select the dino-logo layer in the Layers panel.

2   In the Properties panel, click Edit Contents to edit the original logo in Illustrator.

As you arrive in Illustrator, notice the filename of the currently open file. This is different from the name in the previous exercise, where we saw that the filename in Illustrator was different from the original referenced document. In this scenario, we're opening the original file instead.

3   In Illustrator, use the Selection tool ▶ to select the *TERROR* text.

4   Double-click the text to change it. Change the word to **ISLAND**.

● **Note:** This logo is a copy of the logo we used in Lesson 5, which is why we are missing the layers we added during that exercise.

5   Choose File > Save.

6   Return to Photoshop and inspect all three documents; notice the logo has updated.

● **Note:** If the Photoshop file didn't update automatically, consult the Properties panel to manually update the linked file from there.

Note that the Drop Shadow effect and the sharpening filter remain intact and were reapplied to the new logo.

7 Save and close all files, except historyWorking.psd.

Because an Illustrator file can be linked in both InDesign and Photoshop (and other Creative Cloud apps), we can update projects destined for web, print, and video output at the same time.

Placing illustrations

The next step is placing and linking the illustrations of the prehistoric animals.

1 In the Layers panel, expand the Content layer group, and then select the animals group (where we'll place all illustrations).

▶ **Tip:** Assign custom keyboard shortcuts to Photoshop commands you use often (like the File > Place Linked command) by choosing Edit > Keyboard Shortcuts.

2 Choose File > Place Linked.

3 In the Lesson06/Imports folder, double-click geochronological.ai.

4 In the resulting dialog box, select artboard 1.

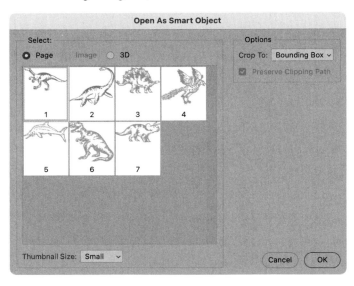

▶ **Tip:** You can also double-click the artboard thumbnail you want to place if that's faster.

5 Leave all options at their defaults, and click OK to place the illustration.

6 In Free Transform mode, move the dinosaur into the first column (Triassic). Scale it down so it fits the space between the column title and the words *First dinosaurs*. Press Return/Enter to confirm.

7 In the Layers panel, drag the linked file (named *geochronological*) into the animals layer group. Expand the animals layer group.

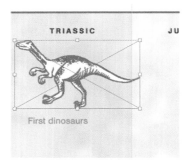

176 LESSON 6   Using Illustrator Artwork in Photoshop

8 Repeat this process to place the second artboard, position it above the text *Ocean-living reptiles,* and make sure it's placed in the animals layer group.

9 Repeat this process to place the third artboard. Position it in the second column between the two text entries.

10 Place the fourth artboard (bird) at the top of the second column.

11 Place the fifth artboard (dolphin-like creature) at the bottom of the second column.

12 Place the remaining two dinosaurs in the third column.

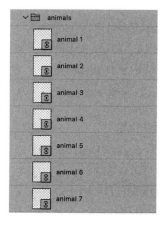

Ocean-living reptiles

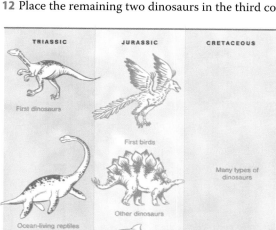

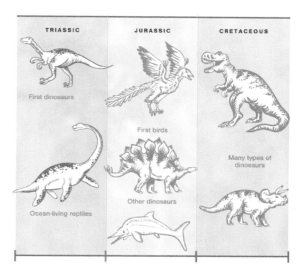

You should now have a total of seven layers named *geochronological* in the animals layer group. In the next step, we'll rename all layers.

13 In the animals layer group, double-click the first of the geochronological layers to edit its name.

14 Enter the text **animal 1**, but instead of pressing Return/Enter, press the Tab key to move to the next layer.

> **Tip:** Pressing Shift+Tab will allow you to rename the previous layer.

15 Name the second layer in the animals group **animal 2**, and press Tab again.

16 Continue your way through the group until you've renamed all layers, ending with **animal 7**, then press Return/Enter to end the series.

Editing and updating placed links

Let's edit the colors of all the illustrations. Because we chose to place the same file seven times, we need to edit only one document to see it update across all layers in Photoshop.

1   In Photoshop, select any of the animal layers.

2   In the Properties panel, click the Edit Contents button to open geochronological. ai in Illustrator.

3   In Illustrator, choose View > Fit All In Window.

4   Open the Swatches panel by choosing Window > Swatches.

5   Press Command+A/Ctrl+A to select all objects in the document.

6   In the Swatches panel, click the New Color Group button to create a new group of the selected colors.

7   From the New Color Group dialog box, select Convert Process To Global and click OK to confirm.

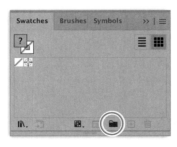
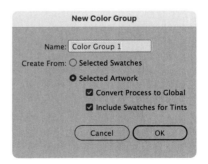

8 Deselect all artwork.

Illustrator has created a color group that contains all the colors of the selected artwork as global swatches (four in total). We can now edit the swatches and see the color updates applied to the artwork. This is very similar to how InDesign uses swatches.

9 Double-click the first swatch in the group to edit it.

10 Change the color values to R **100**, G **75**, B **60**, and click OK to confirm.

11 Double-click the second swatch.

12 Change the color values to R **75**, G **130**, B **75**, and click OK to confirm.

13 Double-click the third swatch.

14 Change the color values to R **215**, G **115**, B **0**, and click OK to confirm.

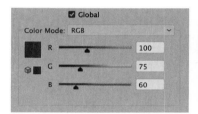 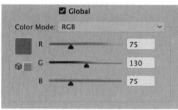 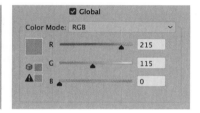

15 Save and close the file.

16 Return to Photoshop and notice that all seven layers have updated.

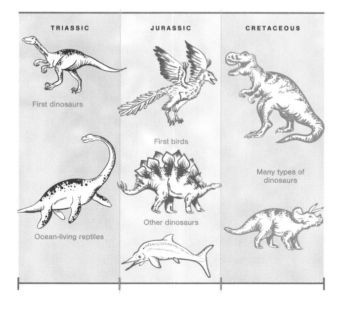

This behavior is different from that of the icons we edited in the previous exercise. Here we can edit all artboards and see all updates in Photoshop, whereas in the previous exercise we needed to edit each individual Smart Object.

17 Save and close your file.

Linking versus embedding

Embedding the artwork in this exercise (as opposed to linking) could have given us the same result. However, there are a few compelling reasons that we chose to link rather than embed:

- The illustrations are quite complex and could potentially import hundreds of individual layers if we chose to copy and paste the artwork into Photoshop (depending on the paste settings).

- We want to keep control over the illustration colors, as we might want to revise them throughout the project. And we need all future color changes to be applied to all historic animals, not just the one we have selected in Photoshop. Remember how using the Place Embedded command in Photoshop creates separate Smart Objects? That would mean we'd need to update all seven illustrations one by one to make their colors match.

- It's possible that these illustrations will be used in other apps, such as InDesign. We can't afford to limit future edits to the realm of Photoshop. Any changes we make to the artwork (when embedding) will not be reflected in InDesign, because we're not updating the original file.

Photoshop's Properties panel offers you the ability to convert the linked Smart Object to an embedded Smart Object by clicking the Embed button. Doing so "detaches" the Illustrator file from the other layers, allowing you to make changes to the original artwork that won't affect the original Illustrator document. This can be a good way of isolating specific instances of the placed file you want to keep separate.

Dealing with a missing link in Photoshop

Linking to a document means we need to keep the link between Photoshop and the referenced file intact, just like the way InDesign and Illustrator work. So we need to be careful when renaming, deleting, or moving the original logo file, as this may cause a missing link error in Photoshop. But the repercussions are not serious.

When a missing link occurs in InDesign or Illustrator, it needs to be resolved before you can properly print the document or convert it to PDF. Otherwise, the low-resolution preview (proxy) of the linked file will be used, causing low-resolution output. Because Photoshop uses rasterized images, the visualization of a linked file (even if the original is a vector file) will always look pixelated (based on the Photoshop file resolution settings). This means that a missing link error will not have a negative effect on the visual quality of the placed file, because it was pixelated already.

But obviously, a missing link error would still have other consequences:

- It would be impossible to edit the original document and see the update in Photoshop, because we wouldn't be able to find the file to begin with.

- The missing link would not be included when creating a Photoshop package.

- Scaling the layer (with the missing link) would have a negative effect on the layer's visual quality, because the original wouldn't be available as a basis for rendering the layer's new size.

In other words, the layer with the missing link will remain visually intact as long as you no longer interact with it in Photoshop. But repairing the link using the Properties panel is always recommended.

Creating a Photoshop package

Just like Illustrator and InDesign, Photoshop offers you a way to package all linked assets within a project, making it easy to back up or share the project with others.

1 Open a Photoshop document that has linked Smart Objects.

2 Choose File > Package.

3 Specify a location, and click Choose.

    Photoshop collects all the linked content, including a copy of the main project, in a separate folder.

Pasting Illustrator artwork into Photoshop

The last method of bringing Illustrator artwork into Photoshop is by copying from Illustrator and pasting into Photoshop. But because Illustrator uses vector shapes and Photoshop uses rasterized content, it's important to understand the choices you have when converting the artwork from vector into pixels. This exercise will help you better understand your choices and when to choose which option.

Embed, convert, or rasterize?

Before you paste content into Photoshop from Illustrator, you need to know the level of control you want to maintain over the pasted artwork in Photoshop. Ask yourself:

- Do I want to *embed* the artwork as a Smart Object, leaving the door open to editing the vectors in Illustrator and updating Photoshop?

- Do I want to *convert* all vector shapes into native Photoshop shape layers, allowing me to change their Fill and Stroke properties in Photoshop?

- Do I want to *rasterize* all content instead of keeping it vector, allowing me to directly edit the pixels using tools that don't work on shape layers or Smart Objects? Common examples are the Clone Stamp tool, Healing Brush tool, Sponge tool, and many others.

Knowing which elements you want to embed, convert, or rasterize in Photoshop is key to moving forward with a project and will help you make the right choices when presented with Photoshop's Paste dialog box.

Photoshop paste options

As you'll see in the next exercise, Photoshop presents you with a Paste dialog box every time you want to paste something from Illustrator.

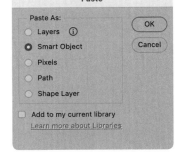

● **Note:** Many Illustrator object types are not supported in Photoshop and may be rasterized. This includes, but is not limited to, certain gradients, symbols, compound shapes, and effects. For a comprehensive list, visit helpx. adobe.com/photoshop/ using/photoshop-and-illustrator.html

- **Paste As Layers** converts all objects to Photoshop shape layers, giving you the ability to edit them in Photoshop using the Properties panel. Photoshop also retains the original layer order, groups, and object names. Be mindful that this can potentially bring hundreds of objects into Photoshop.

- **Paste As Smart Object** converts the selected artwork into an embedded Smart Object. You learned about this earlier in this lesson. Remember that the Smart Object will include only the artwork that was selected in Illustrator (no additional artboards).

- **Paste As Pixels** rasterizes all artwork to a single flattened layer in Photoshop.

- **Paste As Path** pastes the shape as a vector path, similar to the Photoshop paths you used in Lesson 2.

- **Paste As Shape Layer** pastes the shape as Photoshop shape layers, which are editable using the vector tools in Photoshop.

    ● **Note:** This book assumes that Photoshop and Illustrator are using their default settings. If you are unsure of how to return to the default settings, review the steps in the "Getting started" section earlier in this Lesson.

Getting started

You'll start the lesson by viewing an image of the final composition and placed artwork.

1   From the Lesson06 folder, open L06-quiz-end.psd in Photoshop.

    This document represents a different page of the dinosaur website you worked on earlier in this lesson. There are a few white dinosaurs in the file, which were pasted into Photoshop as shape layers. Additionally, there is a small icon next to the multiple-choice answers.

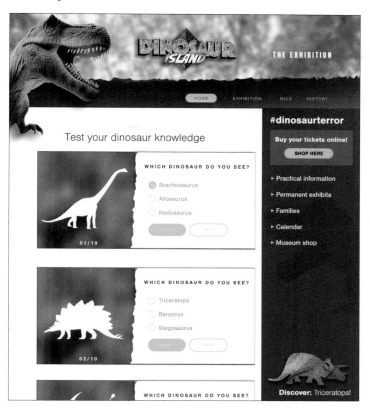

2   In Illustrator, open dinosaurs.ai from the Lesson06/Imports folder.

3   Choose Window > Layers to view the Layers panel.

4   Expand the layer named dinosaurs.

This document includes a series of dinosaur shapes that we want to use on the web page. Note that every dinosaur object is properly named.

5   Close L06-quiz-end.psd, but leave dinosaurs.ai open.

Pasting as shapes and layers

Next, we'll copy the dinosaur shapes from Illustrator and paste them into Photoshop.

1   In Photoshop, open L06-quiz-start.psd from the Lesson06 folder.

2   Choose File > Save As, and save the file as **L06-quizWorking.psd**.

3   Return to dinosaurs.ai in Illustrator.

It's time to ask ourselves the questions proposed in the section "Embed, convert, or rasterize?" The goal is to import the dinosaur shapes into Photoshop and convert them into native Photoshop objects. This allows us to change their color in Photoshop. In this case, there is no compelling reason to keep a link to Illustrator, so we won't be pasting the objects as Smart Objects.

4   Using the Selection tool 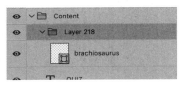, select the brachiosaurus shape on the artboard.

5   Choose Edit > Copy, or press Command+C/Ctrl+C, to copy it.

6   Return to Photoshop.

7   In the Layers panel, select the QUIZ type layer in the Content layer group.

8   Choose Edit > Paste, or press Command+V/Ctrl+V, to paste.

9   In the Paste dialog box, select Layers and click OK.

10 Inspect the Layers panel and notice a new layer group was added. This layer group holds all the pasted objects. Expand the new layer group to view its contents.

11 Because there is only one layer in the group, there is no need to keep the group. With the new layer group selected in the Layers panel, click the Delete Layer button (the trash can icon).

12 When Photoshop asks you which elements you want to delete, click Group Only.

Notice that the name of the object was retained in Photoshop and that the layer was converted into a shape layer.

13 Double-click the brachiosaurus layer thumbnail to open the Color Picker, and select white as the fill color. Click OK.

14 Press Command+T/Ctrl+T to use the Free Transform command on the object.

15 Drag the object into the area to the left of the first "Which Dinosaur Do You See?" block, and scale it up to fit within the available space. Press Return/Enter to confirm.

16 Return to Illustrator and copy the stegosaurus shape.

17 Return to Photoshop and press Command+V/Ctrl+V to paste.

This time we'll select a different option when pasting.

18 In the Paste dialog box, select Shape Layer and click OK.

Note that the shape is brought in as a shape layer, but it is missing the original layer name. That is because this command orders Photoshop to create a new shape layer from scratch, whereas selecting the Layers option in the Paste dialog box causes Photoshop to try to import as much information from Illustrator as possible, including the original name.

19 Using the Move tool, position the new layer in the area to the left of the second quiz block.

20 Press Command+T/Ctrl+T to use the Free Transform command to fit the shape within the available space. Press Return/Enter to confirm.

21 Double-click the layer name and enter **stegosaurus**. Press Return/Enter to confirm.

22 Return to Illustrator and select the pterodactyloidea shape, then copy it.

23 Paste it in Photoshop as layers.

Because it's cumbersome to have to rename layers, we'll revert to pasting as layers rather than shape layers.

24 Remove the layer group that comes with the pterodactyloidea shape, then move and scale it onto the area to the left of the third quiz block (part of it is cut off at the bottom of the screen). Change its color to white.

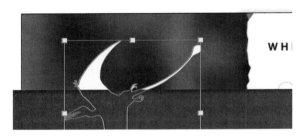

25 In Illustrator, open paleontology-icons.ai from the Lesson06/Imports folder.

26 Navigate to the Dino-Circle artboard by using the Artboard Navigator at the bottom of the Illustrator interface. Select all objects on this artboard and copy them to the clipboard.

27 Return to Photoshop, click the Content layer group, and press Command+V/Ctrl+V to paste.

28 In the Paste dialog box, select Layers and click OK.

29 Photoshop pastes all objects as a group. In the Layers panel, expand the group and its subgroups to view their contents.

This group contains most of the layers in the image. Beneath the expanded <Group> (not visible in the figure) is a separate layer, also named <Path>. This <Path> object is the background circle, and all other objects in the subgroup are the bones of the dinosaur. We want to recolor the circle while keeping the bones white.

30 In the Layers panel, double-click the <Path> object to edit its colors.

31 Move the cursor outside the Color Picker and click inside one of the SUBMIT button graphics on the webpage to copy the orange color. Then click OK.

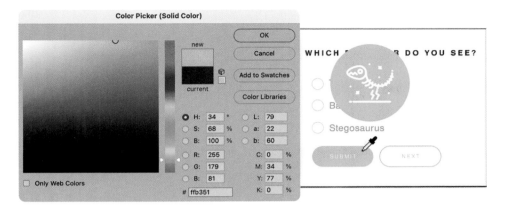

32 In the Layers panel, select the layer group that holds the icon elements (named Layer 301 in the screenshot, but this number might be different in your version).

33 Press Command+T/Ctrl+T to enter Free Transform mode, and scale the icon down until it is barely larger than the multiple-choice radio buttons.

34 Move the icon on top of the bullet to the left of the word *brachiosaurus*, then press Return/Enter to confirm the transform.

35 Double-click Layer 301 and rename it **choice icon**.

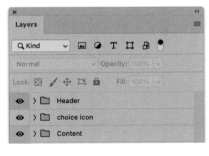

Pasting as paths

We will end with one last variation of the paste options. This time we'll use one of the Illustrator dinosaur shapes as a vector mask in Photoshop.

1 Go to Illustrator and copy the triceratops shape from dinosaurs.ai.

2 Return to Photoshop.

3 Inspect the Layers panel and notice there is a hidden triceratops layer in the Content layer group. Click its eye icon to make the layer visible.

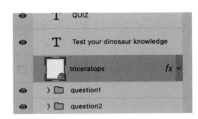

This is a normal image layer with a drop shadow effect applied to it.

4 Select the triceratops layer in the Layers panel.

5 Hold down the Command/Ctrl key and hover the cursor over the layer thumbnail. The pointing hand icon changes to a pointing hand icon with a selection marquee.

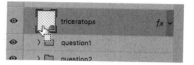

6 Click the thumbnail to load the layer as a selection, and then release the Command/Ctrl key.

7 With the selection active, press Command+V/Ctrl+V to paste.

8 In the Paste dialog box, select Path and click OK.

Photoshop will use the copied shape to create and apply a vector mask to the triceratops layer. Also note that the vector mask is centered on the triceratops layer. This is because Photoshop will always paste to either the center of the canvas or the center of an active selection (if present).

9 Choose Select > Deselect, or press Command+D/Ctrl+D, to deselect.

10 Select the Path Selection tool from the Tools panel.

Notice that selecting the Path Selection tool has selected and highlighted all the control points of the mask in blue. This is because the mask is currently selected in the Layers panel.

11 With the current vector selection active, press Command+T/Ctrl+T to enter Free Transform mode.

12 Scale the vector mask up to fit the width of the green sidebar. Also move it down to position it above the *Discover: Triceratops!* text.

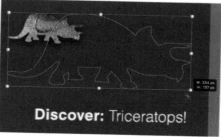

13 Press Return/Enter to apply the transformation.

14 Deselect the shape.

15 Save your work and close the file.

When you want to rasterize everything

This lesson has taught you every possible method for embedding, linking, or pasting content from Illustrator into Photoshop while retaining as much control over vector content in Photoshop as possible.

One method for bringing Illustrator art into Photoshop, however, will rasterize everything in the file while keeping all (rasterized) layers and text intact. This means that once it's converted, you will no longer be able to edit the original Illustrator art from Photoshop. Let's give this a try.

1 Go to Illustrator and open desk.ai from the Lesson06/Imports folder.

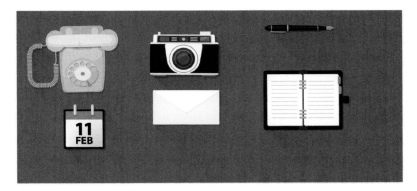

   Inspect the Layers panel and notice the different top-level layers.

2 Expand the calendar layer and notice that there are two text objects.

3 In the Layers panel, click the brown <Rectangle> layer's target icon to target it, then choose Window > Transparency.

   Note that the object's blending mode has been set to Multiply.

4 Choose File > Export > Export As and navigate to your desktop.

5 From the Format menu, choose Photoshop (psd) and click Export.

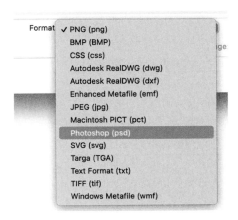

6 In the Photoshop Export Options dialog box, make sure Write Layers and Preserve Text Editability are selected. Set Resolution to Medium (150 ppi). Then click OK.

   By default, Maximum Editability will be selected when Write Layers is selected. This preserves the transparency of non-opaque layers, opacity masks, and blending modes. Leave this option selected.

7 When Illustrator informs you that some containers in the file will be flattened, click OK to continue.

Because you selected Write Layers, Illustrator exports every top-level layer to a Photoshop layer group. And because Preserve Text Editability is on, Photoshop converts all Illustrator type objects into type layers.

8 Go to Photoshop and open the file you just exported, desk.psd.

Note that the canvas size is different. This is because the PSD file that Illustrator created needs to fit all the Illustrator artwork.

9 Inspect the Layers panel and expand the calendar layer.

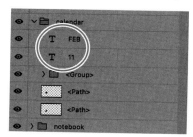

Both type objects were converted to type layers in Photoshop.

10 Expand the background layer and select the layer named <Rectangle>.

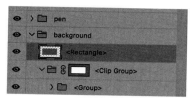

The blending mode of this layer is Multiply, as it was in the original. Also notice that the Illustrator clipping mask (<Clip Group>) that contains the wood texture has been converted to a layer group with a clipping mask in Photoshop.

Despite having to rasterize all artwork during the export process, the layer names, layer positioning, opacity, blending mode settings, and live text were preserved. This makes Illustrator's Export command a good solution for exporting rough sketches, interface elements for UX projects, and basic web layout to Photoshop.

Review questions

1 What is a potential advantage of *placing* an Illustrator file as an embedded Smart Object versus *pasting* the artwork from Illustrator as a Smart Object in Photoshop?

2 Why is it better to place an Illustrator document in Photoshop as a linked Smart Object, as opposed to an embedded Smart Object, when needed in multiple Photoshop documents?

3 Name one potential disadvantage to pasting artwork from Illustrator into Photoshop as layers.

4 What is the difference between the Path and Shape Layer options when pasting Illustrator artwork in Photoshop?

5 Describe what happens to the artwork and layer structure of an Illustrator document when you choose File > Export As > Photoshop (PSD).

Review answers

1 When you place an Illustrator file as an embedded Smart Object, the entire Illustrator file is embedded into Photoshop. This allows you to double-click the Smart Object in Photoshop and access all other Illustrator artboards. Pasting Illustrator artwork into Photoshop requires you to first select the artwork you want to import, which means you are bringing in only that selected artwork and nothing more.

2 Placing an Illustrator document as a linked Smart Object in Photoshop allows you to edit the original Illustrator file later, triggering an update to every Photoshop document where the file is linked. Embedding as a Smart Object only allows you to update one document at a time. You can even link the same Illustrator file to multiple applications, including Photoshop documents, InDesign documents, Illustrator documents, and other Creative Cloud apps.

3 Pasting artwork from Illustrator into Photoshop as layers could potentially bring in dozens or hundreds of individual layers, which would be very challenging to manage.

4 Choosing Path pastes the Illustrator artwork as a vector path, which is managed by the Paths panel in Photoshop. This gives you the advantage of potentially using the pasted path as a vector mask or a clipping mask, or of converting it into a selection. Pasting as paths does not generate any additional layers. Choosing Shape Layer when pasting converts the pasted artwork into a single shape layer whose fill color you can change.

5 The Export As > Photoshop (PSD) command in Illustrator saves the entire Illustrator file to a single Photoshop document while retaining layer structure, names, layer transparency, and type objects.

7 NESTING DOCUMENTS

Lesson overview

In this lesson, you'll learn how to do the following:

- Understand the principle of nesting documents.
- Link multiple Photoshop documents to another Photoshop document.
- Use layer comps when nesting a Photoshop document.
- Link multiple InDesign documents to another InDesign document.
- Nest an Illustrator document to simplify a layout.
- Package nested InDesign, Illustrator, and Photoshop projects.

This lesson will take about 45 minutes to complete. Please log in to your account on adobepress.com/DesignCIB to download the files for this lesson, or go to the "Getting Started" section at the beginning of this book and follow the instructions under "Accessing the lesson files and Web Edition." Store the files on your computer in a convenient location.

Your Account page is also where you'll find any updates to the lesson files. Look on the Lesson & Update Files tab to access the most current content.

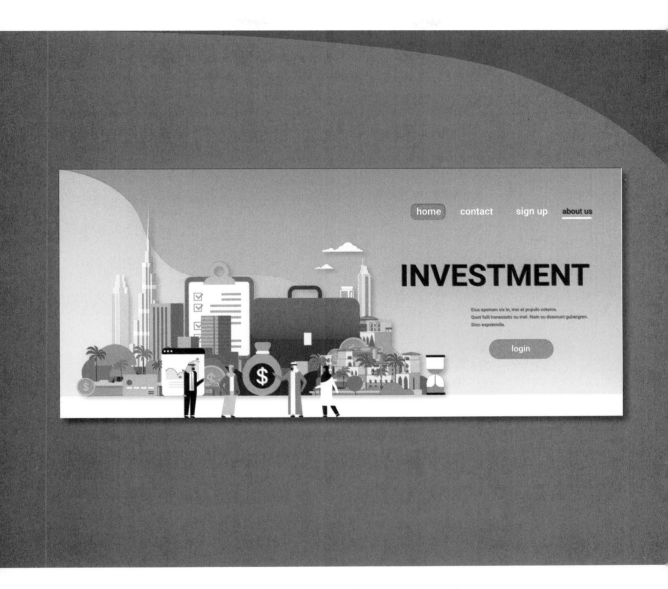

Placing a document from one app into another document of the same app can unlock workflows that allow you to work faster and update projects more easily.

What is document nesting?

So far, you've learned various ways of pasting, linking, and embedding a document from one appllication into another application's document. And now that you've mastered these techniques, it's time to go one level deeper and discover that there truly is no limit to linking documents. *Document nesting* is an unofficial industry term often used for placing a document from one application into a document in the *same* application, as either a linked or embedded file. Let's take InDesign nesting as a basic example. An InDesign layout often contains placed images like Illustrator or Photoshop files, JPEG files, or files in other formats, typically placed as linked graphics. You can take that InDesign layout and place it into another InDesign layout (as opposed to copying and pasting all the elements that make up the layout).

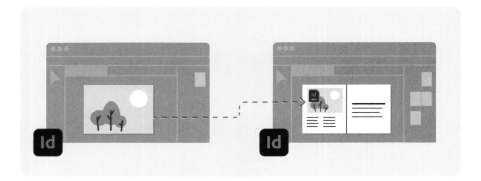

When you nest a document in another document, it is treated just like any other linked file. For example, in InDesign, there are specific import options to choose from while placing, and the Links panel clearly lists the nested file. If you think of the placed files that were in the nested file, you'll realize that these graphics are already two levels deep, because they were placed in one InDesign document and then that was placed into another InDesign document. Think of it as a Russian matryoshka doll, where one doll fits into another, which fits into another, and so on.

Here's another example to illustrate this:

1   Place an Illustrator logo or icon into a Photoshop banner design.

2   Place the Photoshop banner into two different Photoshop documents, each representing different design versions of a web page.

3   Place the web page designs into two different mockup images—for example, a picture of a laptop onto which you superimpose the website design that's on its screen.

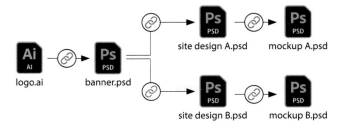

logo.ai banner.psd site design A.psd mockup A.psd site design B.psd mockup B.psd

Updating the original logo or icon triggers an update to the banner PSD, which triggers an update to both website design PSDs, which triggers an update to both mockup PSDs.

Nesting versus copying and pasting

It's clear that nesting multiple instances of a document creates different opportunities than does nesting a single instance of that document. Let's take a look at a few use cases and advantages for each Adobe design app.

InDesign examples

USE CASE	NEST A SINGLE ID FILE	NEST MULTIPLE INDDS
InDesign	Place small ads built with InDesign into a larger InDesign newspaper file.	Create a header or footer in a separate InDesign document, then nest that into multiple InDesign documents that make up different sections of a catalog.
Advantages	Avoids copying and pasting dozens of objects, avoids mixing text styles of the same name, and simplifies document creation.	Links one source to multiple documents, allowing you to update all at once.

Here's why copying and pasting entire pages or layouts from one InDesign document into another can be dangerous:

- Your InDesign document can get very complex very quickly.

- When you select the artwork that needs to be copied, there is the danger of not having included every object in the selection simply because you missed it or it might have been hidden or locked.

- When you paste objects into an InDesign layout that contains text styles or swatches with the same names as those in the target document, InDesign applies the target document's formatting to the pasted objects.

  For example, if in the source document you have a paragraph style named Title that uses Helvetica, and a style named Title in the target document uses Myriad

Pro, the text from the source document will convert to Myriad Pro during pasting. This happens without warning.

- Depending on your InDesign settings, pasting from another document can bring in unwanted layers.
- Objects that extend to the bleed area in the source document might be placed elsewhere in the target document, meaning you'd have to update the object's width and height to compensate for the loss of bleed.

Illustrator examples

USE CASE	NEST A SINGLE AI FILE	NEST MULTIPLE AIS
Illustrator	Place complex Illustrator drawing as a background element in another Illustrator file.	Create decorative element, such as an infographic or graph, that is referenced in multiple other Illustrator documents.
Advantages	Greatly reduces the complexity of the main layout.	Links one source to multiple documents, allowing you to update all at once.

Here's why copying and pasting entire illustrations from one Illustrator document into another can be dangerous:

- Your Illustrator document can get very complex very quickly, potentially adding thousands of vector points (depending on the design) and many layers.
- Pasted objects might overlap with others, causing the need to add clipping masks to help isolate them.
- Pasting objects from the source document that use a swatch with the same name as one in the target document will create a swatch conflict.

Photoshop examples

USE CASE	NEST A SINGLE PSD FILE	NEST MULTIPLE PSD FILES
Photoshop	Place a Photoshop document with a complex layer structure in another Photoshop document. To take one example, add dozens of layers to retouch a picture of a painting, and then nest that file in a Photoshop file depicting a gallery of paintings. You can scale and change the painting's perspective to make it look as if it's framed and hanging on the wall.	When designing graphics for screen and social media, create a header or footer that will be present in every document—for example, saved on a server and used by multiple designers.
Advantages	Greatly reduces file complexity, saves memory, and gives you an easy way to return to the original painting project.	Links one source to multiple documents, allowing you to update all at once.

Here's why copying and pasting (or dragging and dropping) a stack of layers from one Photoshop layout into another can be dangerous:

- The file size of your Photoshop document can get heavy very fast.

- Copying a lot of content might result in an error telling you the clipboard is full.

- If there is a large difference between the canvas of the source and that of the target document, it might be difficult to locate objects that were lost beyond the smaller canvas border.

- When you move and scale multiple layers that use masks at the same time you risk getting unexpected results when masks are not linked with the layers to which they are applied.

Nesting InDesign documents

The next two exercises will help you better understand how easy it is to nest a document in InDesign and how it can be advantageous to your workflows.

Linking to a single document

Here you'll learn how to place an InDesign ad in a magazine. The ad we'll use is the food and wine pairing project we used in Lesson 5, "Using Illustrator Artwork in InDesign." You should be familiar with these Illustrator and Photoshop files.

You'll start by inspecting both InDesign documents in order to better understand the project details.

1   Start InDesign, and then press Control+Option+ Shift+Command (macOS) or Ctrl+Alt+Shift (Windows) to restore the default preferences.

2   When prompted, click Yes to delete the Adobe InDesign Settings file.

3   From the Lesson07/01 InDesign/Imports folder, open food-ad.indd.

    Notice the document has a bleed setting applied.

4   Choose Window > Layers.

    The document has two layers, one for the background objects (which is locked) and one for the foreground objects. If we were to copy and paste the ad (instead of placing it) into the magazine, we would probably miss the objects from the locked layer in our selection. Also notice the ad doesn't have any objects that extend into the bleed area.

5   Choose Window > Links.

There are four placed items in the document: two instances of a placed Illustrator file for the icons (each on a separate artboard), one Photoshop document, and one Illustrator file for the logo. The links in this document are located at Lesson07/01 InDesign/Imports/Links.

6   Close the file.

7   From the Lesson07/01 InDesign folder, open L07-magazine-start.indd and navigate to page 4.

Page 4 is reserved for sponsored content and is where we need to place the ad from InDesign.

Placing the ad

1   With L07-magazine-start.indd open, choose File > Save As and save it as **L07-magazineWorking.indd**.

2   On page 4, select the text frame that says *sponsored content here* and delete it.

3   Use the Selection tool ▶ to select the gray graphics frame.

4   Choose File > Place.

5   Navigate to Lesson07/01 InDesign/Imports and select food-ad.indd.

6 Make sure Show Import Options is selected and click Open.

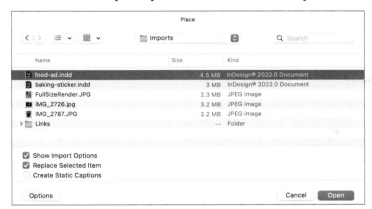

7 In the Place InDesign Document dialog box, click the Crop To menu.

Notice the Crop To options are slightly different than those for placing an Illustrator document. InDesign allows you to place another InDesign document while retaining its original bleed or slug settings. Because the elements in the placed ad don't extend to the bleed area, we can leave this setting on Page Bounding Box.

8 Make sure Page Bounding Box is chosen from the Crop To menu.

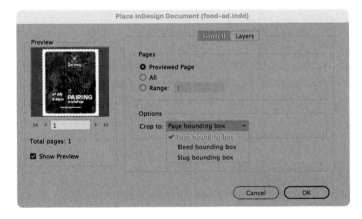

▶ Tip: It is not possible to change the Crop To settings after the InDesign file has been placed. Instead, you'd need to place the InDesign file again. Likewise, if you want to change to a different artboard in a placed Illustrator file, you have to place the file again.

9 Click OK to place the file.

10 In the Properties panel, click the Fit Content to Frame icon (the third from the right) in the Frame Fitting area to fit the content to the frame size. This slightly upscales the placed InDesign document and makes it better fit the available space.

A placed InDesign document acts the same way as a placed PDF document. This means that all elements that are vector (for example, native InDesign artwork or placed Illustrator documents), as well as live text, can be scaled nondestructively. However, all placed raster images in the nested InDesign document might no longer have sufficient resolution when scaled too big.

11 Apply the None swatch to the fill color of the graphics frame.

Inspecting links

1 Open the Links panel to view all placed documents. Notice that food-ad.indd is listed.

2 Click the arrow to the left of food-ad.indd and the arrow to the left of icons.ai to see all the links.

> ● **Note:** It is possible that some links might need to be updated when you open the document. If this is the case, start by using the Links panel to update all links.

InDesign gives you a clear overview of all the links and sublinks that are used in the document. This makes it easy to keep track of every file used in the chain of linked files you've built. However, it's possible to get even more information.

3 Click the Links panel menu and choose Panel Options.

The Panel Options dialog box lists dozens of link characteristics that you can display in the panel. Select options in the Show Column list to display columns of information that will help you better organize your links.

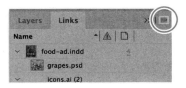

4 Scroll down the list of options, and select the Link Type and # Of Sublinks checkboxes in the Show Column list.

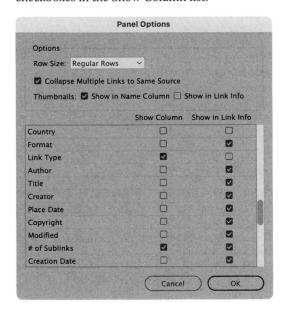

5 Click OK to close the dialog box.

6 Drag the edge of the Links panel to expand it to make the added information visible.

Tip: A *child link* is a link to a file in a nested InDesign document.

InDesign now shows that there are a total of four sublinks in food-ad.indd, and that they are all listed as child links.

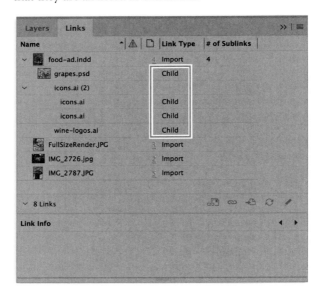

7 Save and close the file.

Why not place a PDF instead?

Designers sometimes create a PDF version of an ad and place it in a magazine, instead of nesting the original InDesign document. The main reason for this is that they are mostly unfamiliar with the nesting technique, and because creating a PDF is the only alternative that allows you to place an entire layout while preserving vector information. The main disadvantage to creating a PDF is that they are very difficult to update. Changes to the original ad will not be reflected in the magazine, meaning you'd need to delete the PDF and create it anew. And as you'll learn in the next exercise, it's very easy to update a nested InDesign document.

On the other hand, one potential advantage to using a PDF is that it is a self-contained file, so you don't need to worry about missing links or fonts.

Linking multiple instances

The next exercise takes a slightly different approach to nesting an InDesign file in another InDesign file. This time, we need to place multiple instances of a layout that all link to a single source. We will reuse the sticker project you built in Lesson 5 and pretend we need to duplicate the design onto a larger sheet that will later be printed on sticker paper.

We must properly place the sticker onto the provided InDesign template and make sure we reuse the bleed settings from the sticker design.

1 From Lesson07/01 InDesign/Imports, open baking-sticker.indd.

The sticker consists of multiple pasted Illustrator objects, a placed Photoshop image, and a pink background that extends into the bleed area.

2 Choose Window > Workspace > Reset Essentials to reset the workspace.

3 Choose File > Document Setup to view the document properties. Notice the file measures 4 in x 2.5 in. Now expand the Bleed and Slug options and notice there is a bleed of 0.125 in applied to the document.

4 Click OK to close the dialog box.

5 Close the file without saving.

6 From Lesson07/01 InDesign, open L07-sticker-template-end.indd.

This file shows you the result of the document imposition. All stickers have been carefully placed and duplicated onto the sheet and link to a single source.

Also pay special attention to the bleed area around the sticker. Notice that there is no bleed edge where the stickers touch at the top and bottom edges, because they share the same background color.

7 Close the file.

Placing the sticker

1 From Lesson07/01 InDesign, open L07-sticker-template-start.indd.

2 Choose File > Save As and save the file as **L07-sticker-templateWorking.indd**.

3 Choose File > Place and select baking-sticker.indd from the Lesson07/01 InDesign/Imports folder.

4 Confirm that Show Import Options is selected and click Open.

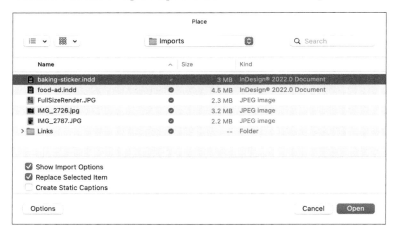

5 In the Place InDesign Document dialog box, choose Bleed Bounding Box from the Crop To menu.

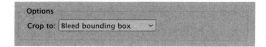

● **Note:** Remember that it's not possible to reveal the bleed by placing the sticker using the Page Bounding Box option and then expanding the frame. Page Bounding Box will not include the bleed at all.

6 Click OK, then click anywhere in the document to place the sticker.

The Properties panel shows that the document measures 4.25 in x 2.75 in. This is the sum of the page dimensions and the bleed around the document. In order to easily place and duplicate the sticker on the page, we need to temporarily hide the bleed of the placed sticker. We'll achieve this by shrinking the size of the frame back to the original document bounds (without the added bleed).

7 In the Transform area in the Properties panel, click the center reference point.

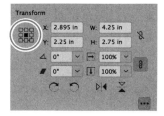

8 Change the nested document's width to **4 in** and its height to **2.5 in**. This represents the sticker's crop area and temporarily hides the bleed area.

9   In the Properties panel, change the reference point to the upper-left corner.

10 Set the sticker's X and Y values to **0.5 in** to position it correctly on the page.

11 Choose Edit > Step And Repeat. Make sure Preview is selected.

12 Set Count to **3**, Vertical Offset to **2.5 in**, and Horizontal Offset to **0 in**.

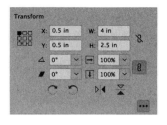

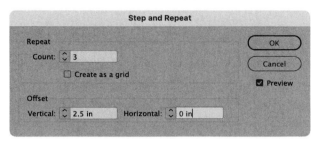

13 Click OK to close the dialog box.

You have now duplicated the object three times, placing one on top of another without any spacing between them. In the next step, we'll duplicate this set of four stickers again and move them to the right, leaving a gap of 0.5 inch between them.

14 Use the Selection tool ▶ to select all four stickers.

15 In the Properties panel, place your cursor after the 0.5 value in the X field, type **+4.5**, and press Option+Return/Alt+Enter to confirm.

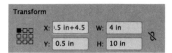

We use a value of 4.5 because the card itself is 4 inches wide and the gap between the columns is 0.5. By adding the Option/Alt key while confirming, we were able to duplicate the cards to those coordinates instead of just moving the cards to those coordinates.

Adding bleed

Now that we have placed all the stickers on the template, we need to account for the fact that we need bleed at the outer edges of the stickers. In previous steps, we've hidden the bleed altogether, but now it's time to selectively bring it back by expanding the graphics frame.

1   Use the Selection tool ▶ to select the top two stickers.

2   Expand the top edge of the selection bounding box to expose the extra bleed area.

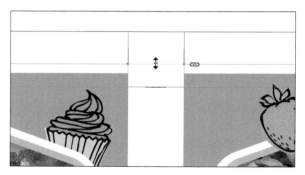

3   Deselect the top two stickers.

4   Select the four stickers in the left column, then expand their frame edge on the left side.

5   Now expand their right edge, exposing the hidden bleed on that side, and deselect them.

6   Select the four stickers in the right column and repeat the previous steps for expanding the frame to the left and right, exposing the hidden bleed area. Then deselect them.

7   Select the bottom two stickers, one on the left and one on the right.

8   Drag the bottom edge down to reveal the bleed area at the bottom, then deselect.

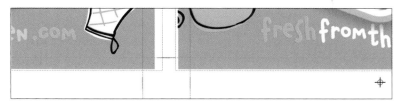

Modifying the sticker

To demonstrate how easy it is to update nested documents, we'll make a small adjustment to the sticker design.

1   Use the Selection tool ▶ to select one of the stickers. It doesn't matter which one, because they all point to the same source.

2   Right-click the sticker and choose Edit Original.

When you choose the Edit Original command, InDesign opens the placed link with its source application (in this case, also InDesign).

3   Use the Selection tool ▶ to swap the positions of the mitt/whisk and the apron. Feel free to scale or rotate the objects as you like.

▶ **Tip:** An even faster way of triggering the Edit Original command is by selecting the image, holding down the Option/Alt key, and double-clicking it.

4   Save the file.

5   Return to sticker-templateWorking.indd and note that all the sticker instances have updated.

6   Save and close all files. Then close InDesign.

Managing nested files' fonts and images

Nine times out of ten a nested InDesign document uses fonts or has placed content of its own. To keep the nested file completely intact, the relationship between it and its fonts and links must not be broken. This is very different from placing a PDF version of a nested file, where both the fonts and placed images are embedded.

You might remember that the Links panel clearly shows the sublinks of nested documents. This is important because you might encounter missing links after the document has been nested. And when that happens, the Links panel will make that clear. However, it's impossible to directly update or relink the sublinks by using the Links panel of the document into which the nested file was placed. Instead, you'd need to open the nested document itself and fix the links from there.

Additionally, it will be more difficult to spot missing fonts within a nested file, without having that file open. But luckily, InDesign is smart enough to notice the missing fonts when you try to package, print, or export the layout.

Packaging a nested InDesign document

Lesson 3, "Using Layered Photoshop Files in InDesign," taught you how to package an InDesign document and told you which information gets collected. The general principle of building a package also applies when documents have been nested. During the package creation process, InDesign gathers all sublinks and fonts used in all nested files, and also in the files nested within the nested files, as long as those deeply nested files are InDesign documents. However, when the package process encounters a Photoshop or Illustrator file, it can't detect the placed links in those files and thus won't include them. The following diagram will help you understand this. The files with a green checkmark will be packaged when annual report.indd is packaged. The files with a red question mark will not be packaged.

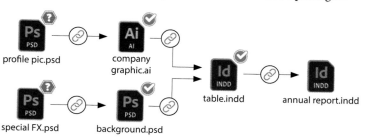

profile pic.psd   company graphic.ai   table.indd   annual report.indd

special FX.psd   background.psd

If you still want to include the files with a red question mark in the InDesign package, you can package company graphic.ai and background.psd files separately using Illustrator and Photoshop and then manually add them to the InDesign package.

Nesting Illustrator documents

Placing an Illustrator document in another Illustrator document might not be something you do every day. But it can really help you simplify complex Illustrator documents. And the placed Illustrator file will remain 100% vector without adding hundreds of objects to your layer stack.

Nesting to simplify artwork

Let's place a complex illustration into another Illustrator file as a background.

1 Start Illustrator, and choose Illustrator > Preferences > General (macOS) or Edit > Preferences > General (Windows).

2 From the Preferences dialog box, click Reset Preferences. Then restart Illustrator.

3 From the Lesson07/02 Illustrator/Imports folder, open city-elements.ai.

4 Choose Window > Layers to view the Layers panel.

5 Option/Alt-click the arrow next to Layer 1 to expand the layer and its subgroups.

This document consists of hundreds of individual shapes and objects. Copying and pasting all these objects into an existing Illustrator document would greatly add to the file's complexity.

6 From the Lesson07/02 Illustrator folder, open 07-site-end.ai.

This document represents the finished version of the exercise. The artwork from city-elements.ai has been placed in the background of this document.

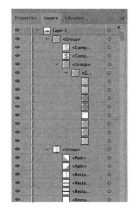

7   Use the Selection tool  to select the placed background illustration.

8   Look at the Properties panel, and note that the currently selected file is listed as a linked file.

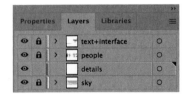

9   Close 07-site-end.ai.

Placing the background file

1   From the Lesson07/02 Illustrator folder, open L07-site-start.ai.

2   Choose File > Save As and save the file as **L07-siteWorking.ai**.

3   Open the Layers panel and note that one layer is unlocked. Click that layer to select it.

4   Choose File > Place.

5   Navigate to Lesson07/02 Illustrator/Imports and select city-elements.ai.

6   In the Place dialog box, make sure Link and Show Import Options are both selected. Then click Place.

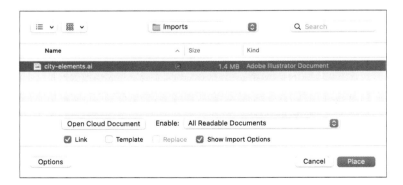

7   In the Place PDF dialog box, choose Bounding Box from the Crop To menu to place only the artwork while ignoring the artboard bounds. Click OK.

8   Click anywhere on the page to place the artwork.

9   Position the artwork on the left side of the artboard and keep it selected.

10 Choose Effect > Illustrator Effects > Stylize > Drop Shadow.

11 In the Drop Shadow dialog box, click the Color box. In the Color Picker, change the color of the shadow to hex #DBB5A1, which works well with the background. Click OK, and click OK again.

12 Open the Layers panel and expand the Details layer; note that it contains only a single object.

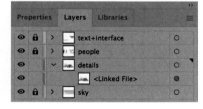

13 Make sure the placed artwork is selected and, in the Properties panel, click the Linked File link to open a temporary Links panel.

14 With the Links panel open, click the disclosure triangle to expand the panel and display information about the file.

15 Click the Edit Original button in the Links panel to open city-elements.ai.

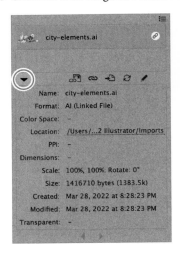

Updating the background file

1 In city-elements.ai, select the clipboard object.

2 While holding down the Shift key, scale the clipboard up until it's about as big as the tower next to it.

3 Save the file and return to siteWorking.ai.

● **Note:** Upon your return to Illustrator, it is possible you'll be prompted with a message asking you to update city-elements.ai. If so, update the link now.

4 Using the Properties panel, reopen the Links panel by clicking the Linked File option.

5 The placed link is outdated and needs to be updated. Click the Update Link button.

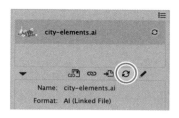

The background illustration updates, keeping the drop shadow effect intact.

6 Save and close all open files, then close Illustrator.

Packaging a nested Illustrator file

As explained in earlier lessons in this book, you can package an Illustrator document to collect all linked content and fonts. However, be careful when working with nested files, as the packaging behavior in Illustrator is more restricted than that of InDesign. In InDesign, all nested files and their respective links are packaged. Illustrator packages only the nested Illustrator file—without its respective links.

To understand this, look at the following diagram, which shows the packaging of website.ai. It contains a nested Illustrator document named background.ai. However, background.ai also has a nested Illustrator file (brush.ai) and a linked Photoshop document (texture.psd). These two will not be included in the package and need to be packaged separately.

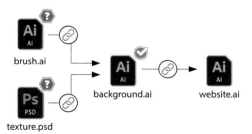

Nesting Photoshop documents

Now let's take a look at a few examples of how nesting a Photoshop document can simplify your documents or create new workflows.

Nesting a document in multiple files

Here you'll learn how to nest a Photoshop document by linking it to multiple other Photoshop documents. This enables you to update the nested file once and see its changes applied everywhere the file is nested. This doesn't just simplify your design (as you have fewer layers to manage in the main composition), but also enables you to point multiple files to a single source of truth.

1   Start Photoshop, and choose Photoshop > Preferences > General (macOS) or Edit > Preferences > General (Windows).

2   In the Preferences dialog box, click Reset Preferences On Quit. Then restart Photoshop.

3   From the Lesson07/03 Photoshop/Imports folder, open footer.psd.

This website footer is made up of three layers that each represent a different website page and will be used in three different Photoshop documents. The file will be linked to these main compositions, instead of copying and pasting individual objects from it, because it will be easier to update all three compositions at once.

4   From the Lesson07/03 Photoshop folder, open L07-exhibition-end.psd.

This document represents one of the three main compositions. The other two are named *history* and *quiz* and you might recognize them from the previous lesson. All three files have the footer element in common.

5   In the Layers panel, notice the layer named *footer*, which is the nested Photoshop composition.

6   Close L07-exhibition-end.psd.

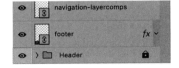

Placing the footer document

1 From the Lesson07/03 Photoshop folder, open L07-exhibition-start.psd.

2 Choose File > Save As and save the file as **L07-exhibitionWorking.psd**.

3 Choose File > Place Linked.

4 Navigate to Lesson07/03 Photoshop/Imports and double-click footer.psd to place it.

> ● **Note:** It is also possible to choose the Place Embedded command instead, which would embed footer.psd into the main composition. However, because we need three compositions to link to the same source, we need to link rather than embed.

5 While the file is still in Free Transform mode, drag it to the far bottom of the canvas. Then press Return/Enter to confirm.

The object appears in the Layers panel with the name footer, and the Properties panel identifies it as a linked Smart Object.

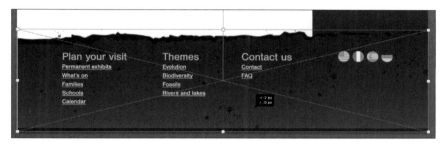

6 Double-click the area to the right of the footer layer name to open the Layer Style dialog box.

7 Click the Drop Shadow effect (be sure to click the name, not just the checkbox) to apply a shadow and display its options.

8 Lower Opacity to **35%** and set Angle to **90°**.

9 Set Distance to **2 px**, Spread to **20%**, and Size to **27px**.

10 Increase the Noise slider to **15%**, then click OK to close.

Duplicating the footer file to other documents

Now we'll duplicate the nested Photoshop document in the two remaining compositions. That way, they'll all reference the same footer.psd document.

1   From the Lesson07/03 Photoshop folder, open L07-history-start.psd and
    L07-quiz-start.psd.

2   Save the files as **L07-historyWorking.psd** and **L07-quizWorking.psd**,
    respectively.

3   Return to L07-exhibitionWorking.psd and make sure the footer layer is selected
    in the Layers panel.

4   Choose Layer > Duplicate Layer.

5   In the Duplicate Layer dialog box, change the Destination Document to
    L07-quizWorking.psd and click OK.

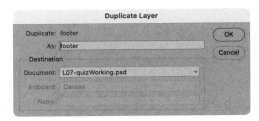

6   Repeat steps 4 and 5, but this time set L07-historyWorking.psd as the
    destination.

7   Inspect all three compositions and use the Move tool to position the footer layer
    at the bottom of each composition.

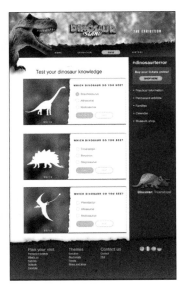

Making updates

Now we'll see how easy it is to update the footer layer in all three compositions by changing the source document.

1 Return to footer.psd.

2 Select the Type tool  from the Tools panel.

3 Click immediately after the word *FAQ* on the canvas. Now press Return/Enter and type **Ask a question**.

4 Save the file.

5 Return to the three compositions and see that all the footers have been updated.

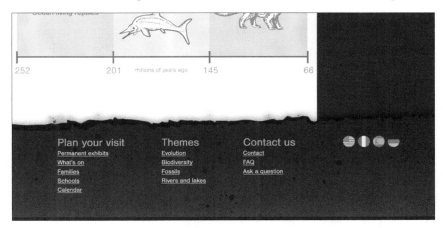

● **Note:** If a linked file isn't automatically updated, go to the Properties panel, right-click the file path, and choose Update Modified Content from the menu.

6 Save and close all files. Don't delete them! You'll need them for the next exercise.

Combining nesting with layer comps

This exercise combines the previous exercise with layer comps, which you learned about in Lesson 3. Nesting files in combination with layer comps is powerful because you can control the layer comp visibility of the nested file from the main composition. This makes it unnecessary to open the nested file every time you want to switch to a different layer comp.

1 In Photoshop, choose Window > Workspace > Reset Essentials.

2 From the Lesson07/03 Photoshop/Imports folder, open navigation-layercomps.psd.

This document displays the website navigation that needs to be placed on the three website compositions you used in the previous exercise.

3 Choose Window > Layer Comps.

4 Click the empty square icon next to any of the custom layer comp names.

With each click, the orange rounded rectangle changes position, and the text in the rounded rectangle turns black while all other text elements turn white.

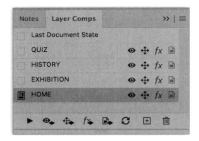

5 From the Lesson07/03 Photoshop folder, open L07-exhibition-end.psd.

The navigation is positioned at the top of the page. The Layers panel shows that navigation-layercomps.psd has been nested in this document. The same file has also been nested in the other two compositions.

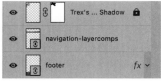

6 In the Layers panel, select navigation-layercomps.

7 In the Properties panel, change to a different layer comp by choosing one from the menu under the path to the original document.

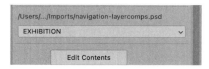

8 Close all files without saving.

Creating layer comps

While building the donut project in Lesson 3, you learned how to record a layer's visibility. You can use layer comps to record a layer's position and layer style.

1   From the Lesson07/03 Photoshop/Imports folder, open navigation.psd.

In the Layers panel, note that each of the four text layers has the Color Overlay effect applied. Using this method to color the text layers allows us to record the layer style properties (of which Color Overlay is one) while creating layer comps.

2   Open the Layer Comps panel (if it isn't already visible) by choosing Window > Layer Comps.

We will now record the current visibility state of the layers as a layer comp. Currently, the button layer (which is the orange rounded rectangle) is sitting behind the *Home* text. Additionally, the color of the *Home* text is black (using the Color Overlay effect), and all other text elements are white (again, due to the Color Overlay effect).

3   Click the Layer Comps panel menu and choose New Layer Comp.

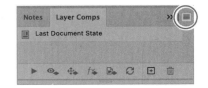

4   Name the layer comp **HOME**.

5   Deselect Visibility, and select Position and Appearance (Layer Style).

Because we only need to change the current color overlay effects for the text and move the orange button to a different location, we deselect Visibility.

6   Click OK to close the dialog box and add the new layer comp.

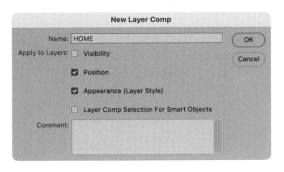
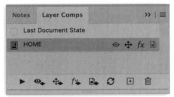

7   Select the button layer in the Layers panel and use the Move tool to center it behind the *Exhibition* text.

Now we will use the Color Overlay effect to change the color of *Exhibition* to black and *Home* to white.

8 Double-click the Color Overlay effect for the Exhibition layer to open the Layer Style dialog box.

9 Click the white color thumbnail and change its color to black.

10 Click OK twice to close all dialog boxes.

11 Double-click the Color Overlay effect for the Home layer and change the color from black to white.

12 Click the New Layer Comp button at the bottom of the Layer Comps panel to create a new layer comp.

13 Name the layer comp **EXHIBITION** and set the same options as before.

14 Click OK to confirm. You now have two layer comps.

15 Repeat the process for the two remaining menu items.

Essentially, you will begin by moving the orange button behind the next navigational item. Then, update the Color Overlay effects accordingly, and finish by saving the setup as a new layer comp. In the end, you should have four layer comps.

 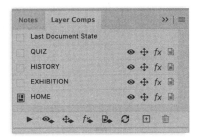

16 Choose File > Save As and save the file as **navigation-layercomps.psd**.

●**Note:** Be aware that there is already a document named navigation-layercomps.psd in the Imports folder. Be sure to choose a different destination folder to avoid overwriting the document that is already there.

Nesting and switching layer comps

Now you'll place the navigation menu in all three compositions and apply the correct layer comp using the Properties panel.

1 From your desktop, open exhibitionWorking.psd.

2 Choose File > Place Linked.

3 Navigate to the folder where you saved navigation-layercomps.psd and double-click it to place it on the canvas.

4 While in Free Transfom mode, move the file up until it sits on top of the white background. Press Return/Enter to confirm.

5 Use the Layers panel to position the navigation-layercomps layer underneath the Trex layers.

6 In the Properties panel, open the menu under the path to the source document and choose the EXHIBITION layer comp.

The navigation updates and the orange button moves to *EXHIBITION*.

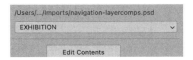

7 From the desktop, open L07-quizWorking.psd and L07-historyWorking.psd.

8 Return to exhibitionWorking.psd and choose Layer > Duplicate Layer.

9 Choose L07-quizWorking.psd as the destination document and click OK.

10 Repeat steps 8 and 9 but choose L07-historyWorking.psd as the destination document.

11 Switch to L07-quizWorking.psd and make sure navigation-layercomps is positioned below the Trex layers in the layer stack.

12 Open the Properties panel and change the layer comp to Quiz.

13 Navigate to historyWorking.psd and repeat steps 11 and 12, but this time, choose History as the layer comp.

Packaging a nested Photoshop file

Packaging a Photoshop document that uses a nested Photoshop document is no problem at all. In fact, Photoshop will search several levels deep to find linked content in the nested document. This makes packaging in Photoshop a lot more thorough than packaging in Illustrator.

This illustration shows you just how far you can go with packaging in Photoshop. In this project we have website.psd as the main project. In website.psd is a nested file called navigation.psd. And this document has two nested Photoshop documents of its own, including a linked Illustrator file and another nested Photoshop document. Photoshop will gather all the documents for you and build one package for the entire project.

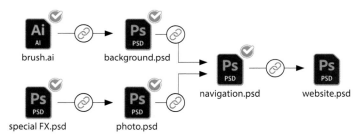

Review questions

1   Why is it easier to nest an InDesign document than to place a PDF version?

2   Is the bleed area of a nested InDesign document maintained during placing?

3   How can you change to a different artboard in a nested Illustrator file?

4   Which Photoshop feature allows you to change to a different variation of a nested document?

5   Are fonts and sublinks in nested documents always included when you build a package?

Review answers

1   Placing a PDF version of an InDesign file, instead of nesting the original, can serve the same purpose as nesting. However, the PDF would need to be re-created each time a change to the original InDesign document is made.

2   Include the bleed area of a nested InDesign document by viewing its Import Options and choosing Bleed Bounding Box from the Crop To menu.

3   The only way to change to a different artboard in a nested Illustrator file is to relink the file to itself and open the Import Options dialog box.

4   By using layer comps in a nested Photoshop document, you can create multiple variations of the same file. You change to these layer comps by using the Properties panel within the main Photoshop document.

5   Not all assets will be included in every design app. This is especially true when nested documents have nested documents of their own. Pay special attention to nested files' sublinks and fonts when building a package.

8 WORKING WITH CREATIVE CLOUD LIBRARIES

Lesson overview

In this lesson, you'll learn how to do the following:

- Understand how Creative Cloud Libraries work.

- Store different types of assets in a Creative Cloud Library.

- Share assets among InDesign, Photoshop, and Illustrator.

- Save assets to a Creative Cloud Library and add metadata to them.

- Place and link library assets between InDesign, Photoshop, and Illustrator.

- Update assets between design apps.

 This lesson will take about 45 minutes to complete. Please log in to your account at adobepress.com/DesignCIB to download the files for this lesson, or go to the "Getting Started" section at the beginning of this book and follow the instructions under "Accessing the lesson files and Web Edition." Store the files on your computer in a convenient location.

Your Account page is also where you'll find any updates to the lesson files. Visit the Lesson & Update Files tab to access the most current content.

Saving and using assets from Creative Cloud Libraries
allows you to build more complex workflows when
combining Photoshop, Illustrator and InDesign.

What are Creative Cloud Libraries?

Creative Cloud Libraries are virtual libraries that are hosted on the Adobe cloud infrastructure. They can contain a variety of design-specific assets that allow you to use your most relevant design assets when you work on projects while using multiple Adobe apps. Most designers store their files and designs on either a company server or in a local folder, so switching to a cloud-based workflow might take a bit of getting used to. However, after this lesson you'll have a better understanding of when and why to use Creative Cloud Libraries instead of a local folder or server. In previous lessons, you learned many of the differences between placing local assets and pasting them; here you'll learn how those techniques change when you're using assets from a Creative Cloud Library.

In Lesson 9, "Integration Through Collaboration," we'll take this concept further as we explore ways of collaborating using Creative Cloud Libraries and cloud documents.

How are they relevant to this book?

Creative Cloud Libraries are supported by nearly every Adobe application that comes with Creative Cloud, even some of the more recent mobile apps. This means that Creative Cloud Libraries enable you to take full advantage of the "Adobe ecosystem," as they allow you to share files, layers, or settings that would otherwise be impossible to achieve using traditional cloud providers.

Imagine the following scenario: you have finished working on an icon, using Adobe Illustrator, that will be used in a large media campaign. Thanks to Creative Cloud Libraries, you can save the icon in a library and reuse it across multiple Adobe design apps:

- You can place it in a document intended for print output, using InDesign.
- You can place it in a web graphic, using Photoshop.
- You can use it as part of an animation or video sequence, using Premiere Pro or After Effects.
- You can use it as part of a UX/UI project, working with Adobe XD.
- You can use it for creating social media posts, using Creative Cloud Express.
- You can even use it within Microsoft Office 365 applications, like Word or PowerPoint, because those applications support Creative Cloud Libraries.

What is unique about this experience is that all the projects mentioned above are created using different Adobe (and even Microsoft) applications, and this allows you to do multichannel publishing. And all those projects will link to the same source, making it very easy to update the icon and immediately make the latest version of the icon available not only to all of your projects, but also to the projects of others. To learn more about sharing libraries, please consult Lesson 9.

This lesson focuses on exchanging assets between InDesign, Photoshop, and Illustrator and on how Creative Cloud Libraries enable you to exchange assets between apps in ways that would otherwise be impossible using the methods described in the earlier lessons in this book.

What makes Creative Cloud Libraries unique?

Many companies are moving to a cloud environment for software solutions and data storage; likewise, designers are increasingly likely to work from remote locations. The design industry in particular has seen massive growth in the adoption of cloud technologies for storing assets and collaborating online. Indeed, it is often more efficient to access design files via solutions like Microsoft SharePoint than it is to access the company server via a VPN connection, which can often be slow. So what is the value in using Creative Cloud Libraries when compared to other cloud solutions for designers? There are two main uses for libraries:

- Reusing assets for your own projects
- Sharing assets with other Creative Cloud users

Creative Cloud Libraries have three main differentiators that make them ideally suited to designers:

- The types of assets they support
- Interoperability among Creative Cloud and Microsoft Office apps
- Sharing and collaboration among groups

Asset types

Traditional cloud solutions allow you to store "normal" files, like PSD, AI, and INDD files, among others, in an online folder. This means that they act the same way as a traditional file server. But Creative Cloud Libraries are not really about *file* management; they're more about *branded asset* management. Let's think about branded assets for a second. What makes up your brand? Is it only your company logo? No, your brand consists of:

- Your logo in different color versions or modes—RGB, CMYK, spot colors
- Company colors
- Icons and other design elements
- Text styles and font settings
- Photoshop layer style settings
- And much more

Looking at these different asset types, you'll realize that many of the items listed above don't have a dedicated file format. This makes it impossible to save them to a server or to cloud storage.

For example, it's impossible to save a text style to your server or cloud storage as a file. Instead, we would save an InDesign text frame using the text style as a separate document. But that is very inefficient when you need to reuse the style across different projects.

So Creative Cloud Libraries were built specifically to store, reuse, and share design assets that don't have a dedicated file format and that are available in nearly any Creative Cloud application. Additionally, you can preview all items in a library when you share them with others via a web browser. Contrast this with traditional cloud storage solutions, which cannot preview InDesign, Illustrator, or Photoshop documents, let alone swatches, text styles, and other asset types.

Interoperability

As mentioned, Creative Cloud Libraries aren't limited to InDesign, Photoshop, and Illustrator. You can use them in nearly any Creative Cloud application and even within Microsoft 365 applications. On top of that, you can also integrate them into third-party solutions like Microsoft PowerAutomate, Frontify, and Zapier, to name a few. This means that you can expand on the Adobe ecosystem by integrating with solutions you might already be using. And this is a great way of sharing branded assets across systems that might be used by other departments—for example, mobile app developers or 3D artists.

Sharing and collaboration

As you'll learn in Lesson 9, it's very easy to share Creative Cloud Libraries with others on your team or outside your organization. This means that you can link a Photoshop layer, an Illustrator icon, or InDesign text not only across your own projects and files, but also across those of others. This ensures everyone is always using the latest version of your logo, or the right version of a specific product image. Additionally, you can share libraries with Microsoft Office 365 users. This is great for sharing assets with those who aren't using Creative Cloud but still need to have access to the latest logo, colors, and images. This is useful whether you're working in marketing or you just need to place native Illustrator, Photoshop, or InDesign assets in, say, a PowerPoint presentation.

What can you store in a library?

You can store a variety of types of assets from different applications in Creative Cloud Libraries. And while several Adobe design applications have some of these asset types in common—for example, color swatches—there are also asset types that are unique to specific apps. This means you can store these asset types in a library, but reuse them in other projects only when you use the same application.

At the time of this writing, there are 23 different asset types you can store in a Creative Cloud Library, and Adobe is constantly adding more as Creative Cloud products evolve.

Commonly used asset types:

- Colors, color themes, and gradients
- Paragraph and character styles
- Text
- Photoshop layers, Illustrator artwork, and InDesign snippets

Specialized asset types:

- Lumetri color looks (for color grading video clips)
- 3D models and lights
- Vector and pixel brushes
- Adobe XD components

Know that it is also possible to save regular files into a Creative Cloud Library. You can achieve this by dragging files from the Finder (macOS) or Explorer (Windows) and dropping them into a library panel from either an Adobe application or the Libraries section in the Creative Cloud desktop app. The file types you can upload into a library include:

- Adobe design app template formats like AIT, PSDT, and INDDT
- Image file formats like JPEG, TIFF, SVG, and others
- Video and sound file formats
- 3D formats like USDZ, OBJ, SBSAR, and others

Can Creative Cloud Libraries replace my server?

The short answer to this question is no. Creative Cloud Libraries are not built to replace your server, hard drive, external drive, digital asset management (DAM) system, or media asset management (MAM) system. Despite the fact you can also store some regular file types in a library doesn't mean it can be used to replace your current storage system. The main purpose of a Creative Cloud Library is to give you an easy way of storing branded assets and using them across projects and teams, not to archive projects or build a database of images. If you do attempt to use libraries as a database, you'll quickly hit the following limitations:

- Every asset you store in a Creative Cloud Library will also be synchronized to your hard drive. This means that adding 500GB of images to a library will also consume 500GB of data on your hard drive, and the hard drive of anyone you've shared the library with.

- The lack of metadata fields for filtering, categorizing, and tagging library assets will quickly prove that Creative Cloud Libraries are not a replacement for a DAM or MAM. The system *does* allow you to use a very basic description metadata field per stored item, which is just enough for searching through branded assets, but nothing more.

- Anyone who needs access to your libraries will require an Adobe Creative Cloud account, via either a Creative Cloud membership or a (limited) free account. This makes Creative Cloud Libraries not very scalable to anyone in the organization who is not part of your design or marketing department.

Where are library items stored?

Creative Cloud Libraries are hosted on Adobe servers and synchronized to your Creative Cloud account. This means that, by default, all your libraries are safely stowed away behind your login and password. When you log in to Creative Cloud on your computer (to use your design apps), your libraries are downloaded and synchronized to your hard drive in order to make them available in all your Adobe applications. This process happens through a desktop application called Creative Cloud (more about this in the next few paragraphs).

When you add an item to a library, via either a design application or the Creative Cloud app, the new asset is synchronized to Creative Cloud. This makes it available across all the applications and services that come with your membership.

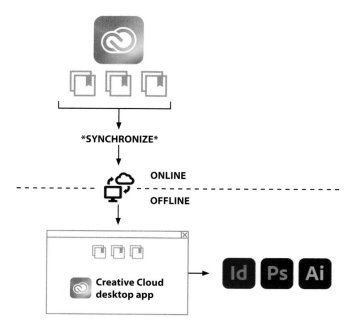

How to view your libraries

Viewing libraries locally

You can view all available libraries, either owned by you or shared with you, by using the Creative Cloud app on your computer. The app launches when you start up your computer and it keeps you signed in to your Adobe account, giving you access to your Adobe products. It's also where you can view, share, and create your Creative Cloud Libraries.

There are two main ways of viewing a library: by asset type and by group. You can define a selection of assets as a *group* and give it a custom name. You can even create groups within groups, called subgroups, allowing you to better organize your libraries. This comes in handy, given that you can store up to 10,000 items per library.

An example of a simple library that uses several subgroups, which are listed in the sidebar on the left side of the window.

Viewing libraries online

Alternatively, you can view your Creative Cloud Libraries online. To do so, open a web browser, navigate to assets.adobe.com, and log in to your account. From there, click the Files tab and then click Your Libraries.

Creating your first library

This exercise focuses on building your first Creative Cloud Library. We won't be reusing the library's assets in a project, so learning how to build the library itself is the purpose of this exercise.

Naming a library and grouping library items

The library we're building is based on the dinosaur brand you're already familiar with. And the library will hold a combination of regular files and assets from documents that you worked on in previous lessons.

1　Launch the Creative Cloud desktop application on your computer by clicking the Creative Cloud icon in your menu bar (macOS) or the Creative Cloud icon at the bottom right, next to the clock (Windows).

   The Creative Cloud desktop application opens.

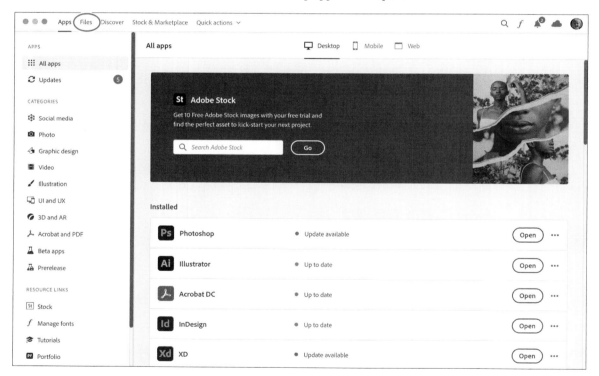

2　In the Creative Cloud app, click the Files tab, then click the Your Libraries category in the sidebar at left.

3 Click New Library to create a new library.

4 Name the library **dinosaur** and click Create.

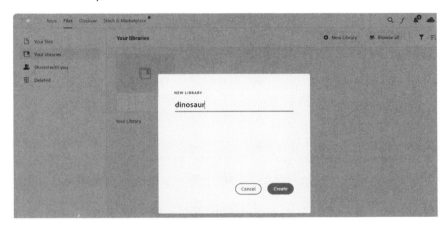

5 Click Upload A File to start the upload process from your hard drive.

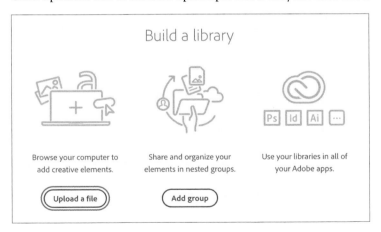

▶ **Tip:** It's also possible to drag and drop files from your hard drive into the library.

6 Navigate to Lesson08/Imports/Library.

7 Select background.jpg, dino-logo.ai, and trex-small.psd, and click Add to start
   the upload process.

8 In the main Creative Cloud app window, make
   sure no files are selected, click the plus icon on
   the right side of the window, and choose Upload
   File from the menu to add more files.

9 Navigate to Lesson08/Imports/Library/icons,
   select all files in the folder, and click Add.

   We have now uploaded a JPEG file, a Photoshop document, and a series of
   Illustrator files. In the next step, we'll categorize the assets into groups and add
   some metadata to them, making them easier to find in the library.

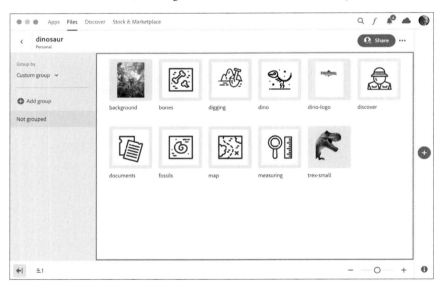

● **Note:** Multi-artboard Illustrator documents can also be uploaded into the library, but in the
thumbnail you can see only the first artboard. To see whether other artboards are present, open
the file from the library.

10 Select all icons in the library by clicking one and Command/Ctrl-clicking
   the others.

11 Click the Add Group button.

12 Name the group **icons**. This creates a group and adds the selected items to it.

13 Select the logo in the library and click the Add Group button again.

14 Name the group **Logos** and press Return/Enter to add the selected logo to the newly created group.

15 Select the trex-small and background items and click the Add Group button.

16 Name the group **Jungle**.

> We've now created three groups with different items in them.

Viewing item information

The Creative Cloud app allows you to see the details of an uploaded asset. This includes the modification date, creation date, size, and file type. To view file details:

1 In the Creative Cloud app, open the dinosaur library.

2 Click the Info button at the lower right of the window to display information about your current library.

> A pane displaying basic information about the library slides in from the right side of the window.

3 Click to select a library item to display information about it.

> It's possible to add a description to the library item from this screen. But for the purposes of this exercise, we'll do so from a design application instead. That way, you'll see that it's unnecessary to leave your design app and return to the Creative Cloud app just to update an item description.

Viewing a library in Photoshop

These steps teach you how to view the contents of a Creative Cloud Library in an Adobe design app—in this case, Photoshop—and add a description to an item.

1 Start Photoshop, and choose Photoshop > Preferences > General (macOS) or Edit > Preferences > General (Windows).

2 In the Preferences dialog box, click Reset Preferences On Quit, and click OK in the confirmation dialog box.

3 Click OK to close the Preferences dialog box, then restart Photoshop.

4 Choose Window > Libraries to open the Libraries panel.

   The Libraries panel lists all your Creative Cloud Libraries, including the dinosaur library.

5 Click the dinosaur library to view its items.

6 Click the Sort Options button. From the Group By menu choose Custom Group to display all items per group instead of per file type.

7 Right-click the background item and choose Add Description.

8 Enter **Always use in combination with trex-small** and click OK.

9 Hover your cursor over the background item.

   The pop-up shows the item description.

Descriptions help you find files, and you can use them to add instructions for use of the file.

10 Click in the search bar at the top of the Libraries panel and type **Trex** to search for that term.

The search returns two items. One is the trex-small item itself because the search keyword is included in its filename, and the other is the background item because the word *trex* is in its item description.

11 Click the x in the search bar to delete *Trex*.

Creative Cloud Library workflows

The following exercises show you how to store design assets in a Creative Cloud Library and reuse them in other applications. There are many more asset types and sharing combinations available than just the ones described in this book. This is why you should experiment with different asset types and applications.

Combining InDesign and Photoshop library assets

In this example, you exchange assets between Photoshop and InDesign. This work-flow is useful because it is difficult to get InDesign assets into Photoshop via the tra-ditional methods of placing or linking. However, thanks to Creative Cloud Libraries we can link content from InDesign to Photoshop.

1 In Photoshop, open L08-billboard-end.psd from the Lesson08 folder.

● **Note:** In this lesson, each of the "-end" files has all of its artwork embedded so that you don't have to deal with broken links. This is because my original Creative Cloud Library is not available with this book.

This Photoshop composition is a mockup of a billboard campaign. The bill-board poster itself is an InDesign layout that is ready for print and linked as a library Smart Object to the Photoshop document. This means we can change the InDesign layout of the original billboard design and see its mockup update in Photoshop.

2 Start InDesign, and then press Control+Option+ Shift+Command (macOS) or Ctrl+Alt+Shift (Windows) to restore the default preferences.

3 When prompted, click Yes to delete the Adobe InDesign settings file.

4 From InDesign, open billboard-end.indd from the Lesson08/Imports folder.

This InDesign document is the billboard design that was placed in the Photoshop composition you just viewed. It consists of multiple images that were originally placed from a Creative Cloud Library created in Photoshop.

5 Close all files.

Saving Photoshop layers to a Creative Cloud Library

We'll first create a library and add items to it.

1 In Photoshop, open summer.psd from the Lesson08/Imports folder.

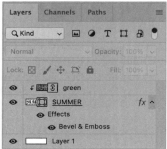

This document contains three layers: a shape layer, a grassy image that is clipped to the shape layer, and a layer filled with white that serves as the background. We need to keep both the grassy image and the shape layer intact in the Creative

Cloud Library. That way, we can always edit the original layers for future updates—by, for example, replacing the grassy image with a different image. The Properties panel indicates that the grassy image has been placed as a linked file, using the Place Linked command.

● **Note:** If you notice a yellow triangle next to a linked layer, choose Layer > Smart Objects > Update All Modified Content to refresh all links.

Additionally, notice the Bevel & Emboss effect applied to the shape layer. We need to save the effect separately from the library for future projects that are part of same campaign.

2   In the Libraries panel, open the panel menu and choose Create New Library.

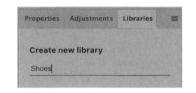

3   Name the library **Shoes** and click Create.

4   In the Layers panel, select both the grassy image layer (named *green*) and the shape layer (named *SUMMER*).

5   With both layers selected, click the plus icon at the bottom of the Libraries panel and choose Graphic to store both layers as a single item in the library.

Both layers are added as a single Photoshop document in the library.

▶ **Tip:** It is also possible to add items by dragging layers from the Layers panel onto the library, or by using the Move tool ✛ to drag items from the canvas onto the library.

6   In the Layers panel, select the SUMMER layer.

7   In the Libraries panel, click the plus icon again and choose Layer Style to add the Bevel & Emboss effect to the library as a reusable asset. (Clicking the plus icon in the Libraries panel shows different options depending on the properties of the selected layers.)

The layer style is added to the library, using the name of the original layer. Let's change this to something that makes more sense for future projects.

8   In the Libraries panel, double-click the name of the newly added layer style and rename it **thin emboss**. Press Return/Enter to confirm.

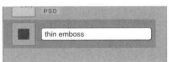

Now that we've added our first Photoshop graphic and layer style to the library, it's a good practice to see what we actually saved. Remember that the grassy image we saved as part of the library item was originally a linked layer. So let's take a look at what happened to it in the library.

9   Double-click the first library asset, named *green*, to open it in its source application (in this case, Photoshop).

Here we notice two things. First, the canvas size is a lot bigger than before. This is because when a library item is created, the total size of all the elements in the layer stack is taken into account, including those hidden in the background. The grassy image extended far beyond the original canvas of summer.psd, which is why we now have a larger canvas.

Secondly, the linked layer has been converted into an embedded layer. This happens to make sure that the library item itself is not dependent on an externally linked image.

10 Close the library item file, then close summer.psd without saving.

Saving Photoshop Smart Objects as library assets

Photoshop has a unique feature that lets you automate the creation of a library and its library items. But in order to accomplish this, we need to convert the artwork we want to save to the library into Smart Objects.

1 In Photoshop, open collection.psd from the Lesson08/Imports folder.

This document consists of images of shoes, each in a separate layer group. Each layer group holds a shoe layer and a shadow layer. We need to add all shoe groups to the library in order to use them in InDesign.

There are two ways of accomplishing this: either we manually add all nine items to the current library, or we ask Photoshop to do the work for us. Admittedly, for some it might be a little bit faster to quickly drag every shoe folder into the library. However, this scenario provides a great learning opportunity for auto-generating a library based on a Photoshop document.

The first step is to convert all items to Smart Objects.

2 In the Layers panel, select the shoe1 layer group.

3 Right-click the group and choose Convert To Smart Object.

> ▶ **Tip:** You can also choose Layer > Smart Objects > Convert To Smart Object, or you can create a custom shortcut for this command by choosing Edit > Keyboard Shortcuts. That way, you can convert all folders with just a single keystroke.

4 Repeat the process for the eight other groups.

5 Open the Libraries panel menu and choose Create New Library From Document.

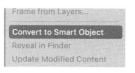

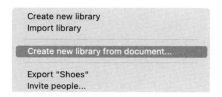

6 In the New Library From Document dialog box, make sure Smart Objects is selected.

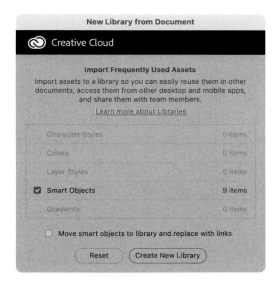

This screen lists all elements from the current Photoshop document that can be automatically uploaded to the newly created library. Note that there is an option to replace and link the original Smart Objects in the Photoshop document to the ones uploaded to the library. Doing so would allow you to update the Photoshop document by editing the library items, a type of "upload, replace, and link" feature. This is interesting, but not useful in the current exercise, so leave that option unselected.

7 Click Create New Library to create a library that includes all objects.

This technique is a great way to quickly create a new library in Photoshop—and it is the only app that allows you to do this. The only problem we have now is that we already have a library for our project. So let's move the content out of this library and into the one we created earlier.

8 Select all nine items in the current library by clicking the first and Shift-clicking the last in the list.

9 Right-click the selected items and choose Move Selected Items To.

10 In the dialog box, click the left-pointing arrow to navigate to the Shoes library we created earlier.

11 Click the Create New Group button at the bottom to add a new group. Name it **collection** and click Create.

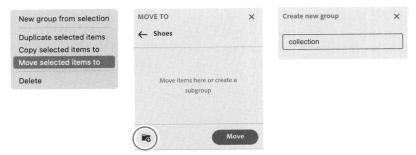

12 Click Move to move all items into the newly created group in the Shoes library. The current library will be empty once this is done.

13 Open the Libraries panel menu and choose Delete "collection" to delete the empty library. Click Delete once more to confirm.

14 Click the Shoes library to navigate into it.

 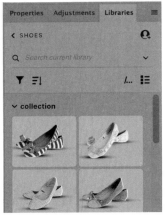

All the shoes are now available in the library and are ready to use in InDesign.

Placing Photoshop library items in InDesign

Now that our library of assets is ready, it's time to reuse the content in other applications. We'll reuse the summer graphic and shoes in InDesign.

1 In InDesign, open billboard-start.indd from the Lesson08/Imports folder.

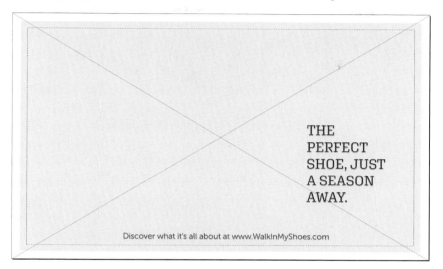

2 Choose File > Save As and save the file as **billboardWorking.indd**.

3 Choose Window > CC Libraries to display the Creative Cloud Libraries.

4 In the CC Libraries panel, navigate to the Shoes library, then click it to open it.

5 Drag the green summer title from the library onto the canvas. This results in a loaded cursor, ready to place the image.

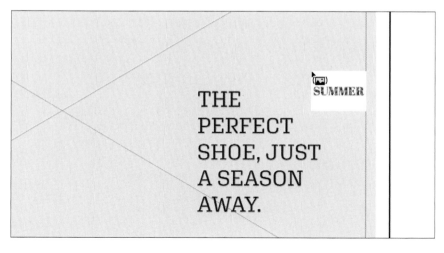

● **Note:** Only InDesign refers to the Libraries panel as CC Libraries. This is because InDesign's native library system already uses the term libraries. You can create these by choosing File > New > Library. However, with today's Creative Cloud Library capabilities, this feature has become outdated.

6 Click inside the gray graphics frame to place the image inside it.

7 Drag the Content Grabber circle to move the image upward within the graphics frame. Then deselect it.

8 Find shoe1 in the CC Libraries panel and drag it onto the page. Place it in the middle of the page.

9 Scale the image up until it takes up approximately half the page.

Now we'll add another asset type by converting the colors in the current shoe image into a color theme and saving it to the library.

10 Press and hold the Eyedropper tool ![eyedropper icon] in the Tools panel and select the Color Theme tool ![color theme icon].

11 Using the Color Theme tool ![color theme icon], hover over the shoe image and click once to convert its colors into a color theme.

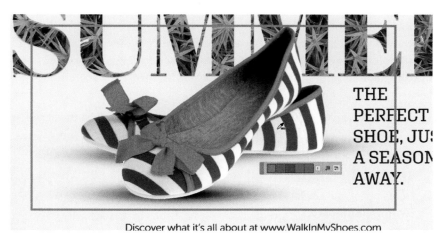

12 Click the Add This Theme To My Current CC Library button.

InDesign adds a color theme of five swatches to the library.

13 Switch to the Selection tool 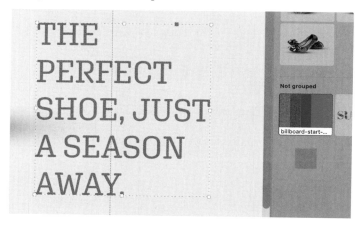 and click the slogan text frame that begins, *THE PERFECT SHOE....*

14 In the Libraries panel, click one of the red colors in the newly created color theme to apply it to the text.

15 Save your file but leave it open.

Placing InDesign library items in Photoshop

Now you'll learn how to place InDesign content into Photoshop—a great way to mock up a print project like a poster, a flyer, or packaging. This is difficult to do without Creative Cloud Libraries. Sure, you can copy and paste content into Photoshop as a Smart Object. But when you double-click the Smart Object in Photoshop as a way of editing the original artwork in InDesign, Photoshop opens the content in Illustrator instead—odd behavior that breaks the relationship between InDesign and Photoshop.

1 In InDesign, press Command+A/Ctrl+A to select all artwork on the page.

2 In the CC Libraries panel, click the plus icon and choose Graphic to add all selected objects as one item to the library.

3 Double-click the newly added item name and rename it **billboard**.

It is important to understand that adding an item to a library adds a *duplicate of that item* to the library. The item we see in the library is not linked to the InDesign layout. They are two separate entities.

By adding all these items to our Creative Cloud Library, we're actually nesting library items, since the title and shoe objects were already library items. So we're now saving library items grouped with other content as a new library item. This means that the summer title and shoe objects in the library are linked to both our InDesign document and the version that was duplicated into the library. The diagram below will help you understand what's going on. Here you can see that the shoe object is connected to both the InDesign layout and the layout in the library. Updating the shoe object in Photoshop will update both items.

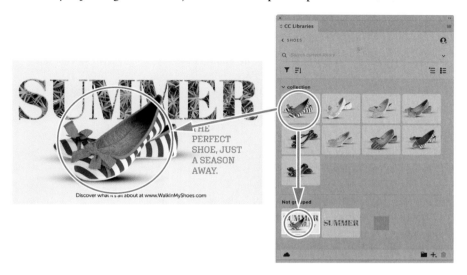

4   Go to Photoshop and open L08-billboard-start.psd from the Lesson08 folder.

5   Choose File > Save As and save the file as **billboard-mockupWorking.psd**.

6   Click the tree layer to select it in the Layers panel.

7   Choose Window > Libraries to display the Libraries panel.

8   Navigate to the Shoes library in the Libraries panel.

9   Drag the billboard object we just added to the library from InDesign. Drop it in the middle of the canvas and press Return/Enter to confirm.

The cloud icon in the layer thumbnail makes it clear this is a linked library item.

10 Right-click the layer and choose Convert To Smart Object.

11 Press Command+T/Ctrl+T to enter Free Transform mode.

12 Lower the opacity of the layer to roughly 50% so you can see the background through the billboard image.

13 Move the billboard image so its upper-left corner is aligned with the upper-left corner of the white billboard placeholder. You may need to nudge the layer using the arrow keys.

14 Hold down Command/Ctrl to apply a perspective transformation, and drag to align the lower-left corner of the billboard to the lower-left corner of the white billboard placeholder.

15 Repeat this process for all corners until the billboard image aligns with the background. Then press Return/Enter to confirm.

16 Set Opacity for the billboard image to 100%, and change its blending mode to Multiply.

17 In the Layers panel, drag the billboard layer down the layer stack until it is underneath the contrast layer.

You have now created a mockup of the billboard in Photoshop.

18 Save your work.

Updating the design

These steps show you the order in which to update nested items that originate from a Creative Cloud Library.

1 Return to InDesign.

2 Option/Alt-click the library icon in the upper-left corner of the shoe frame.

The Links panel opens and the link whose icon you clicked is selected. This is a great way to quickly open the Links panel to find the link you need. Both links in the panel display the library icon.

3 With the shoe image selected in the Links panel, click the Relink From CC Libraries button to relink the image to a different library item.

The CC Libraries panel opens and asks you to choose a replacement graphic.

4   In the CC Libraries panel, select shoe8 and click Relink at the bottom of the panel.

This is a great way to update a design with a different asset from any Creative Cloud Library. This ability to relink an item to a different library graphic is also available in Photoshop and Illustrator.

However, since the shoe graphic and shadow effects are not the same size, you might see some clipping occur around the edges.

5   With the shoe image selected on the page, open the Properties panel and click the second icon under Frame Fitting to adjust the shoe image proportionally to fit the frame.

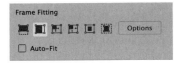

We've now hit a crossroads in our workflow: we need to update the billboard design that we used in Photoshop. We could repeat the same steps for the library graphic by double-clicking it in the CC Libraries panel to open it in InDesign. Or we could save the new layout as a second billboard item.

For flexibility, we'll choose the second scenario, as it is just as easy switching library items from Photoshop as it was from InDesign. And we'll always have a backup of the other shoe version in case our customer changes their mind and prefers the previous version after all.

6 Press Command+A/Ctrl+A to select everything on the page.

7 In the CC Libraries panel, click the plus icon and choose Graphic.

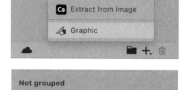

8 Double-click the graphic name and rename it **billboard2**. We now have two billboard versions to choose from in Photoshop.

9 Return to Photoshop.

10 Double-click the billboard Smart Object thumbnail to open its contents in a separate window. (If an explanatory dialog box opens, click OK.)

11 In the separate file window, right-click the billboard layer (displaying the cloud icon) and choose Relink To Library Graphic.

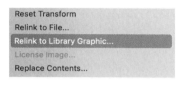

12 In the Libraries panel, select billboard2 and click Relink to update the layout.

13 Save and close the file to return to billboard-mockupWorking.psd.

● **Note:** Note that the perspective transformation and blending mode were retained. This is because we created a Smart Object from the original layer before applying the perspective transformation.

14 Save and close your Photoshop document. Then do the same for InDesign.

You could even go another level deeper by selecting all the layers in the mockup file and saving the Photoshop layers as a library asset, only to place the library asset back in an InDesign layout (for a magazine, for example). As you can see, working with Creative Cloud Libraries is very powerful, but it can be confusing because of the endless nesting possibilities.

Combining Photoshop and Illustrator library assets

In this scenario, we'll save Photoshop artwork into a library and use it in Illustrator. Then we'll add a few elements from Illustrator to the same library and place both Photoshop and Illustrator content in InDesign.

You'll start by inspecting the final Illustrator and InDesign documents in order to better understand the project details.

1 Start Illustrator, and choose Illustrator > Preferences > General (macOS) or Edit > Preferences > General (Windows).

2 In the Preferences dialog box, click Reset Preferences. Then restart Illustrator.

3 From the Lesson08 folder, open L08-travel-banner-end.ai.

4 Choose View > Trim View to hide all objects that extend beyond the artboard.

This document uses Photoshop layers in the foreground and vector artwork in the background.

5 Return to InDesign, then choose Window > Workspace > Reset Essentials.

6 From the Lesson08 folder, open L08-oslo-end.indd.

This layout reuses several of the Photoshop layers used in Illustrator, and also some of the vector artwork from Illustrator.

7   Close all files.

Creating a Creative Cloud Library

The first step is creating a library and adding content from Photoshop.

1   Return to Photoshop.

2   Choose Window > Workspace > Reset Essentials.

3   From the Lesson08/Imports folder, open oslo-layers.psd.

This Photoshop document used to be a single image, but it has been split into several layers. We need a way to bring the Photoshop document into Illustrator with full transparency and full control over the separate layers, while still having the ability to go back to Photoshop and make changes.

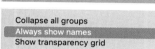

Based on the exercises from Lesson 2, we know that we could place the Photoshop document in Illustrator. However, we can retain separate Photoshop layers in Illustrator only if we choose to embed the document, which makes it impossible to update the file in Photoshop. And if we place and link the file in Illustrator instead, we'll be able to update the file in Photoshop, but we won't have access to the individual layers from Illustrator. Creative Cloud Libraries to the rescue!

4   Choose Window > Libraries to open the Libraries panel.

5   Open the panel menu and choose Create New Library.

6   Name the library **Oslo** and click Create to confirm.

7   From the Layers panel, click to highlight the boat layer. Now click the plus button at the bottom of the Libraries pane and choose Graphic to add the layer to the library.

8   Repeat the same step for the remaining three layers.

9   Open the Libraries panel menu and choose Always Show Names to see the names of all objects.

Placing Photoshop library items in Illustrator

Now we'll import the library items we just created into Illustrator and reconstruct the composition.

1   In Illustrator, open L08-travel-banner-start.ai from the Lesson08 folder.

2   Choose File > Save As and save the file as **L08-travelWorking.ai**.

3   Choose Window > Libraries to view the Creative Cloud Libraries.

4   Click the Oslo library to open it.

5   Open the Libraries panel menu and choose Always Show Names to see the names of all objects.

6   Drag the sky layer from the library and click the upper-left corner of the artboard to place it.

7   In the Properties panel, click the Horizontal Align Left and Vertical Align Top icons in the Align section to align the sky to the top left of the artboard.

8   In the Libraries panel, drag the foreground object onto the artboard and click the lower-left corner of the artboard to place it.

9   In the Properties panel, click the Horizontal Align Left and Vertical Align Bottom icons in the Align section to align the image to the bottom left of the artboard.

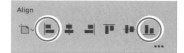

10 Place the boat object from the Libraries panel onto the artboard.

11 Use the Selection tool ▶ to position the boat so it perfectly overlaps with the boat in the image.

12 Drag and drop the cloud image onto the artboard, and place it in the middle of the image.

13 With the cloud image selected, go to the Properties panel and click Opacity to see more options. Then change the blending mode from Normal to Screen to blend the cloud into the background.

14 Open the Layers panel and drag the boat object to the top of the layer stack.

15 Drag the sky object to the bottom of the layer stack.

16 Drag the foreground object so it's directly below the boat object.

17 Drag the cloud object on top of the OSLO layer.

18 Make the vectors1 and vectors2 layers visible.

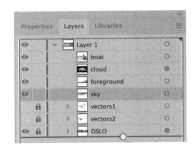

Your layer stack should look like this.

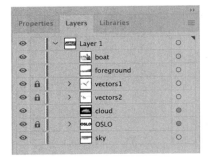

Keep in mind that anytime you need to update any of the Photoshop layers, you only need to double-click the item in the library and make your edits. When you save your file it will trigger an update to the library, which will then trigger an update to the linked copies in the Illustrator document.

19 Choose View > Trim View to hide all objects that extend beyond the artboard.

20 Click the lock icons on the layers vectors1 and vectors2 to unlock them.

21 Click the selection rectangle of the vectors1 layer to select all objects on the layer.

22 With the selection active, go to the Libraries panel and click the plus icon. Now choose Graphic to add it to the library.

23 Repeat this process for the vectors2 layer.

24 Save your file.

Placing Photoshop and Illustrator library items in InDesign

Now we'll place the artwork we saved to the library in an InDesign document.

1 Return to InDesign and choose Window > Workspace > Reset Essentials.

2 From the Lesson 08 folder, open L08-oslo-start.indd.

3 Choose File > Save As and save the file as **L08-osloWorking.indd**.

4 Choose Window > CC Libraries, then open the Oslo library to view all items.

5 Drag the foreground object onto the layout. Scale it down by dragging it from the left side of the spread to the right until it matches the width of the spread.

6 Now drag vectors1 onto the right-hand page.

7 Scale it so it partially overlaps with the text.

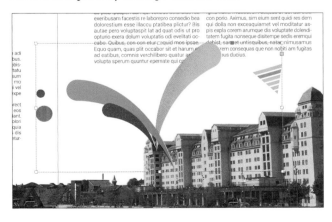

Note: If the Subject Aware Wrapping pop-up appears, click OK.

8 With vectors1 selected, choose Window > Text Wrap.

9 Click the third Text Wrap option to wrap text around a shape, and enter **0.5 in** for the Top Offset Value.

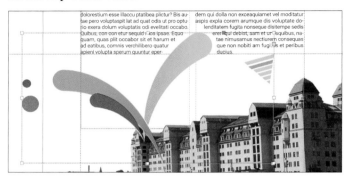

10 From the Contour Options Type menu, choose Detect Edges to wrap the text around the Illustrator artwork.

11 Using the Selection tool ▶, select the foreground object.

12 In the Text Wrap panel, apply the third Text Wrap option and enter a value of **0.375 in**.

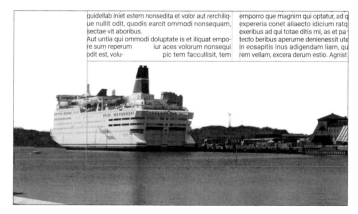

13 Change the Contour Options Type menu to Alpha Channel.

InDesign detects that this layer is partially transparent, so we can leverage the layer's transparency by choosing Alpha Channel when applying text wrap.

Relinking Photoshop layers and updating

To finish, we'll replace one of the original Photoshop layers with the linked version from the library. That way, a layer used in Photoshop, Illustrator, and InDesign will link to the same source.

1 Return to oslo-layers.psd in Photoshop.

This file has the original layers that we saved to the library. However, when you save assets to a library they will always be unlinked copies of the original. This means that the current foreground layer in Photoshop is not linked to the library source.

We could just delete the foreground layer and place a fresh (linked) version from the Libraries panel. But that would require us to place it at exactly the same location, which is time consuming.

A better way is to use the Relink To Library Graphic command, which we've used before. However, you can't use this command with normal layers. To make this work, the layer we want to relink to a library asset must first be converted into a Smart Object.

2 Right-click the foreground layer and choose Convert To Smart Object.

3 Right-click the same layer again and notice that we now have many more options available. Choose Relink To Library Graphic.

4 In the Libraries panel, select the foreground asset and click Relink to replace the original with the cloud version in the library.

Now the foreground asset in the Oslo library is linked to Photoshop, Illustrator, and InDesign projects at the same time. It would have been impossible to achieve this the traditional way, at least not with this level of control. Let's trigger an update to see how all projects update.

5 In any application's Libraries panel, double-click the foreground asset to edit it.

This library asset is actually a fully functional Photoshop document, which means we can add as many layers as we want.

6 Use the Layers panel to add a Hue/Saturation adjustment layer.

7 Increase the Saturation value to **+50**. (We'll exaggerate a little bit to make easier for us to spot the updated version of our library asset.)

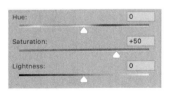

8 Select the Spot Healing Brush tool . from the Tools panel.

9 Click the brush settings at the top of the screen to change the brush Size to **20px** and Hardness to **100%**.

10 With the foreground layer selected, paint over the six yellow poles in the water by dragging from the top of each pole to the bottom, removing them from the picture.

Photoshop replaces the painted area with neighboring pixels to camouflage the painted area. One or two additional paint strokes might be required to make it look flawless.

11 Save and close the file.

The thumbnail in the Libraries panel updates to the latest version. All files in which we used the asset, oslo-layers.psd in Photoshop, osloWorking.indd in InDesign, and travelWorking.ai in Illustrator, update as well.

Backing up library items

Once you have a finished project that uses one or more linked library items, you'll probably think about archiving your project. So how do you back up and collect cloud-based assets? There are two possibilities.

Creating a package

Just as with any other project in InDesign, Photoshop, or Illustrator, you can package your project to collect all linked project assets into a separate folder. The library items will be extracted from the library and stored locally in the package. This means that the packaged copy of your project will link to locally saved versions of the original cloud assets.

The following diagram will help you understand how linked library assets are converted to local assets when you package your project:

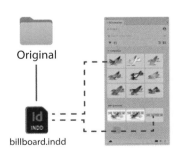

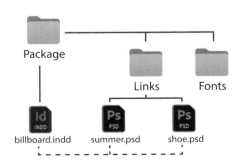

Exporting the library

It is possible to export a Creative Cloud Library, including all assets, to a local file. This allows you to save a local copy of a library to back up a project or share a library with others offline.

To export a library, follow these steps:

1   In Photoshop, Illustrator, or InDesign, open the Libraries panel menu and choose Export *name of library*.

▶ **Tip:** You can also export or import libraries using the Creative Cloud app.

▶ **Tip:** It is also possible to export a single item from a library: view the library using the Creative Cloud app, right-click the item, and choose Export A Copy.

2   Choose a destination folder for the library, click Save to confirm the location, then click Export.

The Creative Cloud Library is exported locally as a CCLIBS file. To import a library file, use the Libraries panel menu and choose the Import Library command.

For backup purposes it is recommended to apply both techniques: First, package your documents; and then, export a local copy of the Creative Cloud Library. It is a good idea to include a copy of the Creative Cloud Library because the package command can include only linked graphics; branded elements that were part of the campaign but remained unlinked—swatches, paragraph styles, and others—would be lost once the library is deleted.

Review questions

1 How are Creative Cloud Libraries different from more traditional cloud repositories?

2 Do you need to be online to use Creative Cloud Libraries?

3 Are Creative Cloud Libraries a good alternative to my file server?

4 Where can you view all assets stored within a Creative Cloud Library?

5 When you use assets from a Creative Cloud Library, are they always linked?

Review answers

1 Creative Cloud Libraries are unique because they offer a way for designers to save design assets that don't have a dedicated file format, like InDesign text styles, colors, or Photoshop layer styles.

2 You don't need to be online to use assets from existing Creative Cloud Libraries. But an active internet connection is required when updating assets, creating new libraries, or collaborating with others.

3 Creative Cloud Libraries are first and foremost intended to store and exchange design assets across multiple apps and teams. They are not built for long-time archiving and are not a replacement for a company server, a data drive, or a DAM or MAM system.

4 You can view all Creative Cloud Libraries stored in your Creative Cloud account either by using the Creative Cloud desktop app or navigating to assets.adobe.com.

5 Photoshop and Illustrator graphics are linked to the document in which they are placed by default, unless you right-click and choose Place Copy instead. Other asset types—like colors, text styles, and layer styles—are not linked.

9 INTEGRATION THROUGH COLLABORATION

Lesson overview

In this lesson, you'll learn how to do the following:

- Share Creative Cloud Libraries by a variety of methods.

- Understand the difference between sharing libraries privately and publicly.

- Understand personal versus team libraries.

- Learn about the advantages of cloud documents.

- Share and receive cloud documents.

 This lesson will take about 75 minutes to complete. Please log in to your account at adobepress.com/DesignCIB to download the files for this lesson, or go to the "Getting Started" section at the beginning of this book and follow the instructions under "Accessing the lesson files and Web Edition." Store the files on your computer in a convenient location.

Your Account page is also where you'll find any updates to the lesson files. Look on the Lesson & Update Files tab to access the most current content.

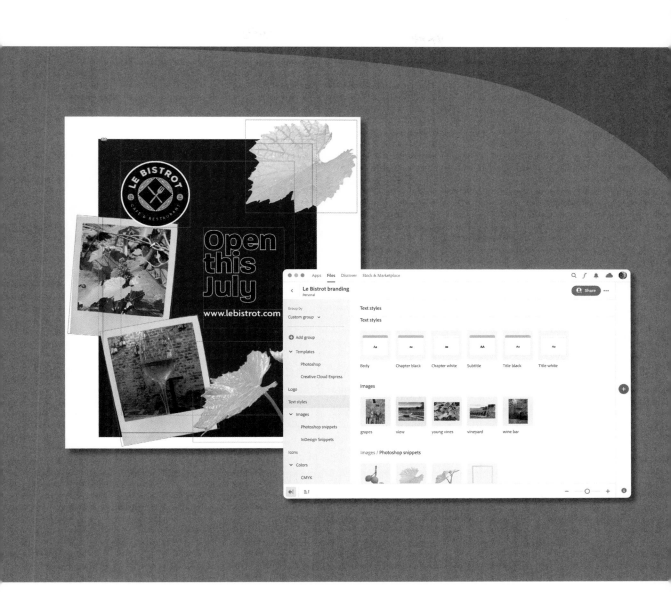

Collaborating with others using Creative Cloud Libraries and cloud documents allows you to share assets at scale and get instant feedback on projects.

Collaborating using Creative Cloud Libraries

In the previous lesson, you learned that Creative Cloud Libraries can store branded assets and other file types unique to Adobe applications in a cloud-hosted environment. You learned how to create a library, add assets and files to it, and reuse the assets in various applications.

An example of a Creative Cloud library, organized using groups and subgroups.

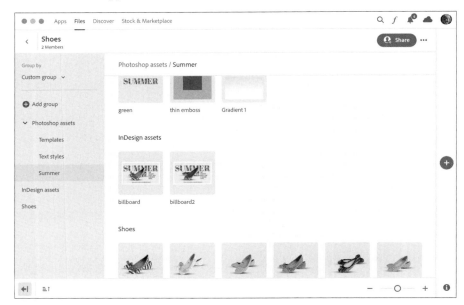

In this lesson, we'll explore how to share Creative Cloud Libraries with others. You'll learn how to set library permissions and what the differences are between sharing with an individual and sharing with a larger group of people. The goal of this lesson is to help you understand how to use shared library assets in Photoshop, InDesign, and Illustrator. Having a better understanding of how library sharing works will empower you to take full advantage of all the library functionality within Creative Cloud. It will also allow you to think creatively about setting up workflows with stakeholders such as a team member, a freelancer, or someone from marketing. Keep in mind that the primary purpose of a Creative Cloud Library is to let you store and share branded assets with collaborators who can use the assets in their projects across multiple apps. Keep in mind that every collaborator who needs to use assets from the library will need some sort of Creative Cloud membership, either paid or free.

All assets in your Creative Cloud account are safely stowed away in your Creative Cloud storage. This includes your libraries, cloud documents, synced folders, and documents shared via apps such as InDesign Publish Online. This means that, by default, no one except you has access to these assets. When you share a Creative

Cloud Library, you're creating an opening for others to view and interact with the assets you have stored in your personal cloud storage. It is up to you to decide how you allow access to your library:

- Do you want to share the library with one or more named recipients? If yes, you'll need to know the email address they use for their Creative Cloud membership.

- Do you want to share the library with a larger group of recipients, whose email addresses you may or may not know? If so, you can generate an open URL that can be shared publicly, granting access to the assets.

Whichever method you choose, know that a shared library consumes space only in the cloud storage of the asset owner. For example, if you create a library and add a 100MB Photoshop document to it, it will take up 100MB of your total cloud storage, but it will not take up any cloud storage space of the users with access to that library.

Sharing a library publicly

The sharing mechanism behind Creative Cloud Libraries allows you to give access to a specific URL that is available to anyone inside or outside your organization. Leaving the door open to anyone to view, use, or copy your branded assets takes away a lot of friction when working with multiple stakeholders, as it takes away the repetitive task of manually having to share the library with individual email addresses.

With this concept in mind, you have the ability to create different libraries based on different uses or stakeholders. This allows you to create a curated gallery of branded assets:

- For each brand or subbrand you work with

- For each product or product line

- For each language or region

- To create a mood board while collaborating with team members or clients

The advantage to this system is that it creates a way for you to cater to different target groups and allow them to use these assets and integrated workflows across their Adobe applications.

Uses

Sharing a library of colors, text styles, Photoshop layers, and other branded assets with designers using Adobe software is the primary use case when sharing libraries. This means that any designer can access a shared URL that leads to the online library and choose to "subscribe" to it in order to get the latest updates. This shared

URL can be included as part of a specific project briefing or can be referenced in a corporate style guide PDF.

However, there are other potential workflows that go beyond the traditional designer-to-designer collaboration use case. For example, let's say you are a designer working in a small company. You know apps like Photoshop, InDesign, and Illustrator well and you're in charge of creating and maintaining all branded assets and designs. However, your co-workers don't know Photoshop, Illustrator, or InDesign but still need to use, apply, and follow the branded assets and guidelines. A typical example of someone who might require this is someone who works in marketing or communication. They don't need to be a designer, but they still need access to the latest logo, icons, colors, and text styles in order to be successful at their jobs. Luckily for them, they can use a Creative Cloud plug-in for Microsoft Office 365 that allows them to view and use Creative Cloud Libraries within the Microsoft environment.

▶ **Tip:** You can even use Creative Cloud Libraries within Microsoft solutions (Word and PowerPoint) but this is beyond the scope of this book. Please consult Microsoft documentation to learn more.

In practice, this means that a designer can build a library with design assets and share it as a read-only library with Microsoft product users within the organization for use in PowerPoint, Word, and other applications. And whenever a library asset is updated by the designer, who acts as a curator, all users of that library will receive the latest version of it.

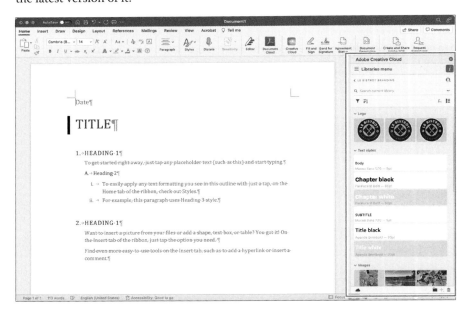

What do you need?

If you want to collaborate with other designers, it is required that everyone has an active Creative Cloud membership. This makes sense, because the collaborators would use Adobe apps to access the assets from the shared library. Users of older

Adobe applications, like those included with Creative Suite 6, can't use Creative Cloud Libraries.

Those who don't use Adobe applications but want to use shared assets in Microsoft applications, to take one example, can simply register for a free account via Adobe. com. Free accounts come with 2GB of storage, which should be enough to receive a Creative Cloud Library with logos, icons, and colors.

► **Tip:** In Word or PowerPoint, choose Insert > Add-Ins > Get Add-Ins. In the Office Add-Ins window, search for Creative Cloud and then click Add next to the add-in.

Following public libraries provided by Adobe

Adobe wants to give you a head start when working with Creative Cloud Libraries by giving you access to a few libraries created by professional designers. These libraries include collections of gradients, UX elements, fonts (synchronized via Adobe Fonts), icons, and much more.

1 Open the Creative Cloud app on your computer.

2 Click the Stock & Marketplace tab.

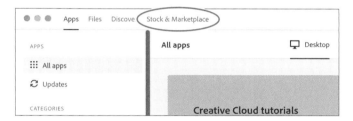

3 Click Libraries to access Adobe's online collection of Creative Cloud Libraries.

4 Click any library to view it in a web browser or click the Add To Your Libraries button to subscribe to the library and add it to your account.

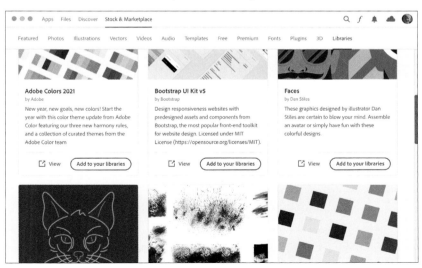

These are what we call open libraries, meaning that anyone that knows the URL to the library can add it to their Creative Cloud account by clicking the Add To Your Libraries button. This button subscribes you to the library by giving you read-only access to all assets in the library. This is a similar experience to following a user on streaming services like YouTube or Spotify. It gives you read-only access to all content in the list and all newly added content the moment it is added by the owner.

Viewing and following a public library provided by another user

A public library has been created for you in order to complete the first part of the exercise. Imagine this shared library comes from a designer who acts as the brand manager for a customer called Le Bistrot. You need to use the library assets for an upcoming design for the same customer.

First, you'll add the shared library to our own Creative Cloud account.

If you encounter any technical issues during this operation, a local copy of the library has been provided in the Lesson09/Imports folder as a backup. Look for the file Le Bistrot branding.cclibs and consult the importing steps described in the "Sharing a library publicly" section later in this lesson. Once it's imported, continue with this exercise.

● **Note:** The original URL has been shortened using Bitly.com.

1   Open a web browser and navigate to adobe.ly/3OiHJdz.

2   Scroll through the library, inspecting all items.

The library order is set to View By Type by default. This sorts all library assets by asset type—for example, graphics, colors, 3D models, and so on. At the top of the

page, you can see the total number of assets in the library and the library owner.

3   Click the View By Group button to view all assets by custom group. This displays items using custom categories created by the author (if present).

This library contains the following:

*   Photoshop and Creative Cloud Express templates
*   Paragraph styles from InDesign (located in the Text Styles group)
*   InDesign snippets
*   Objects on transparent backgrounds from Photoshop
*   Illustrator logos
*   Various colors

4 Click the Add To Your Libraries button to start following the library. This adds it to your account as a read-only library (you might be asked to log in to your Creative Cloud account).

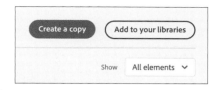

> **Note:** Clicking the Create A Copy button would place a copy of the library in your account, giving you full editing rights. However, you would no longer receive asset updates because you chose to work with your own copy of the library instead of subscribing to the original.

An open URL is a great way of sharing assets with large groups of users.

5 Return to the Creative Cloud app on your computer.

6 Click the Files tab to view all your cloud assets, then click Your Libraries.

The newly added library has a label that clearly identifies it as public.

> **Note:** If you imported Le Bistrot branding.cclibs instead of using the provided URL, the library will be listed as personal instead of public.

Le Bistrot branding
Public

Applying text styles

You'll start the exercise by inspecting the finished InDesign document to better understand the project details.

1 Start InDesign, and then press Control+Option+Shift+Command/Alt+Shift+Ctrl to restore the default preferences.

2 When prompted, click Yes to delete the Adobe InDesign Settings file.

3 From the Lesson09 folder, open L09-flyer-end.indd.

This design uses various assets from the shared library, including a paragraph style, an Illustrator logo, and multiple Photoshop assets.

> **Note:** To avoid broken links, all artwork in this file has been embedded in the InDesign document.

4 Close the file but leave InDesign open.

Now we'll reuse the library assets to re-create the project you just viewed.

5 From the Lesson09 folder, open L09-flyer-start.indd.

The document includes a background image and two text frames.

6 Choose File > Save As and save the file as **L09-flyerWorking.indd**.

7 Choose Window > CC Libraries to display the Creative Cloud Libraries panel.

8 In the CC Libraries panel, navigate to the newly added library, Le Bistrot Branding.

● **Note:** If you locally imported Le Bistrot branding.cclibs you will not see a globe icon and you will have editing rights.

Notice the globe icon next to the library name if you hover your cursor over it in the CC Libraries panel. This makes clear it's a public library.

9 Using the Selection tool ▶, select the top text frame in your InDesign document.

10 In the CC Libraries panel, click the name of the Le Bistrot Branding library to display its contents. Scroll through the library to the Text Styles section and click the Chapter Black text style to apply it to the selected text frame. The lock icon at the bottom right of the panel indicates that the library is read-only and can't be edited.

Applying a paragraph style from the CC Libraries panel not only applies the style but also displays the Paragraph Styles panel and adds the style to the panel.

11 Use the Selection tool ▶ to select the second text frame, with the website address.

12 In the CC Libraries panel, click the Title White style to apply it.

13 With the frame still selected, switch to the Properties panel and in the Paragraph section, click the Align Left button to align the text to the left.

14 Deselect the text frame.

Placing graphics

1 Switch back to the CC Libraries panel and open the panel menu. Choose Always Show Names to display the names of all items.

2 Scroll through the library until you reach the Images/Photoshop Snippets group. Drag the item named Leaf from the library onto the page.

3 With the loaded cursor, drag to place the image at approximately 22% of its original size. Position it at the upper-right corner of the page.

4 Drag the item named Photo Frame from the library onto the page and place it at approximately 6% of its original size.

5   In the CC Libraries panel, scroll up to the Images category. From there, drag the Young Vines images onto the page to load the cursor with the image. Drag to place the image on the page, but don't place it too large, as its size should fit the height of the photo frame image just placed.

6   Select the Photo Frame object, right-click it, and choose Arrange > Bring To Front to place it above the Young Vines image.

7   Use the Selection tool ▶ to crop the Young Vines image in such a way that it's completely hidden behind the photo frame, giving the impression it's part of the photo frame.

8   Select both the image and photo frame and group them by pressing Command+G/Ctrl+G.

9   Slightly rotate the group at an angle of −8°, and place it next to the main title.

10 Repeat the photo frame process by dragging a second copy from the library. This time, use the image named Wine Bar. End by grouping the image and photo frame.

11 Slightly rotate the new photo frame group to give it a more casual look, and position it below the first photo frame, slightly overlapping the corner of the first photo frame.

12 In the CC Libraries panel, drag the Logo CMYK item onto the page. Scale it to 50% of its original size and place it in the upper-left corner of the page margins.

13 Lastly, drag the item called Twig from the library onto the page. Position it in the lower-right corner at 30% of its original size. Allow it to overlap with the second photo frame.

14 Save your file and close the document.

Sharing a library publicly

Sharing a Creative Cloud Library publicly allows others to follow it. For obvious reasons, it's not possible for a user to follow or subscribe to a library they already own. This means that you won't be able to share a library with yourself unless you have two different Adobe accounts.

This exercise provides you with a library to get started: an exported copy of the dinosaur library you created in Lesson 8, "Working with Creative Cloud Libraries." If you still have that library in your account, you can skip these steps. If you deleted the dinosaur library, follow these next steps to add it to your account.

● **Note:** Importing a local library file always synchronizes it to Creative Cloud, making it available from all your applications.

1 In InDesign (or any other Creative Cloud app), open the CC Libraries panel menu and choose Import Library.

2 In the Import Library dialog box, click the folder icon to open a file browser window.

3 Navigate to the Lesson09/Imports folder and select Dinosaur.cclibs.

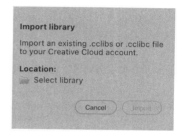

4 Click Open to import the local library into the panel, then click Import and then OK in the confirmation dialog box.

Now it's time to create an open URL that we can share with others. That way, anyone with the URL can follow the library and use its assets.

Make sure you're viewing the Dinosaur library contents before continuing.

▶ **Tip:** You can also drag a CCLIBS file into the Libraries section of the Creative Cloud app to add it to your account.

5 In the CC Libraries panel in InDesign, open the panel menu and choose Get Link.

The Creative Cloud app opens and presents you the Share Link To *Dinosaur* dialog box.

We need to decide how much freedom we want to offer to the recipients of the URL. Allow Save To Creative Cloud prevents users from creating their own copy of the library with full editing rights. Allow Follow enables users to subscribe to a read-only version of the library.

▶ **Tip:** You can trigger the Get Link command from any Creative Cloud app that uses libraries, or directly from the Creative Cloud app.

Typically, you use Allow Follow only in scenarios in which brand guidelines need to be strictly followed and the library owner oversees changes. You would typically use Allow Save To Creative Cloud in situations in which you trust the recipient to maintain and update their own version of the library or you grant them the freedom to make edits as they please.

6 Deselect Allow Save To Creative Cloud, then click Copy Link and click the X in upper-right corner of the dialog box to close it.

We deselected the Save To Creative Cloud option so that recipients can only save a local copy of the library to their own account. This is a good practice when you want your version of the shared library to be the only source of a shared branding.

● **Note:** As long as a URL is listed in the Share dialog box of a library, it will remain accessible for anyone to use. If you want to deny access to a previously shared library, click Remove Link in the Share dialog box. Access the Share dialog box by clicking the More Options button (labeled with an ellipsis, or three dots) and clicking Get A Link.

7 Open a new browser window and paste the URL into the address field to load the library.

If you can see your Creative Cloud username in the upper-right corner, click it and click Log Out to log out of your account in order to simulate what a user without a Creative Cloud account would see.

All assets are displayed in the browser and the Add To Your Libraries button is made available.

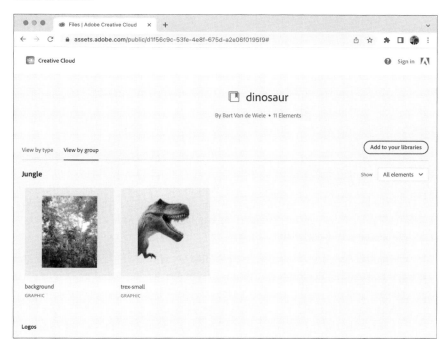

Sharing a library privately

Sharing a Creative Cloud Library privately is a great way of setting up a collaborative system that allows you and your collaborators to create, share, and update assets. To complete this exercise you need two different Adobe accounts: one for sharing assets and one for receiving assets.

The most direct way to share a library is by inviting the recipient into the library. You do this by choosing a command in either the Libraries panel within a design app or the Creative Cloud app on the desktop. Once the invitation is sent, the recipient needs to accept the invitation in order to view and interact with the library.

This gives you full control over who is invited and who is not. If necessary, the recipients can save a private copy of the shared library into their own Adobe cloud storage.

Inviting users to a Creative Cloud Library also allows you to set privileges for each collaborator:

- **Editing rights** allow the user to use, edit, or delete assets in the library. Additionally, they can add assets to the library, making them available to everyone who is part of the active collaboration.

- **Viewing rights** allow the user to use all assets in the library. All assets that allow you to link to the library—for example, artwork from Illustrator or Photoshop— are linked as read-only instances. It is not possible to delete or edit existing library assets or to add assets.

Keep in mind that these editing and viewing properties are there to help you set up a collaborative workflow, not for the purposes of data protection. Sharing a read-only library still allows the recipient to duplicate a local copy into their own account, just as invited collaborators can invite other collaborators.

Uses

The most common use case of sharing a library privately is to allow designers to share branded assets. We like to think of a Creative Cloud Library as "the one" library that holds *all* materials that make up your brand. However, keep in mind that you are free to create as many libraries as you like, as long as you have online storage available. This means you can create a separate library for specific stakeholders—for example, external freelancers.

When organizations hire an external freelancer to work on a particular assignment, the organization's IT department often needs to share a login and password with them so they can access the company server to find and use the branded assets and project files required for the assignment. Providing access to the server might require some time, as the freelancer is allowed to access only the server project files and nothing else. Because this might prove to be a hassle for some organizations, they often end up sending a "briefing" package to the freelancer using a file transfer system.

However, as you learned in the previous lesson, cloud providers (or file transfer systems) are only able to share "normal" files and not colors, text styles, and other brand elements specific to Adobe software. Sharing and briefing a freelancer on which assets, layers, styles, or colors to use can be challenging, especially if they're working remotely.

This is why creating and inviting a freelancer into a dedicated library that holds all branded assets and project building blocks is a great alternative to opening your company server or sending files via a file transfer system. Not only does this enable you to collect specific design assets, but all assets will appear directly within the Adobe applications of the freelancer.

If the recipient of a shared Creative Cloud Library has a free Adobe account, without a subscription, they will still receive the invitation to join the library. Because they don't have the software to use it, there is not much they can do with the library apart from viewing it inside a web browser. This might be useful in scenarios in which stakeholders need to view or approve a collection of assets.

Sharing, receiving, and using a private library

You'll start the exercise by inspecting the finished Photoshop document to better understand the project details.

1 Start Photoshop, and choose Photoshop > Preferences > General (macOS) or Edit > Preferences > General (Windows).

2 In the Preferences dialog box, click Reset Preferences On Quit. Then restart Photoshop.

3 From the Lesson09 folder, open L09-banner-end.psd.

4 Photoshop greets you with an error message explaining there are currently missing links in the document. Click Cancel to ignore this message.

Several elements in these banners are linked to a Creative Cloud Library to which you currently don't have access (yet). And even the banner itself is based on a Photoshop template (PSDT file) that was saved in the same library. This exercise will teach you how to accept a shared library and use design elements from it. Both banners use the same assets: a shoe, a logo graphic, and text.

5   Close the file.

Importing the library

A local copy of the library has been provided in the Lesson09/Imports folder. For this exercise, we'll reuse a slightly altered version of the Shoes library you created in Lesson 8. And because this library differs from the one you created in Lesson 8, it's important to follow these steps.

1   In Photoshop, choose Window > Libraries to display the Libraries panel.

2   If necessary, delete the old Shoes library from your account: click the library to display it, open the panel menu, and choose Delete "Shoes." Click Delete in the confirmation dialog box.

3   To import the new version of the Shoes library, open the Libraries panel menu again and choose Import Library.

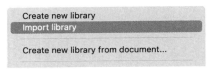

4   Click the Select Library button, navigate to the Lesson09/Imports folder, and select Shoes.cclibs.

5   Click Open, then click Import and then OK in the confirmation dialog box to import the local library into the panel.

The sharing experience

This exercise requires us to wear two different hats. On one side, you'll learn how the owner of the Shoes library can share a library privately. And on the other side, you'll learn what the collaborator (that is, the receiver) of the library experiences when receiving the invitation.

In the "Sharing a library publicly" section in this chapter, you learned how to create an open link to grant anyone with the link access to the library. And, we used the Get Link command from the CC Libraries panel menu in InDesign to make that happen. In the following scenario, we want to invite *specific* users to collaborate. While we could theoretically use another command from the same panel menu in Photoshop to privately invite a user, we'll use the Creative Cloud app instead to better understand that these commands are available from multiple locations.

1 Open the Creative Cloud app.

2 Click the Files tab.

3 Click the Your Libraries category to display all libraries in your Creative Cloud account.

 The Shoes library is listed there.

4 Click the Shoes library to access it.

 This library comes with custom groups of various asset types. The sidebar on the left displays the hierarchy of groups and subgroups created by the person who set up the library.

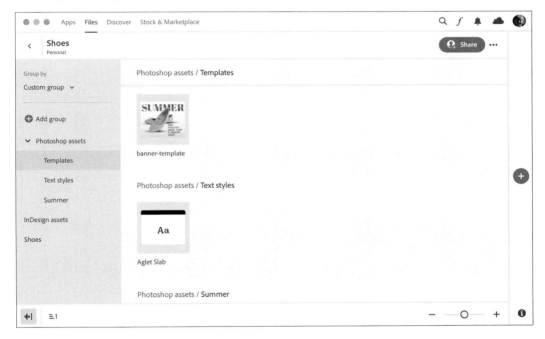

5 Click the blue Share button at the top right of the screen to start the sharing process. This displays the Invite dialog box.

 ▶ **Tip:** Clicking the More Options button instead of the Share button allows you to use the Get A Link command.

6 Enter the email address of the first collaborator with whom you'd like to share the Shoes library. For the sake of practicing this workflow, enter your personal email address. That way, you can see what the invitation email looks like. You won't be able to accept the invitation unless you have a second Creative Cloud subscription or a free Adobe account.

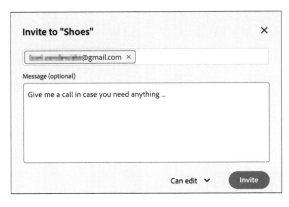

The menu in the lower-right corner of the dialog box determines whether this individual has editing or only viewing rights when working with the library:

- **Can Edit** means the collaborator has the same editing rights as you. This includes editing the library assets and structure, adding new items, and deleting existing items. However, it is not possible for them to delete the library. Deleting the library would result in the collaborator un-inviting themselves from the collaboration, which will result in them losing access to the library.

- **Can View** offers an experience similar to using the Get Link command. However, the main difference with Get Link is that this experience is based on invitations only, which means you have better control over who gets to see and use the assets in the library. Remember that you have less control when publishing an open URL using the Get Link command.

Leave all settings at their defaults.

● **Note:** You can always change these settings for individual contributors by re-visiting this dialog box again at a later stage.

▶ **Tip:** Return to this screen to revoke pending invitations.

7 Optionally, include a message that will be sent alongside the invitation. For example, add details about the project or library or provide contact details in case there are questions.

8 Click the Invite button to send the invitation.

Once the invitation is sent, you can see the status of every collaborator. As you've not accepted the invitation yet, the current status is Pending.

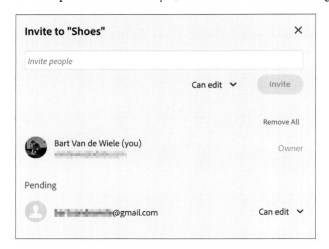

9 Click the X in the upper-right corner to close the Invite dialog box.

Receiving a library invitation

These next few steps will help you understand what the recipient of your invitation will see when invited into a Creative Cloud library. This means we are switching roles and are moving from the library owner's experience to the receiver's experience (i.e., the collaborator). Obviously, you'd only carry one of these roles per library in a real-life sharing scenario.

1   In your email inbox, open the library invitation email (sent to you as the collaborator).

The email clearly states the name of the initiator and the name of the shared library.

2   Click the Start Collaborating button.

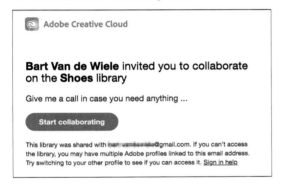

Your Creative Cloud online account asks if you want to accept the invitation. You may need to log in to your account first.

3   Accept the invitation to join the library.

A notification is sent to confirm that the invitation was accepted.

4   As the initiator, return to the Creative Cloud desktop app.

5   Click the Notifications icon at the top right of the screen and notice the notification of acceptance.

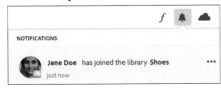

Using the shared library

These last few steps will allow you to build a small project using the library that was just shared with the collaborator. This means that we are switching hats again and are pretending to be the collaborator once more. But because most of us don't have a second Creative Cloud subscription, we'll keep working with the library owner's account instead.

Using a template from the shared library

1 Go to Photoshop.

2 Open L09-banner-end.psd from the Lesson09 folder.

This time you didn't receive an error message that reported missing links. This is because the Creative Cloud Library to which the layers were linked is now available within your account. So for future projects, be sure to first have the library available before opening files in order to avoid missing link errors. Note that multiple layers have a cloud icon in their thumbnails.

This document contains two web banners. You'll learn how to recreate one of the banners in the next few steps.

3 Close the file.

4 Choose Window > Libraries to display the Libraries panel.

5 Open the Shoes library in the Libraries panel.

6 Open the panel menu and choose Always Show Names to clearly see the names of all items.

7 In the Templates subgroup within Photo-shop Assets/Templates, right-click the banner template and choose Open New Document to create a new document based on it.

This Photoshop template was created by saving the design as a regular PSD document on the desktop and then manually renaming the file to a PSDT document. This creates a Photoshop template document, which was then dragged into the Shoes library, just as you did during the first exercise of Lesson 8. Note that the document uses artboards instead of a locked Background layer. This allows you to add additional artboards to bundle multiple designs or sizes within the same Photoshop document.

Saving Photoshop templates (PSDT), InDesign templates (INDDT), and Illustrator templates (AIT) that reference linked items from the same library is a great way of interchanging assets. Also, you will never have any missing links, because the referenced library assets exist in the same library in which the templates are saved.

▶ **Tip:** When sharing a document in a more traditional way—such as via email, servers, or cloud providers—share the referenced library with the collaborator first and then share the document itself. That way, you'll avoid missing links when they first open the document.

8   Choose File > Save As and save the file as **bannerWorking.psd**.

9   Click the artboard name on the canvas to view its properties in the Properties panel.

10 Click the plus symbol on the right side of the artboard to add a second artboard on the right.

11 Using the Properties panel, change the artboard's dimensions to **850 by 160 px**.

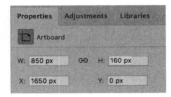

12 Double-click the Artboard 1 name in the Layers panel and rename it **banner 850x160**. Press Return/Enter to confirm.

Placing shared assets

1   In the Shoes library, drag the item named *green* onto the new artboard. You can find it in the Summer group.

2   Scale the graphic up until it's about as large as the canvas height, but leave a little bit of room at the bottom to fit a line of text. Press Return/Enter to confirm.

● **Note:** If Photoshop prompts you with a message about how Smart Objects are linked to libraries, click OK to continue.

3 In the Layers panel, create a new layer. Place it underneath the green layer.

4 With the new layer selected, click the Gradient 1 library item in the Summer group. This converts the new layer into a gradient fill layer.

5 In the Layers panel, double-click the thumbnail of the new gradient fill layer to open the Gradient Fill dialog box.

6 While the Gradient Fill dialog box is open, move your cursor outside the dialog box and drag slowly upward on the canvas to move the gradient up slightly. Stop when the slightly darker part of the gradient is positioned in the middle of the canvas.

7 Click OK to close the Gradient Fill dialog box.

8 Select the Type tool T. and click inside the canvas to create a new type layer. By default, Photoshop adds a few words to the type layer.

9 Before entering any text, change the font size to **5.5 pt**.

10 Use the Move tool ✛. to position the text underneath the SUMMER graphic, left aligned.

11 In the Shoes library, click the Aglet Slab text style to apply it to the text.

12 Use the Type tool 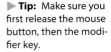 to enter the campaign slogan on a single line: **THE PERFECT SHOE, JUST A SEASON AWAY.**

To save time, we'll duplicate the shoe layer from the other artboard into our new artboard.

13 Option/Alt-drag the selected layer into the banner 850x160 artboard layers to duplicate it, dropping it above the green layer and gradient layer.

▶ **Tip:** Make sure you first release the mouse button, then the modifier key.

14 Press Command+T/Ctrl+T to enter Free Transform mode.

15 Move and scale the shoe layer to the right side of the banner. Make sure most of the image is visible. Press Return/Enter to confirm.

16 Save your file.

Relinking assets within a library

To demonstrate that all assets are linked to the same source, we'll now update both banners by switching to a different shoe image.

1　In the Layers panel, right-click the name of either of the two shoe layers and choose Relink To Library Graphic.

2　In the Libraries panel, click shoe2, then click the Relink button at the bottom of the Libraries panel.

▶ Tip: If you want to convert a linked library item into a regular (unlinked) Smart Object, first select the layer in the Layers panel and then click the Embed button in the Properties panel.

Both layers update using the new shoe image. This is because they both link to the same source. Remember that linked library assets are actually Smart Objects in Photoshop, meaning that any duplicate of an object will link to the same source.

3　Save and close the file.

What happens when you revoke access?

No matter how a user gains access to a library (whether through private or public sharing), any asset they use in a file will always link to the original shared library. And any change made to that library will ripple through to all followers, regardless of sharing method. However, this means that revoking access to the library can have grave consequences.

▶ Tip: You can change the viewing or editing rights of any collaborator at any time, or choose to revoke their access completely.

When you revisit the sharing options, either via the Invite or Get Link command, you have the ability to stop sharing access to the library. This means that all collaborators and followers will see the library in question disappear from their account, often leaving behind missing links in existing projects. This is why you need to be very careful when sharing libraries. In the end, this is about setting up a collaboration, and collaboration requires communication.

When you consider removing your shared library or removing access to it, communicate your decision to all stakeholders (if possible) before you pull the plug.

This gives them the opportunity to save a local copy of the library into their own account (if that privilege was enabled), or to embed all linked content in their projects. If they chose to save a local copy of the library, they will still need to relink all assets to the newly created copy by using the Links panel in InDesign and Illustrator, or by right-clicking a layer in Photoshop and choosing Relink To Library Graphic.

Sharing via the Creative Cloud mobile app

The previous exercises have taught you how to share Creative Cloud Libraries privately and publicly using any of the design apps, via the Creative Cloud app, or directly from the web.

You can also use the Creative Cloud mobile app, available for iOS, iPadOS, and Android, to create, view, and share libraries. This is a great way to manage your branded assets on the go. It also gives you a way to view your other online assets, browse and synchronize Adobe fonts, and watch tutorials.

1   Launch the mobile app on your device.

2   Tap the Sign In button to log in to your account and access your libraries.

3   Tap the Files icon.

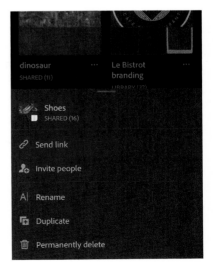

4   On the Files page, tap the Libraries tab to view all your libraries.

5   Tap the More Options button underneath one of your libraries to open a menu that includes the Send Link button. Tap this button to share the library publicly, or tap the Invite People button to share it privately.

Sharing a library offline

There is one more way to share a library. As you learned in Lesson 8, you can export a local copy of your library to your hard drive as a CCLIBS file. While most users think of exporting a local copy of a library as a means to back up a library for long-time archiving, this method can also be used to share a library. Because a CCLIBS file is a local document, you can place it on a server, put it on a USB stick, or send it using third-party cloud providers. All the recipient needs to do is import the offline library into their account to get started.

However, keep in mind that sharing a library using this method takes away the control you have when you share an online version of the library. You take the risk that the library will be acquired by those who have no business using your assets. And it may lead users to keep using outdated assets without your knowing. Because of this, it is recommended that you use the online sharing capabilities offered by Creative Cloud—that way you'll stay in control of the sharing mechanism and you'll be sure the recipients will always have the latest version of your design assets.

Viewing and filtering libraries

Over time, you might accumulate a large number of libraries in your Creative Cloud account. So finding ways to properly filter and structure your libraries and assets will be a necessity. Try to keep good library hygiene:

- Properly name your libraries by including, for example, references to project names or to customer names.

- Add metadata to assets by adding a description (as you learned in Lesson 8).

- Clear out libraries you no longer need by saving a local copy. To do so, export the library to a CCLIBS file and then delete the library from Creative Cloud Libraries.

You can also use the Creative Cloud app to get a better overview of the complete set of libraries you currently have under your control. However, the default view settings in the Creative Cloud desktop app don't always provide you with the best way to get your bearings as you navigate through a long list of libraries. In that case, follow these steps to make things easier:

1 Open the Creative Cloud app.

2 Click the Files tab to access your cloud assets.

3 Click Your Libraries in the left sidebar.

4 Toggle List view by clicking the list icon at the upper-right corner of the window.

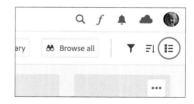

The Sharing column in List view displays the sharing status of your libraries.

5 Optionally, click the Filter button to include or exclude specific libraries from the current view, based on their sharing status.

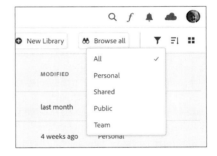

Summing up

Now that we've explored all online sharing options when working with Creative Cloud Libraries, it's important to return to the main question stated at the beginning of this lesson.

How do you want to share your library?

• I want to share the library with one or more named recipients.

• I want to share the library with a larger group of recipients, whose email addresses I don't know.

The answer to this question will determine which sharing method will work best for the library at hand.

Sharing a CC Library

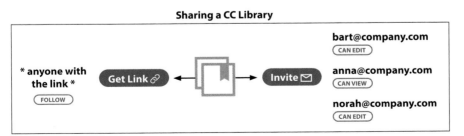

If you want to learn more about the current limitations when sharing libraries, how many active collaborations you can have, how many assets can be stored in a library, or how many collaborators you can invite, please consult the online help pages at helpx.adobe.com.

Personal versus team libraries

Now that you're familiar with the possibilities of sharing Creative Cloud Libraries, it's important to understand the principle of library ownership and the ownership of the assets within that library. Depending on the type of Creative Cloud membership you have, the ownership of a library might lie with either the individual or your organization.

PERSONAL LIBRARIES

Libraries created using an individual Creative Cloud license are referred to as *personal libraries*. This means that every library is automatically stored within the user's account, and it remains private until the user decides to grant access to it by using any of the methods described in this lesson. Also, the owner of a shared library can't be removed from the collaboration by other collaborators.

When a user or a member of an organization uses a Creative Cloud for Teams or Enterprise license, additional options become available when creating a library. These options allow the user to choose whether the library (together with its future assets) is owned by the user or by the entire organization. Libraries owned by the organization are called *team libraries*, and saving a library as a team library automatically enables everyone in your organization to follow it, without having to use the Get URL command. This accelerates the collaboration process, as this is a great way to push assets into a shared space within the organization, just like saving a file to a company server to which everyone has access. To grant editing rights to certain individuals, you can still use the Invite command as before.

► **Tip:** Individual members of Creative Cloud will always have an individual account. If your account was granted to you by your employer, there is a good chance you are using a Teams or Enterprise membership. To verify, talk to your IT department or visit account.adobe.com.

Team libraries also ensure that links to shared files remain intact in case anyone leaves the organization.

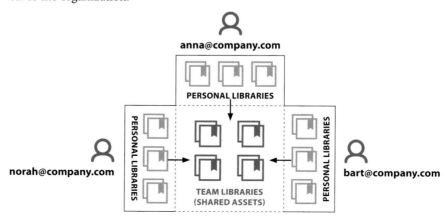

Creating a team library

Adding assets to a personal library makes them available only to yourself. But adding assets to a team library immediately makes them available to everyone else in the organization. The only choice you need to make is whether your teammates can edit or only view the assets in the library.

Consider the following scenario. You work for a local ad agency and start working on the Summer Shoes brand assets you used in the previous exercise. But because you suspect other designers will also work for this client, you need a central store for the various libraries you created. Creating, storing, and giving access to regular design files is easy, as you can just store them on a shared company server. But how do you share the Creative Cloud Libraries that go with the design files? This is exactly why team libraries exist. By creating all libraries as team libraries, anyone in your organization (using Creative Cloud) can look through a database of shared libraries and access the ones they need.

1   Open the Creative Cloud app.

2   Click the Files tab to access your cloud assets.

3   Click Your Libraries in the sidebar.

4   Click the Browse All button on the right to open the library browser.

5   From this screen you can view and browse all shared libraries within your organization, and choose to follow the ones you need. To follow a library, hover your pointer over it and click Add.

Don't put all your eggs in one basket

But what if the owner of a shared library decides to leave the team?

Imagine you are part of an organization that employs five designers, with Alex as the team leader. Alex has created a library with branded assets. They know the branding very well and are in charge of curating and maintaining the library. Their organization purchased Creative Cloud for Teams licenses, which Alex is using. But because Alex doesn't know the differences between a personal and a team library, they decide to create the library as a personal library.

They share the library with others by creating an open URL, using the Get Link command in InDesign. The URL is created and then shared with the rest of their team. Over the course of the next few months, multiple projects are created in Photoshop, Illustrator, and InDesign, all linking to the library created under Alex's Creative Cloud account.

Then Alex decides to move into a different role in the company. Because they will no longer be actively using their Creative Cloud membership, their IT co-worker removes their Creative Cloud membership. This means all of Alex's libraries and shared URLs will disappear, resulting in missing links for all of their co-workers' projects. This happens because Alex created their libraries as personal assets instead of company assets. If Alex had decided to create and share their libraries as team libraries instead, there would not have been an issue when their Creative Cloud membership was removed.

Converting from personal to team and back

If you have a Creative Cloud membership that allows you to create both personal and team libraries, it's important to know how to move between both types of libraries. If you want to learn more about team libraries, consult the documentation at helpx.adobe.com.

1   Use the Creative Cloud app to view your libraries.

2   Make sure the libraries are displayed in Icon view.

3   Click the More Options button in the upper-right corner of a personal library thumbnail to display a menu.

4   From the menu, choose Move To Team.

Collaborating using cloud documents

Let's spend a little time further exploring cloud documents. You should already be familiar with them because you used them in Lesson 2, "Enriching Illustrator artwork with Photoshop content." If you skipped that lesson, go back and read the section "Photoshop cloud documents in Illustrator" before proceeding.

What are cloud documents?

Creative Cloud is rapidly evolving into a solution that enables you to save native Adobe documents directly into the Adobe cloud infrastructure. A cloud document is saved in a special version of an Adobe native format that provides additional capabilities and features when collaborating. At the time of this writing, you can save the following as cloud documents:

- Adobe Photoshop files, identified as PSDC files
- Adobe Illustrator files, identified as AIC files
- Adobe InDesign files, identified as INDDC files
- Adobe XD files, identified as XDC files (beyond the scope of this book)

Solutions like Adobe Fresco and Adobe Aero use cloud documents as their native file format.

Saving cloud documents consumes online storage within your Creative Cloud account but also makes the file available from the Creative Cloud app, the Creative Cloud website, the Creative Cloud mobile app, and individual Adobe design apps such as Illustrator, Photoshop, and others.

Cloud documents versus Creative Cloud Libraries

Cloud documents are different from Creative Cloud Libraries. A library allows you to save individual assets and snippets from Creative Cloud applications. It also allows you to save files in formats such as PDF or JPEG or as native Adobe documents, all with the intention of using these assets in one or more projects. A cloud document is complete in itself—like an AI, PSD, or INDD, it's a native Adobe file format that is saved to the cloud and offers specific advantages.

▶ **Tip:** It is not possible to save a cloud document into a Creative Cloud Library.

You can use Creative Cloud Libraries in almost every desktop and mobile app that comes with your Creative Cloud membership. And with the ability to add Microsoft integrations or third-party automation capabilities, libraries are a key component of the greater Adobe ecosystem.

Cloud documents, on the other hand, are specific to individual Adobe apps, which sometimes limits their use to single-app projects. Recent updates to cloud documents, however, have started to bring certain cross-application functionalities, as you experienced in Lesson 2 when you placed a linked Photoshop document into Illustrator.

Advantages of cloud documents

The most obvious advantage to saving a file as a cloud document is the fact that you have it available whenever you log in to your Creative Cloud account. This makes it easy to work on a cloud document from different computers, as when switching from your desktop to your laptop, or when you need to place a cloud document into another file, as you did in Lesson 2.

You can also save different versions of a document to the cloud as a single document. This makes it easy to view or revert to previously saved versions of your design. Consult the Adobe Help pages for more information on this subject.

Lastly, you can share and collaborate on cloud documents with others. Sharing offers you the ability to place files created by others directly from the cloud into your documents.

Working online versus offline

Cloud documents are saved online, so you need an internet connection to view or edit them. When you open a cloud document from Photoshop or Illustrator, a local copy of the file will be downloaded before you are able to work on it. Any changes you make to the file will be saved and synchronized to the original file that is hosted on the Adobe cloud servers.

If you want a specific cloud document to be available every time you start your computer without having to download it first, tell the Creative Cloud app to keep a copy of the file available offline:

1 Open the Creative Cloud app.

2 Click the Files tab.

3 In the Your Files category (which is selected by default), right-click the document you want to keep offline and choose Make Available Offline Always.

● **Note:** Changes made to an offline version of a cloud document will still be synchronized to Creative Cloud, as long as an internet connection is available.

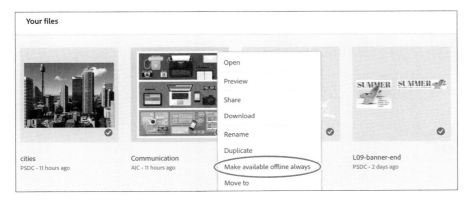

Sharing cloud documents

The two main purposes for sharing a cloud document are coediting and commenting. Let's explore these options.

Sharing for coediting

Coediting means giving others privileges to directly edit your document using their Creative Cloud account. This means that multiple designers can work on the same original file without having to create a duplicate for every user. This is very much the same behavior as saving a document on a server to which multiple team members have access. And just like on a server, only one user can access the document at a time. This means that the file needs to be closed in order to make it available for editing by others with whom the file was shared.

Sharing a cloud document with the intention of coediting allows you to exchange assets with others without having to manually send the documents via file transfer systems, send them via third-party cloud solutions, or exchange USB drives. And because your cloud documents live within your Creative Cloud storage, they're readily available the moment you start apps like Photoshop or Illustrator.

▶ **Tip:** The only exception to the limitation of one user working on one file at a time is Adobe XD, where multiple users can edit a live document at the same time. To learn more about coediting in Adobe XD, see www.adobe.com/products/xd/features/coediting.html.

Coediting a document is a great way to extend access to your work when you're not around. A few examples:

- When you want a remote co-worker to access your document while you're away on holiday
- When you need to share an entire document with others
- When others need to reuse or copy a portion of your design
- When someone needs to place your shared file into one of their designs, either by linking or embedding

Sharing a cloud document

Sharing a cloud document is as easy as sharing a Creative Cloud Library.

1 Start Illustrator, and choose Illustrator > Preferences > General (macOS) or Edit > Preferences > General (Windows).

The Preferences dialog box opens.

2 Click Reset Preferences, then click OK to close the dialog box.

3 Click Restart Now in the confirmation dialog box to restart Illustrator.

4 From the Lesson09/Imports folder, open communication.ai in Illustrator.

5 Choose File > Save As.

6 In the dialog box, click Save Cloud Document to save it as a cloud document.

7 Click Save to save the file to your Creative Cloud storage.

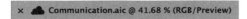

At the top of the document window you'll notice a cloud icon next to the filename and the altered filename extension. This has become an AIC document that is ready to be shared with others.

8 In the upper-right corner, click the Share Document button to start the sharing process.

9 In the Share Document dialog box, click the gear icon at the top right to view the available settings.

The sharing principles you learned when sharing libraries are also used when sharing cloud documents: do you want to invite specific, named recipients into the document, or do you want to create an open URL that anyone can view? Let's share the document with a specific individual.

10 Make sure Only Invited People Can Access is selected. Click the back arrow next to the word Settings to return to the main screen.

11 Click in the Invite People To Edit field and enter an email address. This should be an address that differs from the one you use for your Creative Cloud membership. Remember that we're doing this only for demonstration purposes.

12 Optionally, add a few words to help the recipient understand why the document is being shared with them.

13 Click Invite To Edit to send the invitation.

Viewing a shared invitation

Because the recipient of this demo requires a Creative Cloud membership in order to use the file, it's possible you won't be able to follow these steps. If that is the case, please read through them to better understand the procedure.

1 Click the Open button in the invitation email to view the file in a web browser.

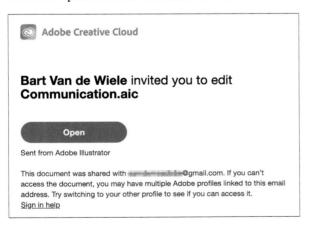

2 Using the recipient's Creative Cloud account, launch Illustrator.

3 Choose File > Open.

4 In the Open dialog box, click the Open Cloud Document button.

5 In the Open From Creative Cloud dialog box, click the Shared With You category to view the received document.

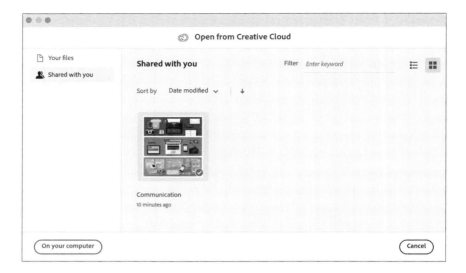

You can now open and edit the received document. Also know that you can place the shared document in other Adobe apps—for example, Photoshop. But whatever you do, keep in mind that this is the original document, not a shared copy. So every edit you make to this document will be visible to anyone that is part of the collaboration.

6 Close the file.

Commenting on a document

Sharing a cloud document with others as an open URL lets them comment on your document from a web browser. This is a great way of gathering feedback from important stakeholders.

1 Make sure you are using the same Creative Cloud account that was used to save the original communication.aic document.

2 Click the Share Document icon in the upper-right corner, and then click the gear icon.

3 In the Settings, select Anyone With The Link Can View and make sure people with the link are allowed to comment.

4 Return to the main Share Document screen and click the Copy Link button to copy the shared URL to the clipboard.

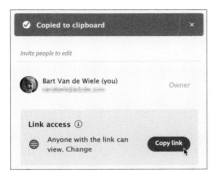

Viewing a shared document

The invited guest can comment on your document and the comments will appear in Illustrator.

1 Open a web browser window and navigate to the copied URL.

The document is visible in the user's web browser, allowing anyone with the URL to comment on the document.

2 Click the Comment option on the right and add the text **Change calendar date to 11th of Feb**.

3 Click the Pin icon and click the calendar artwork to place the pin. Then click Submit to confirm the comment.

4 The system prompts you to log in. Choose whether to use an existing (potentially free) Adobe account, or to comment as a guest.

The comment is placed on the document and the designer is notified via the Creative Cloud app and email.

Viewing shared comments in Illustrator

Let's view the received comment in Illustrator.

1 Return to Illustrator and make sure communication.aic is still open.

2 Choose Window > Comments.

The comment is displayed in the Comments panel, and the pin appears directly in the Illustrator document.

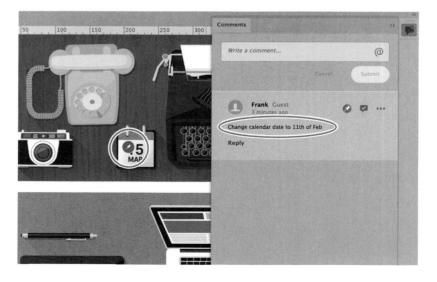

Once you view comments in Illustrator, you can reply to the commentator using the Comments panel. Or you can click the Resolve icon to mark the requested change as resolved.

Sharing restrictions

If you're a Creative Cloud for Enterprise member, your organization can limit sharing capabilities when using Creative Cloud Libraries or cloud documents. Security policies or project confidentiality are the typical drivers behind a policy of limiting a designer's sharing capabilities within an organization. The limitations you can impose on designers include deactivating the ability of sharing via open URLs (the Get Link command), limiting the Invite People command to users of the same email domain, and whitelisting additional email domains when inviting into a library people who use a different email domain from your own. Trying to use any of these limited sharing commands will result in a user error that redirects you to your IT department. These settings can be used only when your organization is using Federated or Enterprise Creative Cloud accounts.

● **Note:** For more information on the details of setting up these sharing restrictions be sure to consult Adobe's help pages.

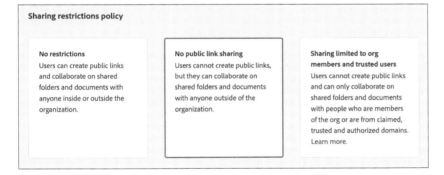

Sharing restrictions policy

No restrictions
Users can create public links and collaborate on shared folders and documents with anyone inside or outside the organization.

No public link sharing
Users cannot create public links, but they can collaborate on shared folders and documents with anyone outside of the organization.

Sharing limited to org members and trusted users
Users cannot create public links and can only collaborate on shared folders and documents with people who are members of the org or are from claimed, trusted and authorized domains. Learn more.

Review questions

1 What is the difference between the Get Link and Invite commands when sharing a Creative Cloud Library?

2 What are the advantages of viewing a Creative Cloud Library by group compared to viewing by asset type?

3 What does it mean to "follow" a Creative Cloud Library?

4 Name two advantages of working with cloud documents.

5 Does the recipient of a cloud document need to have an active Creative Cloud membership in order to comment on a document?

Review answers

1 The Get Link command can be used when sharing a library as an open URL to unnamed recipients. It gives all recipients a read-only view of the library. They can also save a local copy of the library into their own Creative Cloud account. The Invite command allows you to invite named recipients by typing in their email address. This offers the advantage of having control over who has access to the library, including setting view and edit privileges.

2 Viewing a Creative Cloud Library by group allows you to view custom asset categories created by the author.

3 Following a library is a way of subscribing to it. This means you have read-only access to the original shared library. All changes or additions to the original library, as applied by the owner, are automatically pushed to its followers.

4 Working with cloud documents provides version control, online collaboration, and shared commenting, and it makes the file available from anywhere.

5 A recipient of a cloud document must have a Creative Cloud account, either free or paid, to comment on a shared document.

INDEX

Contributor

Based in Belgium, **Bart Van de Wiele** started his career in 2002 as a graphic designer with a strong focus on print production and image retouching. His career quickly evolved into a life as an Adobe trainer, a consultant, and an author for InDesign Secrets and *CreativePro Magazine*. As a worldwide public speaker, he can often be found as a presenter at conferences like CreativePro Week and Adobe MAX covering a variety of design subjects and Adobe technologies. He is also a LinkedIn Learning instructor with a growing library of creative courses. In 2015, Bart joined Adobe as a Principal Solutions Consultant, specializing in Adobe design workflows and solutions. In 2022 he moved into a manager role at Adobe, currently supporting his own team of Solutions Consultants.

Production notes

Adobe Photoshop, Illustrator, and InDesign Collaboration and Workflow Classroom in a Book ®, was created electronically using Adobe InDesign. Art was produced using Adobe InDesign, Adobe Illustrator, and Adobe Photoshop.

References to company names in the lessons are for demonstration purposes only and are not intended to refer to any actual organization or person.

Images

Chapters 01, 07, Front Matter, checklist survey investment property business concept money graph buildings finance investments: ProStockStudio/Shutterstock

Chapters 05, 07, 09, Front Matter, set of badges, banner, labels and logos for French food restaurant, foods shop, bakery, wine and catering. Design Elements: Pat Poseh/Shutterstock

Chapters 05, 07, Baking kitchen icons doodle vector set: Ohn Mar/Shutterstock

Chapters 06, 07, Front Matter, dinosaur: Viktorya170377/Shutterstock

Chapters 06, 07, 08, outline black icons set in thin modern design style, flat line stroke vector symbols - archaeology collection: Meowu/Shutterstock

Chapters 06, 07, Geochronological scale. Part 4 - Mesozoic Eon. International chronostratigraphic units, ranks, names: alinabel/Shutterstock

Chapters 06, 09, Past, present and future of technology and devices, from typewriter to computer and touch screen desktop, business communication improvement concept: elenabsl/123RF

Chapters 08, 09, Back Cover, collection of woman fashion slip on shoes: dean bertoncelj/Shutterstock

Chapter 08, Vector of modern abstract background: Passion artist/Shutterstock

Typefaces used

Adobe Myriad Pro and Adobe Warnock Pro are used throughout this book. For more information about OpenType and Adobe fonts, visit www.adobe.com/type/opentype.

Special thanks

This book would not have been possible without the help, guidance, and learning opportunities offered by so many people throughout my personal and professional life. I want to thank everyone in the Adobe community that hired me as a designer, sat in my classes, attended my presentations, or watched any of my online courses. I would also like to extend a special thank you to a few exceptional people.

My lovely family: Tessa, thank you for your love, support, and patience during this project and others. Anna, for your curiosity and encouragement. And little Norah, never stop sparkling.

Everyone from the CreativePro community, with a special shout-out to David Blatner and Anne-Marie Concepción. Thank you for your never-ending enthusiasm, knowledge sharing, and friendship.

The kind folks at Pearson that helped make this book a reality, including Laura Norman for helping to launch this project and Victor Gavenda for his guidance and invaluable input that has helped shape the lessons in this book. And all the reviewers, editors, proofreaders, compositors, and designers that have helped make this book what it is today.

My amazing friends within the Adobe community, including Mike Rankin, Nigel French, Chad Chelius, Tony Harmer, Dave Clayton, Rob de Winter, Dimitri Stevens, Melinda Grant, Ren Reed, Joanna Shindler, Pamela Sparks, and so many others.

My managers and co-workers at Adobe for challenging me and being an inspiration: Lionel Lemoine, David Deraedt, Corinne Masson, Waldo Smeets, Ross McGuire, Mark Hawes, Alexander Meyers, Jamie Ragen, and the broader solutions consulting community.

And last but not least, the good folks at LinkedIn Learning.